Truth to Power

The Journalism of a Benedictine Monk

Truth to Power

The Journalism of a Benedictine Monk

Andrew Murray Britz, OSB

Edited and Introduced
by Dennis Gruending

Kingsley
PUBLISHING

Copyright editorials © 2010 *Prairie Messenger*
Copyright other articles © 2010 The authors

First published in the United States in 2011 by Kingsley Publishing.

All rights reserved. No part of this publication may be reproduced, stored in a retrieval system, or transmitted in any form or by any means, electronic, mechanical, recording, or otherwise, without the prior written permission of the copyright holder, except in the case of a reviewer, who may quote brief passages in a review to print in a magazine or newspaper, or broadcast on radio or television. In the case of photocopying or other reprographic copying, users must obtain a licence from Access Copyright.

Cover and interior design by Rob Muench, Lucille Stewart
Project management by Kingsley Publishing Services
www.kingsleypublishing.ca

Library and Archives Canada Cataloguing in Publication

Britz, Andrew, 1940-
    Truth to power : the journalism of a Benedictine monk /
    Andrew Murray Britz ; edited & introduced by Dennis Gruending.

Includes index.
ISBN 978-0-9784526-8-1

1. Catholic Church. 2. Catholic Church — Doctrines.
3. Church and social problems — Catholic Church. I. Title.

BX1753.B75 2010   230'.2   C2010-903117-2

Printed in Canada by St. Peter's Press

2010 / 1

Ordering information: www.kingsleypublishing.ca

All proceeds from the sales of this book are donated to the *Prairie Messenger* Sustaining Fund.

This book is dedicated
to two great mentors in my life

Rev. Leonard L. Sullivan
a priest for the church in Regina
(1929-1999)

Rev. James Gray
a monk of St. Peter's Abbey
(1927-2009)

Cover art by Greg Schulte

In stark black, a Greek cross stands as the mark of Christian paradox over the Maltese cross often associated with the Benedictine community. This cross, with its rounded arms, signifies the openings to the north and the south, to the east and the west, openings to the absolutely surprising humanity of the kingdom. Seeing the world as Jesus did makes us realize that everything opens for those seeking the kingdom.

Biblical references printed in concentric circles connote the Good News pulsating outward to the ends of the earth. This is not dissimilar to the manner in which North American Native elders treasure the whole earth — for them everything in time reveals the Holy. — GS

Table of Contents

Foreword   xiii
By Joan Chittister, OSB

Introduction: 1
Andrew Britz and the *Prairie Messenger*
By Dennis Gruending

Chapter 1: The Catholic Press   11

A prophetic vocation, February 6, 1989	11
Role of the Catholic press, February 20, 2002	12
The *Messenger* is 100, February 11, 2004	14

Chapter 2: Magisterium: People, Bishops, Pope   17

Ecumenism a weathervane, July 25, 1988	17
The Word was made flesh, December 19, 1994	20
The bishop as leader, June 19, 1995	23
Ministry and authority, April 8, 1991	26
We are an Episcopal church, June 13, 1988	28
Papal primacy, November 11, 1998	30
A living magisterium, April 3, 1989	32
Simple Gospels, July 20, 1987	35
Celebrating Pentecost, May 8, 2002	36
Dream for the church, March 12, 1997	39
Cardinals differ, February 9, 2000	41
Theological debate, July 7, 1999	43
The new catechism: Maintaining orthodoxy, January 15, 1990	45
Runcie prepares for Rome visit, October 2, 1989	46
Papal office, June 27, 2001	48
The Spirit given to all, May 8, 1989	49
Post-Vatican II church, September 8, 1986	50
A sinless church, April 8, 1998	51
United in charity, July 5, 2000	54

Chapter 3: The People of God — 57

World Synod on the Laity, September 14, 1987	57
Secularity and the synod, October 19, 1987	59
Gospel and the world, January 31, 2001	60
Faith and culture, November 2, 1987	61
Inculturating the faith, July 15, 1985	62
Recognizing holiness, March 23, 1992	63
Ordinary time, January 15, 2003	64
New lay spiritual movements, October 26, 1987	66
The synod on the laity closes, November 9, 1987	67
Devotion to Mary, July 17, 1983	68
Knights of Columbus (Fourth Degree), February 16, 2000	70
Cookie monitor, October 15, 1997	71
One with the earth, April 23, 1997	72

Chapter 4: Women and the Church — 75

Women's voice needed, August 28, 1995	75
Women's gifts essential, March 14, 2001	78
First witness to the Resurrection, April 9, 2003	80
The language of liturgy, November 7, 1994	82
Powerful scrutiny, March 4, 1998	84
Pointing out sin — at home, April 18, 1988	86
Women's ordination, April 2, 1997	87
Women hearing confessions, September 10, 2003	88
Dysfunctional church, July 19, 1993	91
Neither male nor female, September 30, 1985	93
Women and the faith, November 3, 1999	94

Chapter 5: Religious, Priestly Vocations — 95

Specialized vocations, April 25, 2001	95
A prophetic call, April 9, 1997	98
Vocations to the religious life, May 4, 1992	99
Bishops seek married priests, September 27, 1993	100
Priests for the North, October 22, 1997	102
Regularizing the Czech church, April 27, 1992	104
Crisis in priestly vocations, January 23, 1993	105
Receiving disgruntled Anglicans, May 3, 1993	107

Roman fever revived, November 30, 1992 — 108
Priests for the community, February 4, 1985 — 109
Corpus Christi, June 7, 1993 — 111

Chapter 6: Pope John Paul II — 115

Pope is *PM* churchperson of the year, January 2, 1989 — 115
John Paul and the papacy, January 30, 2002 — 117
Pope as ecumenist, May 23, 2001 — 118
Unity with the East, May 15, 1995 — 120
That they may be one, June 12, 1995 — 121
Pope an Orthodox Christian, January 16, 1995 — 123
Prophetic journey, May 9, 2001 — 124
Pope on the attack, June 4, 1990 — 126
Does the pope have Parkinson's? January 10, 2001 — 128
Should popes retire? November 5, 2003 — 129
Cheering the pope, September 3, 1997 — 131

Chapter 7: That They May Be One — 133

Proclaiming the kingdom, June 20, 2001 — 133
Catholics today need ecumenism, January 23, 1989 — 135
The faith of Peter, August 10, 1984 — 137
Unity of Christians, January 22, 2003 — 139
Healing the churches, January 16, 2002 — 142
Pope serious about ecumenism, January 21, 1998 — 143
Christian unity revisited, January 21, 2004 — 146
Christian unity sought, January 22, 1997 — 149
Catholic/Lutheran healing, November 22, 1995 — 151
Diversity in the church, October 7, 1998 — 152
Eucharist in ancient "Iraq," October 31, 2001 — 153
A 1,500-year misunderstanding, November 28, 1994 — 154
Ukrainian Catholic Church, June 9, 1984 — 155
Vocation of Ukrainian Catholics, May 2, 1988 — 157
Salvation of non-Christians, October 30, 1995 — 159
Jewish brothers and sisters, July 13, 1987 — 160
Ghetto mentality, September 18, 1989 — 162
Christendom and Islam, December 12, 2001 — 163

Chapter 8: The Ethic of Life — 165

Immaculate Conception, December 7, 1987	165
Need for "seamless garment," July 1, 1984	166
Gospel of life, April 10, 1995	168
Birth control and the Gospel, January 30, 1989	171
Differing on birth control, March 22, 1993	172
Humanae Vitae: 25th anniversary, August 2, 1993	174
Condoms, February 26, 1996	177
When does life begin? March 27, 2002	178
Accepting human sexuality, July 10, 1989	179
Strengthening marriage, May 26, 1999	181
Changing laws, changing hearts, February 8, 1988	182
Abortion as violence, March 14, 1988	184
Addressing sexual abuse, June 12, 2002	186
Dignity in dying, February 28, 2001	188
Sue Rodriguez, February 21, 1994	190
Honouring the dead, March 6, 1995	191
Capital punishment revisited, February 23, 1987	193
Applying capital punishment, April 27, 1987	194

Chapter 9: Call to Justice — 197

A spirituality for justice, September 12, 1994	197
Ten Days for Development, February 3, 1986	199
The Berlin Wall comes down, November 20, 1988	200
Cold War camouflages neo-colonialism, November 20, 1988	202
Progressive taxation, May 27, 1985	202
U.S. farm subsidies, May 15, 2002	204
Feeding the hungry, June 19, 2002	206
Same dignity given to all, April 15, 1998	208
Racism in the church, June 18, 1983	210
Futility of violence at Oka, September 10, 1990	210
Ovide Mercredi's tears, December 18, 1995	212
Tracy Latimer, November 28, 1994	215
Penal reform, April 15, 1996	216
Turning play to violence, April 11, 2001	218
Events of September 11, September 19, 2001	221
Waging a "just" war, September 25, 2002	222
Nuclear weapons, June 5, 2002	226
Depleted uranium weapons, January 17, 2001	227

Protesting in the streets, April 18, 2002   227
Morality of the marketplace, August 28, 2002   230
An alternative to capitalism, June 21, 2000   231

Chapter 10: Heroes of Faith   233

Pope John XXIII, June 6, 2001   233
Canonization of Dorothy Day, September 4, 1983   236
Karl Rahner: Where he needed to be, April 15, 1984   237
Canonizing Archbishop Romero, March 26, 1990   238
Who is a martyr? March 22, 2000   239
Cardinal Henri de Lubac, September 16, 1991   241
Christiane Brusselmans, November 18, 1991   242
Dom Bede Griffiths, May 24, 1993   243
Cardinal Yves Congar, July 13, 1995   246
Cardinal Joseph L. Bernardin, January 8, 1995   248
Rev. Bernard Häring, July 15, 1998   251
Cardinal Basil Hume, June 23, 1999   253
Dom Helder Camara, September 1, 1999   254
Rev. Jean-Marie Tillard, November 22, 2000   256
Mother Teresa beatified, October 22, 2003   258
Mother Teresa's demons, September 12, 2001   261
Cardinal Franz König, March 24, 2004   261
Sparring cardinals honoured, January 2, 2002   263

Chapter 11: Revolution by Tradition   267
By Dr. John Thompson

Chapter 12: Discerning the Signs of the Times   275
By Dr. Mary Jo Leddy

Epilogue: 277
Pessimism too easy an out, March 20, 2002

Appendix: *Prairie Messenger* Editorial Policy   281

Index   283

About the Authors   291

Foreword

Truth to Power

"One man with courage," Andrew Jackson wrote, "makes a majority." Father Andrew Britz, OSB, is a man whose courage and commitment to the truth has helped all of us to be more courageous. He gave us material we could trust, with integrity we could swear by. Readers everywhere knew that what they read in the *Prairie Messenger* came with a hallmark.

What's more, it came wrapped in sharp argument and fair dealing — tasting of justice, sounding like the Gospels, and rooted in faith.

And just as importantly, these essays bear reading for the sake of the writing alone. William Zinsser, well-known writer, editor, and teacher — master of the craft — teaches that there are "four basic premises of writing: clarity, brevity, simplicity and humanity." If ever those criteria applied to a body of writing, it certainly applies to this one. The writing in this collection will carry you to new heights of understanding and evaluation if for no other reason than they are, first, crafted so well.

The pieces ring with a kind of sparkling clarity. There is no attempt to drown a topic in words and phrases to the point that by the time you finish reading it, you have no idea of what it is supposed to be about. Andrew Britz says of the church in an essay on the laity, "While it is true that the church is not a democracy, it is equally true that it is not a hierarchy according to the principles of the world." Clearly, he is to the point and starkly clear. If readers have any problem at all with these pieces, it may well be that there is no escaping the point that's being made. Britz's arguments demand attention, which, of course, is where the reader's own conscience and conviction come in.

More than that, each of the pieces presents complex ideas with incisive economy. The very brevity has its own impact. By reducing each topic to its marrow, it focuses the idea and holds it in a veritable laser beam of light to such an extent that no one, least of all readers, can say they did not know and had never heard of such possibilities. "Without the effective voice of women," Britz wrote in 1995, "the church has not been able to keep its balance in many, many areas — not just in its understanding and appreciation of women."

With great simplicity, with disarming honesty, these essays wrestle their way into our hearts until we, too, find ourselves poised on the teeter-totter of truth, forced to determine which way to fall: for or against the oppressed; in favour or not of the collusions; uncertain or decided about the justice of commonplace injustices; open or closed to information we would have preferred to avoid. "Fundamentalism," he wrote in 1984, "has become very appealing. Rather than parables and paradoxes (good enough to carry the message Jesus meant to leave us), we want simple dogmas that can be written in stone. Rather than preach the cross of Christ, we want moral answers in black and white. Rather than find the kingdom in the necessarily ambiguous signs in our midst, we are prepared to run halfway about the globe to witness miracles that do not challenge our basic value systems." It is precisely the honest, open, and searingly simple presentation of naked truth written too artlessly to ignore that stays with the reader for a lifetime.

In the end, Britz's humanity and the ongoing relevance of the situations he wrote about to the humanity of the reader makes this collection an enduring part of the spiritual literature of our period.

But there is even more in this book to be wondered at, to be emulated. The fact is that these essays spare no one and nothing from the glare of truth and the impulse to grow.

There are those who would say that the very term "Catholic journalism" is an oxymoron, the mixture of two unlike and equally contradictory terms in the same concept — like white chocolate or bitter sweet or square circle. But not here. Not in these essays. As Cicero said, "A man of courage is also full of faith." It is the faith of Andrew Britz that underlies this book.

Andrew Britz, OSB, the former editor of one of the best Catholic newspapers on the globe, has the kind of faith it takes to turn the best skills of his craft — the edge of sharp questions and the grace of doubt — on the church itself, on the unexamined ideas of the Catholic tradition, on our own distortions of those ideas. As a result, the written pieces in this collection are far and beyond the level of the local church bulletin board.

Britz does not confuse public relations and journalism. He does not write commercials and call them analyses. He does not barter truth for favour. He does not fall victim to the kind of loyalty to the institution that by failing to write the truth makes the growth of that institution impossible. He does not swear the kind of fealty to the church that is more sycophancy to the system than fidelity to the best of its ideals.

That kind of writing from the very centre of a system is more than skilful; it is lovingly dangerous and dangerously loving.

That kind of commitment, however, is neither easy to come by nor easy to achieve without failing in one direction or the other. After all, how can the communication arm of any centrally controlled organization really tell its own story? How can writers who are dedicated to the very organization they're writing about turn the light of truth into corners whose illumination might very well seem to damage the truths it purports to defend? "Whether we like it or not," Britz writes, "there is a great variety of opinions in the church at large. A Catholic paper must reflect this reality to its subscribers — it is the only reality there is…. Readers of the Catholic press must come to accept this."

Britz does great Catholic journalism by being true to the essence of Christianity and to the Gospels upon which it is built. He also does it by being true to the image of the Jesus who walked from one end of Israel to the other, contending with the Pharisees, questioning the laws, recalling Israel always to the meaning of the Covenant and its implications for both synagogue and state.

These pieces are not only the best of reflections. They are also, as a consequence of that, as spiritually relevant for readers today as they were when they were written.

Read them for the sake of your religious development. Relish them for the honesty of heart they offer. Reflect on them for the sake of the future of the church in this new age to come.

Joan Chittister, OSB
March 21, 2010
Co. Kerry, Ireland

Introduction

Truth to Power:
Andrew Britz and the *Prairie Messenger*
By Dennis Gruending

Truth to Power presents much of the best from 21 years of journalism by Father Andrew Britz, a Benedictine monk at St. Peter's Abbey at Muenster, in the hinterland of rural Saskatchewan, far from the centres of ecclesiastical and political power. From 1983 to 2004, he was editor of the *Prairie Messenger*, a Catholic weekly published by the monks since 1904. He was fearless in speaking truth to the powerful — to popes and politicians, capitalists and clerics. "It is not easy producing a prophetic paper year in and year out," he writes in one of the editorials published in this book. "Prophets call us to a new age."

The new age for him is one that resists an imperial papacy, one in which his church honours and takes seriously the gifts of all the baptized — lay people as well as clerics, women as well as men, and the poor, especially the poor. That new world is also one where the abuses of liberal capitalism are held in check, where militarization is curtailed, where the earth and all of its peoples are treated with respect, and where all religions act in unity for the common good. Although he is best known for his provocative editorials, Andrew Britz also has a deeply contemplative dimension to his writing, the legacy of his life as a monk and a trained liturgist, who is well educated and deeply steeped in church history. A planned second volume will stress the interior life while this volume deals much more with the institutional church.

I first met Andrew in 1965 when I was a student at St. Peter's College, a boys' boarding school that was opened by the monks in 1921. Between 1960 and 1966, Andrew had been away, taking seminary training at St. John's Abbey, in Collegeville, Minnesota, where he received a Master of

Arts degree in liturgy in 1965. He and the other seminarians would come home to Muenster when their university year ended in April or May. Since our high school year at St. Peter's didn't finish until late June, we students had some contact with the junior monk seminarians. Andrew was a big, sturdy-looking guy in his long monk's habit, who wore black-framed glasses and kept his thick, dark hair in a crewcut.

He was ordained to the priesthood in June 1966, and that autumn he began to teach at the college, later serving as its principal until the high school closed in 1972. He left that year to pursue doctoral studies in church history at the Toronto School of Theology. The abbot called him home in 1974 to resume his work as principal, this time of the university program at St. Peter's, which was affiliated with the University of Saskatchewan. He held that post until 1982, and most years he also taught courses in biblical literature or religious studies in Muenster and at the university campus in Saskatoon.

Andrew was born in March 1940 into a large farming family near the town of Lake Lenore, less than 30 kilometres from the monastery. He was by the 1960s among a cadre of monks who had been born and raised within the abbacy. By contrast, when the first monks arrived with settlers from Minnesota in 1902 and the years following, they considered St. Peter's to be a mission field. The settlers were virtually all German American Catholics who could not purchase or expand farms in Minnesota because most of the arable land was already settled. They considered a variety of locations for a move and a number of them decided on the parklands in east-central Saskatchewan, land that had been used from time immemorial by Indian peoples for hunting and gathering. The region had also been an important outpost in the fur trade and for Métis buffalo hunts. But by the late 1800s, the Indians had been forced onto reserves and the Métis who fought to preserve their traditional lands had been defeated by Canadian militia at the Battle of Batoche in 1885.

The new settlers wanted priests, churches, hospitals, and schools in their new homeland, and they got them. The monks who accompanied the Minnesota farmers in 1902 were transplanted from a failed abbey on the southern tip of Illinois and were associated with St. John's (Benedictine) Abbey at Collegeville, Minnesota. Later, Elizabethan sisters came to build a hospital and Ursuline sisters to create a school for young women. The government's settlement regulations held that all homesteaders had to reside on their piece of land, but the monks received permission in 1904 to combine their individual parcels into one block held in common. They created a farm to support the monastery, had churches built, and organized parishes where they served as priests. It was a situation born of duty and circumstance; traditionally, monks lived a cloistered existence that followed the 1,500-year-old rule of Benedict, where they bracketed their days with communal prayer. It was a lifestyle that included work, prayer, and hospitality, along with a strong intellectual tradition. Monks at St. Peter's lived a kind of hybrid existence, combining their contemplative monasticism with the more public roles of parish priests and teachers.

The farm was there from the beginning in 1902. A German-language newspaper called *St. Peter's Bote* began publishing in 1904. Later it became *St. Peter's Messenger* and later still, the *Prairie Messenger*. Andrew was the editor when, in 2004, the monks at St. Peter's observed the paper's 100th anniversary. From the last months of the First World War until 1923, the federal government prohibited the *Bote* from publishing in German. Undeterred, the monks began publishing *St. Peter's Messenger* in English. The war meant that the earlier tide of settlers slowed to a trickle, and by the 1920s, most of the nearby land was occupied in any event. The Great Depression, which began in 1929, coincided with almost a decade of drought in Saskatchewan. Although the situation was somewhat less severe in St. Peter's Abbacy than elsewhere, it did create poverty and hardship and led to a rural exodus from which Saskatchewan has never fully recovered. The *Messenger* began to report and to editorialize to a much greater extent on political and social developments during this decade.

The editors had a close-up view of the economic carnage. Their rural parishioners were hit hard, and the monks would have endured economic setbacks on their own farm. Hard times in Saskatchewan and elsewhere led to the promulgation of new social and political movements, to farm co-operatives, such as the Saskatchewan Wheat Pool, and to the birth of the Co-operative Commonwealth Federation (CCF), a democratic socialist movement led in significant degree by members of the Protestant clergy. These were trying but also vital times for an editor. Father Wilfrid Hergott, who was born in the abbacy and attended St. Peter's College, served as editor from 1931 to 1955. He set a high standard for intellectual rigour and excellence, but as editor he often found himself out of step with the Catholic hierarchy, as well as with many readers and even members of his own monastic community. Most likely, although it has not been proven decisively, he was eventually forced to resign as editor because he was considered too political, and he spent his later years serving as a hospital chaplain in nearby Humboldt.

The Catholic Church had an established role in feudal society and found itself on the wrong side of history as the enlightenment, capitalism, and liberal revolutions swept over Europe in the 18th and 19th centuries. It was not until 1891, in Pope Leo XIII's encyclical *Rerum novarum* (Of new things), that the church attempted to speak out about emerging economic and political developments, including industrialization and the resulting exploitation of people. In 1931, Pope Pius XI delivered an encyclical called *Quadragesimo anno* (In the fortieth year) to mark the anniversary of Pope Leo's earlier document and to update the church's social teaching. Both popes were critical of the abuses of capitalism, a papal tradition that has continued to this day, although arguably they were not opposed to it as a system, particularly if it were to be anchored in smaller enterprises. The church was, however, entirely opposed to socialism. Although Pius XI did appear in his encyclical to understand the distinction between communism and democratic socialism, he chose to condemn socialism in all of its forms.

The pope's message was picked up by Canada's Catholic bishops, who condemned not only Marxism but also the movement advocated by people such as J. S. Woodsworth and Tommy Douglas, both Protestant clergy who found their inspiration in Great Britain's Labour Party, as well as in the Scriptures. Bishops in Quebec issued a pastoral letter in 1933 condemning every form of socialism, and Saskatchewan's bishops produced a similar letter in 1934. There is some argument about whether they actually forbade Catholics to vote for the CCF, but the code was clear. As my father was to tell me, local priests in the 1930s and 1940s warned parishioners from the pulpit against voting for the new party.

Gregory Baum, a well-known Canadian sociologist, writes that editors of the *Prairie Messenger* — and chronology indicates this would have been Father Hergott — evolved in their views about socialism and maintained "a critical dialogue with the CCF." Baum notes that initially the paper's editorial stance followed Pope Pius XI in warning against any form of socialism. But the *Messenger* came to argue editorially that society needed "radical change, not palliatives" and that Catholic social teaching provided the norms with which to evaluate the programs of all political parties. The editor wrote that the Saskatchewan bishops' condemnation of socialism did not mention the CCF by name, that the party's program contained many policies in keeping with Catholic teaching, and that Catholics should be free to support the party of their choice. It was a controversial position to have taken at the time.

Equally controversial was the paper's editorial stance on the divisive issue of public medical-care insurance introduced into Saskatchewan in 1962 by the social-democratic CCF government. That led to a political standoff and a bitter 23-day strike by the province's doctors. Emotions ran high — much as they did in the United States when President Obama attempted to introduce a more modest plan in 2009 — and there was even fear of violence in the streets. Former Saskatchewan Premier Allan Blakeney, who was a young cabinet minister in 1962, has said that only two newspapers in the province gave editorial support to the introduction of medicare — and one of them was the *Prairie Messenger*. The editor of the day, Father Augustine Nenzel, faced harsh criticism for his stance from many Catholics who tended to support the provincial Liberal Party, which vociferously opposed the plan.

Father James Gray was appointed editor in 1962, the year in which Pope John XXIII convened the Second Vatican Council, which was to hold four sessions and to last until 1965. This gathering of bishops from around the world set out to update the church, to prepare it for greater service to the world, and to promote Christian unity. Not much had changed in the church for hundreds of years, and Vatican II was the pope's attempt to open the doors and windows. Despite initial widespread optimism, there was also division among the bishops and opposition to change, much of it embedded within the bureaucracy of the Vatican's stone walls. Changes were significant and swift in a church that had existed for 2,000 years. Soon, altars were turned so that priests faced their congregations. The Latin Mass gave way to the vernacular in readings and songs. The sacraments were updated and changed. Priests, sisters, and brothers changed the way in which they dressed.

One of the most important debates to take place was about the role of bishops in guiding the church. Was this to be done collegially, with the Bishop of Rome as first among equals, or was it to remain a papal monarchy governed from the centre? Another key question revolved around the role of lay people — those whom Andrew frequently describes as the People of God who comprise more than 99 percent of the church's members. These were questions for the universal church but often were felt most keenly and directly in the lives of parishes and individuals. Do lay people have a meaningful role in their churches? Or are they expected to do as told by the clergy? Do women have a meaningful role? The question of collegiality also extends to other Christian churches and world religions. Traditionally, Catholics defined themselves as the one true church and believed they had little, if anything, to learn from others. Now the church was being challenged to open dialogues with other churches and with non-Christians.

Pope John readily admitted that he did not know where the process, once unleashed, would lead, but he believed it must be done and he trusted in the outcome. Many Catholics had been comfortable in the old church and now felt they had lost their moorings. There has been bitterness, acrimony, and criticism about how the council has been interpreted. Some felt it had all been a big mistake, while others shuddered at what would have happened if the church had attempted to stand still and remain aloof from contemporary history. Vatican II was the most momentous development in the church in centuries, and the debate over its meaning and implementation was to fill the pages of the *Prairie Messenger* and remain the preoccupation of James Gray and every subsequent editor. A former monk says, "During Wilfrid Hergott's editorship, the *Prairie Messenger* explored and promoted the social teachings of the encyclicals. During Andrew Britz's editorship, it explored and promoted the teachings of Vatican II."

Andrew likes to say that he was installed as editor on April Fool's Day 1983 and that he left on the same day in 2004. It was, despite his humorous aside, an impressive tenure. A former monk who had attended seminary with him says, "Andrew developed, from the country bumpkin novice I saw at St. John's Abbey, to a mature individual and theologian — a man of profound insight as well as faith." He was intelligent and learned. He appeared as comfortable talking about church councils in AD 400 as he was about contemporary debates on euthanasia or American farm subsidies. His earlier studies in theology and philosophy, as well as in liturgy and church history, gave him an impressive breadth and depth. One former associate says, "This was a continuation of his life as a teacher, except in this position he was teaching the faithful." In fact, this book will be a useful reader or textbook for students in university, seminary, or even high school.

Andrew was driven by the idea that the post-council church must be at the service of the world, particularly those whom he called the "little people" — the poor, the oppressed, the defenceless — indeed, all the marginalized. He was highly focused and he expected others, including those with families and other responsibilities, to be as dedicated as he was to the paper and its cause. As an editor, he could be blunt but he never took himself too seriously; good humour remained his defence against the many challenges he faced. A former associate says, "He would slip things into the paper when I was doing proofreading just to see how I would react when I read it. One of his favourite such lines was 'the devil she made me do it.'" But his was a firm hand at the helm. Another former colleague says that Andrew "was unafraid to confront the church's flaws but was enthusiastic in celebrating its richness and diversity." He had his detractors, particularly among those who believed that in challenging the church and the hierarchy he was being disloyal.

Andrew writes in one of his editorials about the "hate mail" he received, mainly from those who believed he was not taking a strong enough stand against abortion. He responded by adopting from Cardinal Joseph Bernardin of Chicago the image of a "seamless garment," in which all questions of respect for life are woven into one mental and spiritual fabric. According to this ethic, any abuse of the defenceless is unacceptable — in war, prisons, hospitals, workplaces, and, as Andrew believes, in the womb. He was stung by the direct attacks on him and of those made against him to the bishops, to Rome, and often to his abbot, but the abbots held firm in their support.

Andrew did not enjoy the angry letters but they did not deter him. A former colleague says, "If negative letters were not coming in, he thought that perhaps he was not being sufficiently challenging to his readers." John Thompson, who writes a chapter in this book describing Andrew's work, says that his critics misunderstood him. Thompson says that Andrew was practising revolution by tradition: "Living out the meaning of the Incarnation in today's world is revolutionary, grounded in the Second Vatican Council's return to the early Christian tradition. Revolution by tradition in 'simple Gospels' speaks truth to power in lives lived differently." Andrew pushed and goaded people. He wanted them and his church to be, or to recapture, what it had been in its early days, before there was an obstinate Curia, an imperial papacy, a cult of bishop-as-CEO, and a clerical class.

He had capable help in editing the newspaper, but he also wrote two and at times three editorials a week for 21 years. Throughout most of his tenure as editor, he continued to serve as a Sunday pastor in several of the abbacy's parishes, and he never lost his common touch. The *Prairie Messenger* was read in the abbacy but also in Saskatoon, Regina, Winnipeg, and much farther afield. The paper's Benedictine roots played a part in its maintaining a modest but loyal base of American subscribers.

The paper won many religious press awards and Andrew won awards as a writer and an editor. He was in demand as a speaker and conference leader, particularly among educators. He was instrumental in setting up the Canadian Catholic News, a co-operative service that shares news among Catholic papers, and in placing a CCN journalist to report from the Parliamentary Press Gallery in Ottawa.

The *Prairie Messenger*, while much admired, was never a financial success and it remained a drain upon the Benedictine community. The monks considered closing it down but it was so important to their ministry that they could not bring themselves to do so. Andrew was unfazed by the economic challenges. He said that monks should be poor. The paper's readers had never been all that numerous and the unrelenting depopulation of rural Saskatchewan meant that many of them had to leave. Andrew became effective at raising money for the paper, relying increasingly upon donations from grateful readers for its survival.

There was only one pope throughout Andrew's years as editor. John Paul II was elected to that position in 1979, and when Andrew stepped aside in 2004, John Paul was still in the chair, although frail and suffering from Parkinson's disease. The pope was a powerful and charismatic personality. Andrew admired him greatly for his courage and his commitment to social justice but that did not prevent him from offering criticism when he thought it was warranted. He felt, for example, that the pope centralized too much authority in his office, that he was complicit in preventing the implementation of reforms called for by Vatican II, and that he was too fiercely resistant to allowing women to use their gifts fully in the church. As the pope became ever more incapacitated, Andrew asked in a November 2003 editorial whether John Paul should consider retiring. Sadly, Parkinson's had by then struck Andrew as well, and the disease made it increasingly difficult for him to continue as editor. The attacks upon him continued as well and they may have been heard in the higher reaches of the church. On April 1, 2004 — April Fool's Day — he stepped down as editor. He continued to serve as the pastor in Lake Lenore, his hometown, and in some nearby parishes. Poor health forced him to retire from full-time ministry, and in 2009 he moved back to the monastery.

But he remains engaged. When we decided to do this book, Andrew agreed to work on the first selection from the approximately 2,000 editorials that he had written over the years. He enlisted the expert help of Sister Marian Noll, OSU, who had been his assistant editor from 1984 to 1998, and of Maureen Weber, who is an assistant editor today. We have all been in frequent contact as I winnowed the pieces down to a manageable number. In addition, I asked two prominent and knowledgeable Catholics to read the selection and to comment on its relevance for today. Dr. Mary Jo Leddy is a well-known author, activist, and a former sister of Our Lady of Sion. Dr. John Thompson, a sociologist, is the former principal of St. Thomas More College at the University of Saskatchewan. Leddy and Thompson provide a dialogue with the text, placing Andrew's work into context and describing how it continues to speak to our age.

I have read the *Prairie Messenger* for all of my adult life, and I have always understood Andrew's writing through the lens of social justice. He was strong on justice to be sure, but as Leddy and Thompson point out, Andrew's consuming interest is the church, past and present. It was his fate to come of age during Vatican II. He has immersed himself in that great reforming project, not yet completed, and in it he finds the keys to justice and to right relationships.

Chapter 1

The Catholic Press

A prophetic vocation
February 6, 1989

Recent sociological studies, including our own a year ago, indicate that a great many Catholics look to the Catholic press as their most important source of information concerning the church. It is an awesome responsibility to be de facto part of the teaching church.

To carry out this function the press must deeply love the church. There is no room for the secular media's predilection for controversy to enliven the news. But there is also no room for the Catholic press attempting to shield its readers from some of the unpleasant things happening in the church.

Most readers will find it unpleasant to read about 163 theologians in Europe roundly criticizing the pope for his appointment of bishops, his treatment of theologians, and his "intense fixation" on the illicitness of contraception. A Catholic newspaper cannot ignore such stories and still maintain its credibility. As with all news media it is important that the news be presented in utter honesty — and without editorial comment within the story itself.

A Catholic newspaper gets its credibility not from carrying only stories that are orthodox, but from honesty and professionalism in its presentation and from its willingness to carry stories not supportive of its own editorial thrust with equal honesty and professionalism.

Readers of the Catholic press must come to accept this. The days are gone — hopefully forever — when the church was so monolithic that one could read every article in a Catholic paper as if it were written in one's catechism.

Whether we like it or not, there is a great variety of opinions in the church at large. A Catholic paper must reflect this reality to its subscribers — it is the only reality there is. This does not mean that Catholic papers are to espouse relativism, a philosophy that says truth is dependent on the mindset of each individual.

A Catholic newspaper is as good as its editorial pages. From the mass of stories that cross editors' desks each week they must choose a representative sampling of the news.

The editor must choose to be fair, not to be perfectly objective. There is no such thing as pure objectivity. To discern what the church is and what lies ahead for it calls for something else — a prophetic vision.

There is no escaping the call. Each editor is called upon to be prophetic. To safeguard against personal deception, the editor must work closely with those especially committed to teaching in our church — the bishops.

We at the *Prairie Messenger* believe we do work closely with our bishops. However, that really is not something the *PM* can take credit for. It is the bishops in Manitoba and Saskatchewan who have made this co-operation so successful. They have understood the purpose and difficulties of the church press — and have been most positive in encouraging the *Prairie Messenger* to take on its prophetic role.

Role of the Catholic press

February 20, 2002

The Catholic press must be unabashedly at the service of the church. It is an integral part of the church's tools for spreading the Good News of Jesus Christ. To do this in an effective manner the Catholic press must love the church deeply.

In this regard its mission parallels that of the hierarchy. In presenting church teaching it must make certain it is in full harmony with the church. Normally Catholic editors and reporters achieve this by working closely with their bishops.

While the Catholic press is not primarily a PR vehicle of the religious institution, its workers and publishers realize how ludicrous it is for anyone to say that they love the church as a force for salvation but hate it as an institution. To be church is to be institution, and thus the Catholic press does not hesitate to play a PR role in the local church.

But we should learn from recent situations that have dominated the secular media. If we are to learn anything from Bill Clinton's zipper and George W. Bush's eagerness for war, it is that we must be wary of spin doctors shaping our information.

Speaking to young Catholic journalists three years ago, Archbishop John P. Foley, head of the Pontifical Council for Social Communication, called the Catholic press the very antithesis of spin doctoring. "It is essential that you report the facts as objectively and as dispassionately as possible," he told them. "People first ask of us: what have we seen; what have we witnessed; what do we know. Only after that might they ask of us: what do we think."

A recent story the *Prairie Messenger* carried that created a lot of stir and considerable criticism was the report on a meeting of six key Vatican administrative departments with the bishops of Australia. They discussed "feminist-inspired demands for gender-inclusive language," and came to the conclusion that feminism leads to a "crisis of faith."

The *Prairie Messenger*, believing it to be the major story of the week, made it the lead story in its next issue. This did not please a great many of our readers.

It's important to look at this criticism. Basically it boiled down to this: critics claimed that the nub of the matter was not that feminism leads to a crisis of faith but that the Vatican said it does. The headline, they insisted, should respect this distinction.

Two families of verbs much stronger than "to say" were suggested: "The Vatican thinks or believes…" or "The Vatican assumes or hypothesizes.…"

In other words, they wanted the *Prairie Messenger* to stand in judgment of the Vatican — and find it wanting. The *Prairie Messenger* was heartened by Archbishop Foley's advice.

From its inception the *Prairie Messenger* (and before it, the *St. Peter's Messenger*) has had the policy of reporting its news as objectively as possible.

If we give space to the expressed opinions of people in the church, whether they are at the "top" (and thus much more likely to be covered) or at the "bottom," we will be as objective and dispassionate as possible and will attempt to give the story a headline that does not stand in judgment of their viewpoint. Not without reason have we moved the editorials, which by their very nature include judgment, to the back section of the paper.

Yes, we report on those at the top. But we also report on those at the bottom. It is not the job of the Catholic press to give a monolithic view of the church — such a view is, of course, not even true for the Roman Curia itself. Deep (and, we believe, healthy) disagreements exist among the pope and the highest cardinals.

Some people might believe there should be no differences of opinion — to say nothing about outright confusion — in the church. We are not called to present such a non-existent church. Nor are Catholic editors to present in technicolour the church they wish would exist.

In choosing what stories to carry, these editors are required to present the church as it is to their readers.

It is not pleasant, for instance, to have to present the story of sex abuse in Boston. Accompanying that story is a brief report on a sociological survey of Catholic Bostonians, which found a great gulf between official church teaching and the people's view on a married priesthood that includes women priests, as well as on premarital and homosexual genital activity.

It might not be what ecclesiastical spin doctors would do, but in the long run — and usually in the short run, too — a dedication to objective truth, with all its human complexities, reassures readers. They know instinctively that they are part of a healthy church if it deals with them honestly, forthrightly, and with that love and sensitivity that comes with respect for everyone.

We believe this editorial policy will lead those who are open to the truth to a deeper love for that flesh-and-blood church in our midst, a church which is ever struggling to be faithful to a Lord who was tested for 40 days in the desert.

The *Messenger* is 100   February 11, 2004

For 100 years, the monks of St. Peter's Abbey have published "the *Messenger*," first in German, then for 24 years in both English and German, and finally, since 1947, in English only.

It has not always been easy for the monks. The *Messenger* has played no insignificant role in keeping the Benedictines poor — as they should be! Already after the very first issue — on February 11, 1904, exactly 100 years ago — Rev. Alfred Mayer was apologizing to the monks for the costs surrounding the newspaper. The type cost $300; the first printing (5,000 copies) cost $55.

Surely the monks are to be commended for their ongoing financial contribution to the *Messenger*. But, over the years, it has not been finances that have tested their mettle. It is not easy producing a prophetic paper, year in and year out. Through it all these Benedictines have stood fast. They are the real ones we should be celebrating.

The monks know that prophets always have enemies: it cost John the Baptist his head, and we all know the story of the Cross. Neither of these great men was able to preach the Gospel without generating anger, without creating resentment.

It's inevitable that prophets who struggle to be on the cutting edge come out bloodied at times. Prophets remind people that they are pilgrims, and as long as they are in this world they always will be pilgrims. Prophets call us to a new age. Jesus had a tremendous gift of giving us glimpses of the kingdom. His parables are as fresh today as they were the first time he uttered them. Yet we know the fear and anger he generated — not among the lukewarm and irreligious but with the religious establishment who were doing their best to be faithful to their understanding of the tradition.

If anything is certain, it is surely that the prophetic tradition cannot be institutionalized. Unlike kings and priests, no one is anointed once and for all as a prophet. "Each morning the Lord awakes me to hear, to listen like a disciple," Isaiah proclaims in the Third Servant Song (50:4). Prophets, too, must be the pilgrim, looking each day for the Spirit that will make them "an altogether new creation" (2 Cor 5:17).

Monastic life, more so than religious life in general, is not about doing good work in the community, and it is certainly not about being holier than people in the world. The Sayings of the Desert Fathers are filled with stories about the young monks needing to learn that they are not better than those married Christians who, through their special sacrament, struggle to reveal the unconditional love of God's kingdom.

Aspirants to the monastic life are usually not impressed when they first study one of the key texts of Benedictine spirituality. Pope St. Gregory the Great, in describing St. Benedict, has him "seeing the whole world in a single ray of light." The would-be monk quite naturally thinks Benedict should see God in splendour divine, or Jesus with his five wounds shining brightly — or at least Mary with a new revelation to the world!

Gregory, like the abbas, the spiritual guides of the desert before him, realized that new monks would have a hard time realizing this goal. So they allowed the beginner to pray "with eyes closed," though they always recognized the inherent danger — that, with one's eyes closed, one could create a world wonderfully according to one's own liking.

They allowed it. Indeed, they encouraged it, recognizing that in the beginning the aspirant had to cut out empty distractions. But they never removed the ideal: the day must come when the monk would be able to pray "with eyes wide open."

This goal marks the meaning of the *Prairie Messenger* to help its readers see the world (church included) as a whole, in a single ray of light. With such a vision comes freedom, the freedom to see ever-new possibilities for individuals, for the church, and for the world itself.

As every editor knows — and the longer I am in office the surer I am about this — the *Prairie Messenger* is the work of the monks of St. Peter's. The paper's development has changed as the monks have changed in their understanding of who they are. Any editor who does not move with the monastic community will not last long; it is the only preventive medicine to burnout.

The *Prairie Messenger* is not the paper a bishop would publish. That is not saying anything disparaging about them. (One of my greatest personal rewards these past 21 years as an editor has been the close association I have had with Prairie bishops.) The *Prairie Messenger* is a product of its religious and monastic roots.

Of course, there is a downside in trying prophetically to be always on the cutting edge. Mistakes will be made — and this editor has made plenty of them! A strong dose of humility is medicine every editor must down. We all must have the faith of Gamaliel, a Pharisee and scholar responsible for saving lives of some early apostles in the mid first century AD: "What is of human origin will die, but what is of God will not be destroyed" (see Acts 5:39). Yes, we need faith for we do not have the answers. It is always a great mistake to doggedly insist that yesterday's answer will suffice for tomorrow.

The monks are proud of their first 100 years on prairie soil; they look forward to — indeed they seek — your trust and support as together we move on to a new history, to new challenges.

Chapter 2

Magisterium: People, Bishops, Pope

Ecumenism a weathervane
July 25, 1988

The central task of the magisterium is most clearly seen in the modern church in a courageous response to the Holy Spirit's call to be ecumenical. Ecumenism, more than anything else, reminds the church that it fulfills its task as teacher, not so much by more closely defining its dogmas as by truly grappling with the parables and paradoxes that were Christ's method of teaching.

In partaking in ecumenism the Catholic Church quickly comes face-to-face with a paradox of its own. Proclaiming dogma seemingly augments the importance bishops feel they have, while on the other hand, grappling with paradox brings the bishop closer to the People of God, who in every age struggle to make their faith a living expression of the dominant culture.

But that is the way it should be, for the bishop gets his power by being so close to his people that he can express the living faith of the church, the *sensus fidelium*, the sense of the faithful.

Most churches involved in ecumenism are declining in membership — especially in the First World. Conversely, most churches that scorn ecumenism are growing.

Before the Second Vatican Council the Catholic Church largely scorned ecumenism. Church leaders reminded Catholics that they had not strayed from the truth and thus had nothing to gain from ecumenical endeavours. Our dogmatism made us scorn study and prayer with other Christians.

Today many Catholics would love to go back to those days of certain answers. Nor should it surprise us in this time of social disintegration that the churches preaching simple black-and-white answers are gaining new converts daily.

It is important for the Catholic Church to address those members who can find no good reasons for ecumenism today and instead want the church to restate in the strongest terms possible all the right answers we possess.

It is important to remind them how Jesus taught. Jesus's religious contemporaries often pushed or cornered him so he would have to give straight answers. Invariably he would answer the religious establishment with parables and paradoxes.

The first are last and the last are first, he said. Rulers in this world rule over people; in the kingdom the slaves will rule. Not the best material with which to establish a church or hierarchy!

One day Jesus would teach, "Blessed are the peacemakers," but lest some thought they understood this, he would proclaim the next day that he "did not come to bring peace, but the sword."

And to those who wanted some religious order in the land, Jesus would tell parables in which the good son who works diligently all day misses out on the feast of the fatted calf, while the prodigal son eats to his heart's desire with a golden ring on his finger.

This teaching style hardly lends itself to simple black-and-white answers. It is hard to imagine that Jesus wanted a church with all the right answers.

Jesus loved to give two truths that were in a paradoxical, creative tension. And it was in accepting the paradox that the follower found the kingdom, discovered a truth that was salvific.

Every Christian truth that is salvific is paradoxical. It is of no saving worth for the young firebrand to espouse Christ's teaching on not coming to bring peace, but the sword. Nor is it helpful for the timid to constantly remember that the peacemakers are blessed.

But the power of the kingdom, Jesus promises, will be with the firebrands who in contemplative prayer come to know the glory of peacemakers. No less prophetic will be the timid who keep before themselves the Lord's saying on minding the sword.

The church must ask itself whether it has preached this paradox, or whether it has preached only the simple answer that lends itself so easily to misinterpretation, to establishment. Does all our Christian art depict the peacemaker? Do any churches — even one — contain a statue of the Lord who said, "I have not come to bring peace, but the sword"? Or, if this is too loaded a question: How many sermons have First World Christians heard on this Jesus with the sword?

To preach one, either one, is not to preach the Gospel. We must preach the paradox. Gospel preaching on salvation is not, as born-again Christians would have it, a matter of full assurance; it's about those who lose their lives finding them, about those saving their lives losing them. The paradox — that the death of Jesus is resurrection — is the basic truth of everything the church knows.

Not surprisingly the ancient church carefully included paradox in its teaching. It did not proclaim Mary the mother of Jesus, but the mother of God — God who was eternal, unborn. It did not proclaim just the humanity or just the divinity of Jesus; it proclaimed them both full and at the same time.

But this did not happen at the time of the Reformation. The Renaissance with its new-fangled ideas shook the world of its time to its very foundations and, much like today, church leaders everywhere were looking for simple, straightforward answers on which they could re-establish the church.

And re-establish it they did — in the Protestant north no less than in the Catholic lands of southern Europe. But they did it at the expense of the paradox; both Catholics and Protestants emptied the Gospel of much of its power.

Instead of struggling in prayer and in service to the world to understand the paradox of Christian reality, each side grabbed on to one pole of the paradox and accused the other of heresy.

To give but two examples. The Eucharist is both a meal and a sacrifice, the celebration of the community remembering the Lord's Supper and the renewal of the Lord's self-gift on the cross. But did any Catholics hear that their sacrifice was to be a grand celebration in the Lord? Were many Protestants taught that their celebration of the Lord's Supper was the sacrifice to which they were called?

No wonder Catholics accepted a eucharist in which the priest did everything, in which his actions alone were significant. No wonder the concept of the people as the centre of the celebration was lost and church architecture turned to the pagan temples of Rome for much of its inspiration.

No wonder Protestants lost the ecclesial, sacramental base for much of their theology of celebration, and of forgiveness and reconciliation.

Christian ministry fared even worse than eucharist. Rather than grapple with the mystery of how the priest could be both the representative of Christ and representative of the people, each side grasped the pole it was most comfortable with.

Catholics feel strongly that their Protestant sisters and brothers have needlessly weakened the order and unity of their churches by limiting the role of the priesthood as it was handed down through tradition. But Catholics, too, got less of the ministry of the kingdom than was offered them by the Lord.

Catholics got a priesthood that was in every way over and above the people. The incomparable glory of the call to baptism was all but forgotten by those called (raised) to orders.

No wonder the maintenance of the priesthood as we know it (male and celibate) has become for many a more important value than the access of the laity to the Sunday table of the kingdom. In ancient times the right to the Sunday Eucharist was the first law of the church.

These two examples from among a great many show us the need for ecumenical theology. By letting our traditions enrich one another we can re-establish in our theology and church practice the paradoxical nature of a faith based on the death of our Lord and God.

It might not give us the simple answers so many are calling for, but it will give us the dynamism of the kingdom, a power none of us will ever understand or be able to control.

The Word was made flesh December 19, 1994

There are surely nicer ways of saying it, of proclaiming that the Son of God deigned to live among us. And it must be said right off: it is not because of any sensitivity to women that the Incarnation was not proclaimed in the much less offensive phrase: "The Word became man."

Flesh is not a positive word in the Old Testament, the only Bible the early church had. Flesh denoted weakness, misguided foolishness. It was the opposite of spirit. Spirit people were strong; they had the wisdom to take full advantage of God's power to save.

Seeing the Word of God as flesh was a scandal many could not get over. To see Christ as flesh would imply that he entered our world without any special prerogatives, that he was fully conditioned by the times which were so profoundly marked by sin.

It would mean he knew weakness on a personal level, knew the beguiling force of temptation, was plagued by ignorance and illness, just as were all his friends and neighbours, and was shaped to a significant degree by the prejudices of a banana republic at the fringes of a decaying empire.

All this seemed to militate against a truly respectable religion. It was not long before proclaiming Christ in the flesh was no longer the principal way of speaking of the Incarnation. With the aid of Greek philosophy — which, by the way, had a strong disdain for the flesh — Christ was now said to have become man.

To be sure, the word in Greek and in Latin was more inclusive than it is in modern English. But something much more fundamental had changed. No longer did we have a Saviour who was fully at home with us on the bottom. With Jesus proclaimed "man," the road was open to speak of perfection. He was the perfect one, untouched by the foibles of ordinary human existence.

Not surprisingly, preachers were soon proclaiming that Jesus simply was the best. He was the smartest. He was the best carpenter. The best in everything.

Today we might find it humorous to learn that a church council was called in Spain just to declare that it was wrong to consider Jesus the best plumber and the best farmer who ever lived.

The debunking of Christ's flesh took its greatest step forward in the Arian controversy (AD 318-81). So completely did the church centre its faith in Jesus in his divinity that his flesh all but disappeared. And what remained of his flesh was so distorted in much of Christian piety that it would have been better had it disappeared altogether.

Jesus became "our divine Saviour"; it was shocking to hear anyone speak of "our human Saviour" — such talk would surely indicate a heresy in the making.

Jesus's humanity now had little about it that we could identify with. Gone was the babe born in the flesh; in his place we had a God filled with all knowledge, even of the future; we now had a Lord overwhelmed at all times, even in the Garden of Gethsemane, with the full splendour of the beatific vision.

There are some marvellous advantages to having a Christ who has been effectively stripped of his flesh. A religion that has to deal with the flesh has to concern itself with change, with struggle, with the anxiety of not having the final answer. It has to acknowledge that its grasp of truth is conditioned by times and places, by cultures and the lack thereof — and, all too often, by small-mindedness and petty political and social intrigue.

By having a divine Saviour filled with absolute truth one could forget all about such scandalous imperfections. One could dream of the church being a perfect society capable of always being able to criticize an imperfect world. One could view it as being capable of interpreting every verse of the Bible with complete accuracy, and of understanding natural law in its finest detail; one could visualize the church's grasp of truth so complete that it is no longer subject to change, no longer conditioned by the flesh.

Today we call such thinking fundamentalism. It is not simply a disease of some evangelical enthusiasts who are not comfortable with the complexities of human existence. Catholics can treat their dogmas every bit as simplistically as the most ardent evangelical. One just has to listen to much of the praise given the new catechism to know that fundamentalism is alive and well in our church.

When Jesus effectively loses his flesh, we lose ours. Truth becomes so absolute that, in everything, only one position is possible. In the world of politics, we call this fascism.

When the flesh of Jesus is unimportant, our sacramental system begins to crumble. There is no need for the cup at the Eucharist; there is hardly any need even for bread — a paste of flour and water will do. There is no need for a symbol of a community meal, because the community itself is no longer a part of the symbolizing process. The "spiritualized" bread — and not the people — has become, first and last, the presence of our God.

Sexuality can no longer be a sign of salvation. The sacrament of marriage now becomes something one receives in church on one's wedding day since the marriage bed can no longer be deemed a fitting reflection of the Eucharist.

The marriage bed is no longer seen as a principal means whereby a new house of God is built. Sex now needs to be justified; the procreation of children comes in handy here.

When we lose the flesh of Christ, when we no longer see Jesus embracing our humanity as it is in the real world, it becomes much easier for us to lose our very meaning as members of the human family.

We should not be surprised that Tracy Latimer could be seen as lacking full human dignity; nor should we be surprised that inconvenient pregnancies are now about fetuses and not about human persons. How long, we must ask, will it be before our elderly begin to fear that, should they become incapacitated, they will be considered meaningless, and then the "merciful" thing to do will be to dispose of them?

Jesus became flesh. That is what Christmas is all about. In so doing he gave infinite value to the lives real people live. The religion of the babe in the manger is about the joys and heartbreaks, the strengths and weaknesses, the beauty marks and the warts of people who know all too well that they are conditioned by time and space, by wisdom and prejudices, by noble aspirations and by embarrassing temptations.

But the Saviour in the flesh reminds us that our religion is not just about wisdom and noble aspirations. It is equally about prejudices and embarrassing temptations — not just in individuals but also in the church itself.

A Saviour who could use only wisdom and noble aspirations would not be of much use to most of us. The Saviour we need to worship in the flesh knows how to touch our prejudices, our temptations — and to empower us to transcend them.

The bishop as leader June 19,1995

The church has long claimed that its leadership policies are of divine institution and thus are in no way a reflection of the world. But history does not bear this out. The church has always to some extent aped the world, modelling its leadership on that of the secular world.

Jesus saw this as a problem right from the start. When the apostles were jockeying for positions, Jesus chided them: "You know that among the pagans their so-called rulers lord it over them, and their great ones make their authority felt. This is not to happen among you. No, anyone who wants to be great must be your servant. The Son of Man did not come to be served but to serve and give his life as a ransom for many" (Mk 10:42-45).

The early church, usually in the midst of persecution, could not have developed much hierarchical order in its underground existence, even if it had wanted to. Its practice of authority appears to have been dictated as much by social conditions as by any teaching of Christ. The theory of authority remained simple: those asked to do the work had the authority to do it.

And they never gave too much work to their leaders. They did not want to expose them and turn them into fodder for the lions.

But with the Peace of Constantine in AD 313, when Christians were accorded complete liberty to practise their religion without molestation, Jesus's dictum of not imitating the pagan rulers was, more often than not, observed in the breach — if not on the personal level, at least on the institutional plane.

In the days of the Roman Empire the actual running of an institution was seen as a burden. And so it was for bishops. While the *paterfamilias* image held sway, bishops disdained the task of actually running their dioceses. Deacons were called upon to sit at the bishop's right hand and become directly involved in the nitty-gritty of administration.

In the days of the divine right of kings, bishops' chairs quickly became thrones and the liturgy around them imitated the courts of the kings.

And when it became fashionable for the wealthy of this world to brag about being top executives of the board, bishops also discovered the joys of actually running their churches.

The church today is deeply involved in a corporate boardroom model of governance. And we have not been able to avoid all the shortcomings that come with this model. The secrecy, the power politics, the facelessness of the everyday exercise of authority, the frantic PR activity to ensure a good self-image for the institution — all these very worldly configurations which we in our better moments disdain have, with the adoption of this board model, found their place in our church.

The poor handling of the sexual abuse scandals that have rocked our church in recent years should bring home to the People of God just how costly it can be to run the church via the secretive, boardroom model.

Giving high priority to the preservation of one's good image, embracing the darkness of secrecy, and favouring "board members" (in this case, the clergy and religious) over the well-being of the general population (the laity) have no place in the Gospel, and the church cannot in truth justify such activity.

The current method employed in selecting bishops also follows this secretive boardroom model. The use of this model for the choosing of bishops is of much more recent origin.

Indeed, a current theology held by many in the highest positions in the church — a theology that does not go back as far as the Council of Trent (AD 1545-63) — sees the bishops alone as the magisterium.

Magisterium: People, Bishops, Pope

The methods for choosing bishops have likely covered the whole gamut of possibilities. Bishops have been chosen locally with only the laity having say (St. Leo the Great, surely one of the greatest popes the church has ever had, believed a bishop should exercise his office only for those who had a say in his selection — a fact conveniently overlooked by those who continually proclaim that the church is not a democracy), and bishops have been chosen in Rome with only the pope having a say.

Bishops have been appointed by Christian kings with the pope having a veto, and they have been chosen by the pope with the local king having a veto.

No one way has completely dominated, but through much of the church's life since the Protestant Reformation the principal method has been canons of the local cathedral making a proposal to the pope.

The very fact that the church has used so many different ways to select its bishops indicates that there is no superior way. The variety of approaches is a clear indication that each procedure has been fraught with difficulties.

Part of the rationale for having the pope select all the bishops in the western church is the removal of "local politics." And this must surely be a concern for all who treasure the church community living together in charity and peace.

The difficulty with this method is precisely that it does not remove the "local politics." The problem with beginning the discernment process with Rome is surely not the pope. It is the thousands upon thousands of miles.

The pope simply cannot know the candidates who would make good bishops in Saskatchewan. But, by using the secrecy of the corporate boardroom, no one knows who is actually doing the discerning. The community does not know if the de facto discerners have the confidence of the people or even of the local bishops.

In current practice, bishops' lists of candidates are easily overlooked; a superior candidate for the office can too easily be blackballed.

The church never found it easy to avoid the worldly pitfalls of the *paterfamilias* or divine-right-of-kings models. Nor is it likely to find healthy ways of using the corporate boardroom model — no matter how perfect and skilful a pope sits on the Chair of Peter. The problem is not the pope but the model itself.

The church today is fast changing its idea of what a bishop is, and as we change our idea of bishop, our ideas about their selection is also likely to change. The pope in his recent encyclical asked theologians and leaders in all the Christian churches to help him discern how the Petrine office must change to be of better service to the church. We must acknowledge right off that we cannot rethink the office of the Bishop of Rome without such a shift in thinking having a profound effect on the meaning of the Episcopal office in the church.

According to the corporate structure, if the pope has total say about the choosing and dismissing of bishops (the French bishops were not consulted in the dismissal of liberal Bishop Jacques Gaillot) then they are, de facto, subordinates to the pope. But the Second Vatican Council, in its document On the Church, has expressly denied that, emphasizing that each local church is a full and complete church, and that all the bishops "together with their head, the supreme pontiff, have supreme and full authority over the universal church."

Bishops play their essential role in the teaching magisterium of the church, not by knowing their theology better than the rest of the church, nor by the magic of an ordination that makes them superior beings, but by their marriage to their church, by being so close to the People of God that they can pray in their name and discern from them the living faith of the church.

With the restoration of the ancient thinking about bishops as the gatherers in prayer of the faith of the People of God, with seeing them as the guardians of the *sensus fidelium* (the sense of the faithful), we will quite naturally look for new ways of choosing our bishops. History has shown us there is no perfect way of choosing bishops; being, as we are, a sinful church, there will always be difficulties, but once the *sensus fidelium* is restored to its proper place as the final authority in the church, it will be difficult to overlook the wisdom of St. Leo who insisted that all the People of God have a say in the selection of the one who is called to make the faith of the community a song to the Lord.

Ministry and authority April 8, 1991

The practice of authority in the early church was simple: those who are asked to do the work have the authority to do it.

This dictum took on some unforeseen results with the Peace of Constantine (AD 313). When the Roman state, as it had long done with its pagan priests, began paying the Christian clergy, thus freeing them from doing other work, Christians naturally expected these suddenly underemployed citizens to do most of the work in the church.

It did not take the clergy long to develop a theology of authority to suit their new position in the church. With little to support any model of authority in the New Testament, they turned to the Old and found there a wealth of handy material. In the ordination rituals the bishops (and to a lesser extent, priests) became the successor, not only of Old Testament priests, but also of the prophets and kings.

All the charisms (divine influences) of authority came to be centred in the sacrament of orders. The priest was not just ordained; to symbolize his complete mastery he was ordained in a sevenfold manner; he was not simply ordained priest but also, among others, Mass server and doorkeeper.

Authority for the clergy was now complete; the clergy not only had exclusive rights in defining dogmas and in determining who could receive the sacraments; they also had full authority to pick the colour of the carpet and to set the church's thermostat.

It took many more centuries, but in time the priest even took over the very title that had originally given all Christians their name — *alter Christus*, another Christ.

With this development, Christian ministry was turned inside out. In ancient times the priest represented Christ insofar as he was the spokesperson for the church, the living body of Christ; now he was a special presence of Christ to the community, and thus its prophet, priest, and king.

In the Second Vatican Council, the church struggled to re-establish the dignity of all the baptized. It reminded Christians that together they were the People of God, constituting God's presence in the world.

But the church has done nothing on an official level to examine the development of orders and the clergy's exclusive right to exercise authority. It has not even begun to face the Lord's dictum that it may not be a hierarchy according to the world, with some on the top and the rest on the bottom.

We in Canada can rejoice in the leadership our bishops have given us. But still we concur with Bishop Albert H. Ottenweller of Steubenville, Ohio, who complains about the "Father knows best" theory of leadership in our church. He states there will be no true church renewal as long as we have laypeople on the bottom and the clergy calling the shots. Changing that model, he declares, "is the hardest nut to crack in church renewal."

It is crucial that we have the honesty and the courage to open up fully the question of ministry in the church. We cannot arrive at satisfactory answers to the questions of priest shortages, priestly celibacy, or the ordination of women with our current practice of ministry.

Could it not be that the Spirit is calling us back to pre-Constantine practices in which the ministries were not centred in a class of people but greatly shared among many people? Need our confessors always be those who perform the Eucharist for us, or those who anoint our sick also be those who decide church policy?

St. Paul often seems to indicate that some are called to be confessors, some administrators, some baptizers, some the visitors of the sick. It never occurred to him that some day the church would be so fortunate as to find all these charisms in the same person.

We are an episcopal church   June 13, 1988

Since at least sub-apostolic times — the early period after the Resurrection — oversight *(episcopé)* in each local church (diocese) has been exercised by a resident bishop. His chair *(cathedra)*, the heart of the cathedral church, was experienced as the unifying focus of the local church.

The church universal was seen as a family of churches joined together. This unity of the churches was symbolized by the college of pastoral concern the bishops formed with the Bishop of Rome who was called to sit on the Chair of Peter.

Thus the Second Vatican Council, recalling the faith of the early church, taught that all the resident bishops, together with the pope, are to exercise *episcopé* over the whole church.

No structures have been developed since the council to put this teaching into effect. In fact much has taken place in the last two decades to undermine this council concern to go back to the traditional ways of governance. And it is no secret that many in the Roman Curia are happy with this. They fear the decentralization which is inherent in the traditional bishop-centred model.

Those favouring centralization have emphasized that the pope can speak in his own name, while ignoring the fact that no pope has ever done so. The Christian community is not reminded that whenever a pope has spoken *ex cathedra* (infallibly), he has made certain that he was speaking in consort with his bishop colleagues.

Several developments have weakened the traditional authority exercised by resident bishops. Some of them find their home right in the Curia. Each department head is automatically ordained a bishop. Thus the head of the Vatican media department or the principal judge in the marriage tribunal is an ordained bishop.

The relationship of a bishop to his local church is largely ignored. In this curial theology the rite of ordination itself, rather than the gathering of the faith community around the bishop, is seen as the essential element. No wonder so little attention is given in this theology to the *sensus fidelium*, the sense of the faithful, as the ultimate discernment of fidelity to the story of Jesus.

The idea of the local church is stretched to the limit in the growing practice of naming special bishops to the armed forces of countries. We tend to see only administrative advantages to such a practice in countries like Canada or the United States. But what happens when the army of Argentina or Chile has its own bishop, a bishop according to its own liking? It has been very difficult and not a little embarrassing for resident bishops in Argentina to experience the army as a church unto itself. No wonder General Augusto Pinochet has asked the pope for a bishop for his armed forces.

Another break with having bishops resident in local churches — and one much more destructive of traditional episcopal governance — has been the creation of personal prelatures. The secretive movement Opus Dei has been given its own bishop, thus making its members virtually independent of local episcopal oversight.

Many lay movements have been asking Rome for models similar to that of the organization Opus Dei. If that is not possible, they have requested to be directly under the pope. (They know he personally will not be able to exercise specific leadership for them; thus they hope to find a powerful, and usually conservative, official among the Curia members who will allow them to follow a way of life they know the local bishop does not approve of.)

The struggle of right-wing lay movements in the church for independence of local oversight was one of the principal struggles of the last world synod in Rome. It is not at all clear if the pope is going to give these lay movements the independence they seek. Resident bishops from around the world have told the pope in the bluntest of terms what they think of the Opus Dei model.

Archbishop Marcel Lefebvre of France is asking for even more. He has given the pope three demands: the formation of a Vatican commission to deal juridically with tradition, the right to three bishops for his society, and the total independence of his priests from local bishops.

There is a terrible irony in these demands. In granting the latter two, the traditional governance of the church would be completely destroyed. Thus Lefebvre, who claims tradition is his great love, sacrifices this very tradition so as to obtain a church he can find himself at home in.

And it is no minor tradition he is asking the church to waive in his special case. It is the founding principle of order, the central role of the residential bishop whereby the community is gathered and God's praises are sung around the table of the kingdom.

As much room as possible must be given to Lefebvre and to others uncomfortable with the Second Vatican Council, especially now that its far-reaching ramifications become more discernible — for laity (women included!), for priests and bishops, for a secular church in a secular world.

But it must not be at the expense of the church's episcopal nature. To be sure, the Office of Peter is a great grace in the church and there are unique moments in history when the Office of Peter is absolutely critical for the church. Yet at all times the local bishop is called to be tied to his people as a sign of unity and love.

This latter ministry will prove critical as we face the issues confronting the church today. With the followers of Lefebvre it is really not an issue of tradition; it is fundamentally a question of whether or not they want to belong to the local church — which, according to the ancients, is the only church there is.

Papal primacy

November 11, 1998

Pope John Paul II has just celebrated 20 years on the Chair of Peter. Editorials in both the religious and secular media marking the occasion have had high praise for his work for the poor and those imprisoned behind the Iron Curtain.

His great influence in social justice affairs was evident when practically all the mainline churches in the First World took up his call to make the

Year 2000 a jubilee year. Rather than see the beginning of the new millennium marked with apocalyptic terror, the pope called for forgiveness of the unjust and often unpayable debt saddling the world's poorest nations.

A good case can be made that never since AD 1054, when Constantinople and Rome severed ties, has a call from the Chair of Peter had such a positive response as did John Paul's call for a jubilee.

Of course, 20 years in the papal office is a long time — and there have been criticisms as well as praise for the one exercising papal primacy. The criticism has focused mainly on the centralization of church governance that has taken place during this pope's tenure in office.

It is important to note, however, that throughout his papacy John Paul seems to have been aware of — and personally troubled by — the exercise of the papal office by his predecessors and by himself.

Early in his pontificate, while in Toronto, he made an extraordinary assertion. He told leaders of the Canadian Christian churches: "I am an optimist about our unity, and I hope the pope is not the biggest obstacle." Then, pensively echoing words first spoken by Paul VI, he added: "We know it is ourselves who are the problem."

Throughout his ministry John Paul has been especially sensitive to the concerns of the East and has left no doubt that he dreams of ending the 950-year split between Constantinople and Rome. In a special apostolic letter to the eastern churches, he speaks most tenderly about his calling as pope. "Peter's task," he writes, "is to search constantly for ways that will help preserve unity. There he must not create obstacles but must open up paths."

Then the pope puts words in the mouth of Christ: "It is as if the Master himself wanted to tell Peter: 'Remember that you are weak, that you, too, need endless conversion. You are able to strengthen others only insofar as you are aware of your own weakness.'"

In 1995 the pope ploughed more new ground. In the first-ever encyclical addressed to all Christians, he called on the leaders of other churches to join him "in a patient and familial dialogue" to find new and better ways of exercising papal primacy.

But he did more than that. He hinted strongly that this study should centre on the first 1,000 years of church history when the churches remained united. Thus he left the door wide open to a critical evaluation of the more recent developments concerning expansion of the papal office.

The pope realizes that developments in travel and communications have in many ways enabled the world to become a global village. These same developments have also enabled the church to centralize its exercise of authority in ways that were utterly impossible even 50 years ago. The papal encyclical *Ut Unum Sint* (That they may be one) expressly asked the churches to help him evaluate that development.

The Vatican document, released by the Congregation for the Doctrine of the Faith, stands out in stark contrast — certainly in the spirit if not in the letter — to this constant theme of the pope.

Whereas the pope strongly suggested that papal primacy may have been adequately clarified in the first 1,000 years (as were the contents of the Scriptures, the formulation of the creeds, and the structure of the ministry as deacons, priests, and bishops), the new Vatican text leaves much room for new developments: "Just the fact that a certain function was not exercised previously by the pope does not authorize the conclusion that such a function never can be exercised in the future as the competence of the primate."

The text adds, "It is clear that only the pope (or the pope with an ecumenical council) has, as successor of Peter, the authority and the competence to have the last word on how to exercise his pastoral ministry in the universal church."

With one of the few hints that this text was indeed written 25 years after the Second Vatican Council rather than after the first council in 1870, the text concedes that "all the bishops must care for the entire church," but it stresses that the pope has the responsibility to do this "with full and supreme power."

At first glance this text does not leave much room for the advice the pope called for in his encyclical. Some maybe will conclude that the Vatican sees this coming of the reformulation process on papal primacy — and come it will — much like labour/management negotiations: both sides always put more on the table than they can hope to get and the bargaining begins.

But this is hardly the way to ask our separated brothers and sisters to help us "find new and better ways for the exercising of papal primacy."

A living magisterium

April 3, 1989

The recent meeting of American bishops with the Vatican dealt with many issues. But behind them all was the meaning and place of the bishop in the church. At the insistence of Cardinal Joseph Ratzinger, head of the Congregation for the Doctrine of the Faith, the teaching office of the bishop became the central issue.

According to the cardinal, the American bishops had in practice, if not also in theory, "abdicated to theologians their role as teachers of the faith." This growing influence of theologians is creating, he said, "increasing uncertainty and confusion" among Catholics.

According to Ratzinger, the bishops alone constitute the magisterium of the church. The cardinal added that only through careful selection of future bishops is the proper balance between bishops and theologians to be restored.

Ratzinger plays down the theologians' role in the development of doctrine. For the cardinal the proper balance between the two offices is to have the bishops be "the voice of the faith" and the theologians to "reflect" on this voice and thus "deepen (our) understanding of the faith."

The cardinal is especially fearful of theologians because they now have access to the media. "These theologians today have influence not just in the world of scientific research and university teaching, but through the mass media they bring into the public arena a concert that frequently is dissonant, to the point that their voices drown out that of the bishop-evangelist."

There is confusion in the church today, but we must not allow that to stampede us into solutions that have the potential of creating even more confusion for the future church.

Painting theologians as the bad guys who are usurping a magisterial role in the church when they in fact should have none makes a mockery of our church history.

No bishop, no pope, gave Thomas Aquinas (whose radical works led to a major book-burning spectacle in Paris) an invitation to the Council of Lyons (AD 1245). He went in his own name, as a magister of theology.

The great Dominican and Jesuit theologians at Trent (AD 1545-47) did not wait for a summons from a bishop to take their place at this council.

We should not forget that the very word "magisterium" derives not from medieval bishops' work in the church but from the leadership role the theologians played in preserving and developing the Christian faith. This happened through long centuries in which bishops enjoyed being lords in this world more than undertaking the gruelling work of making the faith good news to every age and culture.

The idea that bishops alone form the magisterium of the church dates back not even as far as Trent.

Confusion can surely result when theologians expound their work in popular journals and weekend religion pages in secular newspapers. But the alternative of keeping all speculation from the people until it has been judged correct is infinitely more problematic.

In such a theological climate the ancient church's ultimate criterion of judgment, the *sensus fidelium* (the sense of the faithful), is totally lost. In this view bishops can judge the rightness of a doctrine without any reference to or relationship with the people — and there is not one church father who would not condemn such thinking as heretical.

In the years before the Protestant Reformation many bishops — and theologians, too! — tried to preserve the purity of the message of the Scriptures by discouraging the people from reading the Bible. May we not attempt a return to such methods by trying to exclude the Christian faithful from the never-ending struggle to incarnate the word of salvation in modern culture.

The confusion today in theology is not simply a matter of theologians not knowing their place. Much of the fuzzy thinking today centres around the role and power of the bishop.

Today on being ordained, a bishop automatically becomes a member of the magisterium. With his ordination the theological opinions of the ordinand virtually become church teaching. In a certain twist of irony, Cardinal Ratzinger calls for a selection of new bishops "who have a strong theological base capable of re-establishing that balance (between theologians and bishops) which has been lost."

A Leo or an Augustine in the West, a Basil or a Chrysostom in the East, would never judge a bishop's effectiveness to teach with his knowledge of theology. They taught (preached) as pastors, not as doctors. Their power to become defenders of the faith did not spring from their knowledge of theology — even though few if any could match them in this regard. It sprang from their ability to discern the faith of their people, to be in touch with the *sensus fidelium*.

It is not difficult to surmise what any of these great church fathers would have thought of the magisterial power of the whole corps of curial bishops who in reality do not preside over any diocese or church.

It is in being tied to his people that a bishop becomes a defender of the faith. The early church realized that individual churches or dioceses can at times fall into heresy. So they broadened the task of the bishop; as a member of a college of bishops he must take on responsibility for the whole church.

But this latter truth never negated the former. It is in his closeness to the faith of the people that the bishop finds the power of the living word of God.

A living magisterium is theologians challenging and enriching — always pushing the People of God to a deeper commitment in bringing a good word to today's world; it is pastors (pope and bishops together) gathering the faith into a powerful expression of new hope; it is the People of God standing in awe of who they are in God's kingdom.

St. Augustine tells us how important it is for the bishop to be tied to his people. For him it was his strength, his salvation. "What I am for you terrifies me; what I am with you strengthens me. For you I am a bishop; but with you I am a Christian. The former is a title of duty; the latter, one of grace. The former is a danger; the latter, my salvation."

Simple Gospels   July 20, 1987

During the period before Martin Luther, church leaders gave simpler and simpler answers to the faithful. As the church's official theology became immersed in absurd complications of a nominalistic philosophy causing it to lose any real relevance, in almost direct proportion the spirituality fed to the people lost any subtlety. Likely there was no other time in church history when such simple answers were handed to the People of God. While German Dominican preacher John Tetzel's zeal in selling indulgences — in part to build St. Peter's in Rome — was not fully endorsed by the church, there surely was no great effort by church authorities to correct him.

Tetzel was not an anomaly in the church. He did not originate the famous couplet that provided the church coffers with so much easy money:

"As soon as coin in coffer rings

The soul from purgatory springs."

It is hard to imagine a simpler theology — or one with clearer answers.

To the very marrow of his bones Luther experienced the destructive force of simple answers. It was a great relief for him to find St. Paul preaching a Gospel of justification by faith, not by knowledge.

It has always been difficult for the church to remember that Jesus was very hesitant to give answers. Parables and paradoxes were more to his taste. Jesus's teaching never had easy or simple answers. His teaching opened us to the paradox of human existence, never freed us from it.

He spoke about losing one's life to save it. He warned those who tried to make certain of their life that they would end up losing it. For Jesus there simply was no alternative to trust, to faith in his Father.

But there is a part of us that does not want to or cannot trust. We need to know — and so we are ready to prove the Lord wrong and attempt to bypass the paradox which the Father wisely planted in every human heart.

St. Peter's was not the only thing built on this human frailty. Many televangelists today preach a gospel that rivals Tetzel's for a lack of subtlety. And the money has been rolling in to the tune of millions of dollars.

Not surprisingly, these fundamentalist preachers stress the need to know that one is saved. One of the key elements in the born-again experience is the sure knowledge of personal salvation that accompanies it.

This simple religious base cannot handle things that are too complicated. It may be all right for black-and-white issues — and this is how quite a few born-again Christians view such things as abortion, homosexuality, and feminism — but they cannot deal with such muddy issues as social justice and ecological responsibility.

Their politics becomes as simple — and destructive — as their theology. It too is based on knowledge, on simple truths that answer all questions. The Cold-War split between East and West becomes part of God's plan in which the righteous march gloriously to Armageddon.

It is frightening to see how many Americans are buying this gospel. For them, it is the epitome of what it means to be an American.

The philosophy at work in Iran and Nicaragua is no different from the CIA's activity in Chile, Brazil, or the Philippines. The world will not be at peace until this simple Tetzeline gospel of American/Christian righteousness is rooted out of the American soul.

Celebrating Pentecost   May 8, 2002

While it may not bear the endorsement of history, it is fashionable today to see Pentecost as the feast that celebrates the birthday of the church. Pope John XXIII certainly believed this and fervently prayed that the ecumenical council he called would be "a new Pentecost, a birth of a new church."

If one had pressed the pope on what this "new church" would be like, he would have freely acknowledged that he did not know — that's why he called the council! — but he would have assured those questioning him that he was certain of one thing: that we needed to be optimistic if we hoped to drink deeply of the Spirit.

Of course, it is not easy to be optimistic in the face of the unknown. When confronted by uncertainty, human wisdom tells us to stick to the tried and true. Optimistically embracing a Spirit who blows where she will in times of crisis is foolhardy, to say the least.

But Pentecost has a tradition of turning things upside down. Whereas it is normal for young people to get lost in dreams and older folk to find consolation in prayer and holy visions, St. Peter pointed out that when the Holy Spirit was poured out, the young saw visions and the old dreamed dreams (Acts 2:17).

To be faithful to this paradoxical Spirit, the liturgy of Pentecost gives us two images of the Spirit side by side, images that are not easy to reconcile with each other. No church worth its salt can be born of just one or the other image. Unless the church is struggling constantly to be faithful both to a Spirit of wind and fire and to the Spirit of the gentle kiss, it will lose much of its saving power by idolizing its human structures.

In the Gospel for Pentecost we are given a gentle Spirit. Echoing the first creation, Jesus gently breathes on the disciples and creates a church of mutual forgiveness. It is a Spirit of tenderness, of utmost delicacy. It spells the end of chaos by creating, as did the Spirit in the beginning of Genesis, a world of order and meaning.

Those who do not want the church to change, those who had no desire for a pope who was ready to open the windows to let in some fresh air, those who tend to view the church in orderly and hierarchical terms love this Spirit.

At first glance, such a Spirit enables the church leadership in Boston to reject out of hand any notion that more room should be given to the laity in the governance of the church. We get a hint here of what can happen when only one image of the Spirit is chosen.

So the liturgy for Pentecost gives us a second image, an image that could hardly be more different from the first. This time the Spirit comes in the dangerous combination of wind and fire. No structure can long endure when fire fanned by a mighty wind attacks. Even structures long held sacred can be consumed in a flash.

Obviously those who fall in love with this Spirit are worlds apart from those who adore the gentle, peaceful Spirit Jesus breathed forth. But it is important to remember that firebrands within the church who place little value on structures that have been lovingly constructed over hundreds of years can be as harmful to the church as clerics who idolize self-serving canons.

Pentecost reminds us that the church needs both manifestations of the Spirit. We need a Spirit of order. We need a church with a concrete form. We need dogmas. We need a sense of tradition — not only those of a thousand years or more, but some not even one hundred years old. People need a sense of tradition in their daily lives.

But we also need a Spirit who is never satisfied with the church we have built, even though it was built with great love and devout zeal.

We need a Spirit who continues to ask questions — fundamental, painful questions. Are we allowing the church to take on a Native face? Are we allowing our Jewish sisters and brothers a home with us in the New Jerusalem — on their own terms? Are we truly open to the gifts of all religions for our troubled world?

Are we permitting the Spirit to show us concretely that in Christ Jesus there is neither male nor female? Are we prepared to allow the Spirit to make development the new word for peace? How much freedom are we allowing the Spirit to create new structures, new ministries, new expressions of the ministerial priesthood itself?

Do we ask why conservative Anglican priests coming into the Catholic Church can remain married while Czech priests, who risked much to be ordained in a hostile communist territory (marriage was usually a necessary cover since so many "celibate" priests functioned as double agents), cannot, now that the Iron Curtain has come down, function as priests in the Roman Rite unless they renounce their wives?

Why, we must ask, do the American cardinals fail to see that the current crisis is really not one of pedophilia or homosexuality, but rather one of leadership, a leadership accountable to the People of God? Indeed, this crisis strongly reminds us how much the church needs a Spirit of wind and fire who insists that we never absolutize church and clerical structures.

The ancient monastic spiritual directors (abbas) knew well the wisdom of the seemingly contradictory images of the Spirit. For example, should a bishop who wants at all costs peace and order in the church ask for a word, he would get one to meditate on such as: "I have come not to bring peace but the sword." But let a bishop come forward who is not at all uncomfortable in attacking outdated structures and he would be told "to eat" the following word: "Blessed are the peacemakers."

The Spirit of Pentecost promises us salvation — but not without the paradox of the cross of Christ. For the church to renew itself today, for it to have a rebirth of the dynamism of the first Pentecost, a dynamism that undermined the mighty Roman Empire, it needs lovers of meekness, order, and peace who are ready to breathe forth fire. At the same time, it also needs firebrands who can regularly get lost in quiet contemplation.

The bystanders at the first Pentecost celebration could not understand why the disciples were acting as they did. Their activity was beyond human explanation, and thus was understandable only as a work of the Spirit. This is true of all church activity, if it is truly to be the salvific work of the kingdom.

People today will see the Spirit at work in us only if we allow the Spirit to take us where we would rather not go.

Dream for the church

March 12, 1997

All long-standing large institutions find it difficult to change. The church, a mammoth institution with a long history that is both its glory and its cross, is no exception.

Anyone who thinks that the church of Christ himself can, without major difficulties, navigate tidal waves, such as the new dreams created by the Second Vatican Council, certainly has had no lessons in anthropology, psychology, or sociology.

The problems are not new; the council itself certainly had its own share. It is no secret that many in the church's highest positions of authority were never comfortable with many of the council dreams. But the council bishops made an important tactical decision: they never tried to defeat the minority, small in number though it was.

Many might be wont to think this a tragic mistake, since this minority has managed to resurrect itself and now has considerable influence in key Vatican circles.

Others, rightly we think, believe it was anything but a tragic mistake. Without a strong, credible pull in the church to stay with the tried and true, the church would never have the wherewithal to struggle creatively for a new expression of its life in today's vastly different world.

The church institution is called to touch with salvation people's innermost hearts. It is naive to think that this goal can be achieved without a life-or-death struggle. All we have to do is look at our own lives: who would we be without struggles, struggles that call us to examine the very core of our being?

We believe that the final authority in the church is not the pope alone, nor the pope with the bishops. It is the *sensus fidelium*, the sense of the faithful, for what is right and proper.

This is no liberal statement; indeed, it is the most conservative of ideas. If it is difficult to get 2,000 bishops to start seeing things in new ways, try it with a billion people!

It is only in the struggle, in the clash of ideas, that a new church is born. And it is born slowly, painfully slowly. Many things go into the mix — not the least important being an extremely conservative Diocese of Rome.

Rome has always been conservative, always been a bit too ready to rely on law and abstract theology to carry the day.

But Rome was never the whole story, and only in the darkest days of the church — when the pope was both a civil and an ecclesial giant — did Rome think it was called by God to grace the church and world as "the one and only."

No, Rome is not the whole story. We must, for instance, give solid theological weight to the church's (lay and clerical) non-reception of many aspects of the natural law arguments against artificial contraception, to the faithful's voting with their feet regarding the way the sacrament of reconciliation is practised in the church, and, though the jury is certainly still out, to the church's reception of the current teaching on women and the priesthood.

There is no way around the struggle. A new *sensus fidelium* is certainly coming to birth, not despite the struggle but precisely because of it and through it.

We should not be surprised that, in this critically important time of consensus building, many will seek simpler solutions. Catholics of Vision (Canada) centre their petition around "an all-pervading atmosphere of freedom among the People of God." Human Life International, on the other hand, dreams of a church with no struggle. Freedom is exactly what Benedictine Father Paul Marx of HLI cannot stomach. It appears that anything but black-and-white structures elicit his burning sarcasm.

It's surely hard to argue against freedom — where there is no room to make mistakes, there is no room for growth — but there is a lot more at stake than space to form and follow one's conscience.

Without our traditional Catholic way of consensus building, the formation of conscience can easily be reduced to French Revolutionary chivalry or rugged American individualism. (We believe, for instance, that a good case can be made that much of North American Catholic liberalism is based more on American secular individualism than on solid theological principles.)

Catholicism, we must remember, is first and last an Episcopal church. We stand or fall as an institution on the health of the order of bishops. But we must hasten to add: the dogmatism of a carefully selected hierarchy is anything but healthy.

Bishops do not become special persons in the magisterium because of their ordination, nor by virtue of the theology they hold — no matter how orthodox it is. The thinking in vogue today that, on being ordained a bishop, one automatically becomes a member of the magisterium is relatively recent in the church.

Of old, bishops were seen to be so close to the people that the ancients spoke of them as being married to their church. Transfers of bishops from diocese to diocese was anathema.

So for the church today to appoint bishops not known for their listening skills is to systematically weaken the magisterium and to prolong unnecessarily the struggle to a new *sensus fidelium*.

The first and last job of the bishop is to give focus to this sensus and make it at one and the same time the power of the church in the world and the new song of praise in the kingdom.

Once the *sensus fidelium* is restored to its proper place as the final authority in the church, it will be difficult to overlook the wisdom of Pope St. Leo the Great — certainly one of the greatest pastors ever to sit on the Chair of Peter — who insisted that all the People of God have a say in the selection of the one who is called to make the faith of the community a song to the Lord.

Cardinals differ

February 9, 2000

It is not often that cardinals differ publicly in the church, especially not when one of the cardinals is the prefect of the Congregation for the Doctrine of the Faith, Cardinal Joseph Ratzinger.

At the recent Synod for Europe, Cardinal Carlo Maria Martini of Milan criticized the congregation, but without directly referring to Ratzinger by name, when he noted that the church has tied itself in "disciplinary and doctrinal knots."

Cardinal Johannes Willebrands of Holland, in his final visit to North America as president of the curial Council for Promoting Christian Unity, publicly took Ratzinger to task for his interpretation of the Catholic Church "subsisting" in the Body of Christ. Ratzinger, he noted, had practically identified the church with the Body of Christ, while the council saw the Body of Christ as a much larger concept in which the Catholic Church subsists.

Cardinal Franz König of Austria, one of the key leaders at the council and recognized for his part in getting the conclave of cardinals to elect Karol Wojtyla (John Paul II) as pope, publicly debated Ratzinger's understanding of the church ban on "artificial birth control." He pointed out that Ratzinger's pessimistic understanding of nature — a critically important element in any theological use of "natural law" — was not consistent with the traditional understanding of the church, powerfully presented in the 13th century by Saint Thomas Aquinas.

While all three of these "tiffs" among cardinals became widespread news events, they lacked the significance of the current disagreement between the chief watchdog of church doctrine and Cardinal Pierre Eyt of Bordeaux in France.

Eyt, a well-known scholar and doctrinal expert, has the confidence of many people in high places. The pope has personally named him to four synods of bishops and appointed him to the commission that finalized the text of the catechism of the Catholic Church. Maybe most interesting of all, Eyt is a member of the Congregation for the Doctrine of the Faith, and so has an insider's experience of the workings of that zealous custodial team which Ratzinger heads.

Eyt's criticism does not centre on doctrinal decisions made by that curial body which, incidentally, was known before the Second Vatican Council as the Holy Office of the Inquisition. He plumbs deeper, questioning Ratzinger's methodology and the very meaning the prefect gives to church criticism itself.

Eyt believes the congregation does not appreciate the ideas of today's lay Catholics on questions of theology, politics, bioethics — to name but a few areas. The church hierarchy's dialogue with them, says Eyt, "seems to be going nowhere."

Eyt and Ratzinger have radically different interpretations concerning the church's "institutional problems," a polite term used by both cardinals. In fact, this expression is very close in meaning to Martini's now famous expression "disciplinary and doctrinal knots."

Ratzinger sees these "institutional problems" as a reflection of a deeper crisis of faith. For him these "problems" are in fact only secondary. They are "the consequence, not the cause, of a crisis of faith in modern times," Ratzinger notes.

It is such thinking, Eyt argues, that has countered the openness the council brought to the church. No wonder, he adds, that dialogue "seems to be going nowhere."

In his very different view of church life, Eyt does not see these "institutional problems" as necessarily bad. They are, rather, part of an "indivisible whole" prompting the church to urgently address the burning issues of the day.

Ultimately, Eyt intimates, the current absence of that openness which was the gift of the council is really not about safeguarding the purity of the faith; rather, it is about procrastination, about avoiding those issues of the day which are crying out for resolution.

Theological debate

July 7, 1999

Two of today's heavyweight Jesuit theologians, Avery Dulles and Richard McCormick, have tackled from radically different positions one of the key theological issues facing the church. The question: How can one give full weight to the authority of doctrine while at the same time leaving ample room for its development?

Dulles centred his presentation around the radical need in the church for a teaching authority; McCormick chose to focus on the other pole of the issue: if theology is not free to develop, it dies; today's formulation will never fulfill tomorrow's needs.

Of course, both of these theologians have laid claim to an absolutely essential point. If either one of these poles is lost, the other loses its power to lead us to the truth.

Often we would like simple answers rather than undertaking the delicate act of balancing one off against the other, but what else should we expect from followers of the itinerant preacher of Galilee who always refused to give fixed agendas but rather challenged would-be disciples to grapple with his parables and paradoxes?

That two of the church's major theologians should profoundly question each other's theological balance of these two poles should not disappoint us. Rather, we should take it as a sign that today's church is still struggling, and struggling mightily, to achieve the "right balance" for the present moment.

The Second Vatican Council was not afraid to present both poles on various issues and leave it to the Holy Spirit to find the right balance for today — realizing also that today's balance may not be what is needed in tomorrow's church.

We have editorialized on the council's wisdom in emphasizing the importance of both the centralizing tendency of the Petrine office and the decentralizing nature of episcopal collegiality. How these two notions are to balance one another was not something the council members knew — but they did know that the whole church would be tragically weakened if one pole absorbed the other.

The council took a similar approach to the priesthood of Christ. The council reminded us forcefully that the People of God formed the one priesthood of Jesus Christ. But this did not prevent them from teaching that the ministerial priesthood of the church's presbyters was ontologically (to its core) different from the priesthood of the laity. How these two statements can be put together was left by the council to the Holy Spirit. But again, the council members realized that if one came to stand over and above the other, the church's hold on the saving truth of Christ would be jeopardized.

It is interesting to note that, while Dulles and McCormick allowed ample room for the other's position, one issue clearly divided them: the question of birth control. On this issue Dulles was not about to give McCormick any room. *Roma locuta, causa finita:* Rome has spoken and the issue is closed.

But it should seem strange to us that suddenly there exists one black-and-white issue, one issue that rises above the human condition of paradox, one issue that has a simple answer.

It is good for us to look once again at the Canadian bishops' response to Pope Paul VI's 1968 encyclical *Humanae Vitae* (Of Human Life). For too long we have allowed those who believe Christianity can be mapped out in simple, straightforward laws of conduct to imply that our bishops were not as faithful to the pope as they should have been.

The bishops endorsed strongly the teaching of Paul VI that sexual intercourse must be open to life, that a contraceptive mentality would gravely weaken the binding force a couple's sexuality should have in their marriage.

But they also acknowledged that sexual expression in a healthy marriage needs no justification. All true acts of love between marriage partners are to bind them more closely together.

How these two poles find a balance is a wisdom not readily given to celibates. It is in the human struggle, honestly engaged in, that each couple finds its saving truth.

It is interesting to note that Paul VI expressly told Cardinal George Flahiff of Winnipeg that he had read the Canadian bishops' statement and was very happy with it. Not for a moment did he imply that the Canadian bishops were unfaithful; rather, he rejoiced in their nuancing of a critically important moral question.

We as church must, in all the difficult questions facing us, remember with humility that itinerant preacher who so often exasperated his contemporaries by refusing to give any answer other than another parable or paradox.

Maintaining orthodoxy January 15, 1990

Shortly after the Council of Trent (AD 1545-63), the Roman Curia issued its Roman Catechism. This catechism was meant to be the church's mark of orthodoxy. Likely its authors never realized how successful this document would be; it played a major role in freezing the concept of orthodoxy for nearly 400 years.

Having official catechisms is great if one does not want anything to change in the church; much less appreciated if one believes the apostolic tradition must be fluid, ever ready, as new circumstances dictate, to embrace, question, or enrich the developing cultures in which the church finds itself.

Not surprisingly, few official members at the Second Vatican Council wanted a new catechism to follow their work of radically redirecting the church. They were deeply conscious of the changing nature of the church and had no desire to freeze the church in the mould of their work, like the Roman Catechism had done after Trent.

That the new catechism, now issued by Cardinal Joseph Ratzinger in its first-draft form, follows almost exactly the form of its famous predecessor indicates how much has changed since Paul VI closed the Vatican Council. Many in the church now want to give "an official teaching status" to church teachings in virtually every area of dogmatic thought. That this procedure, if successful, will bring about a new freeze in Catholic thought does not appear to be a concern.

The catechism is not likely to bring the peace its authors are hoping for. Too many Catholics today are educated well enough to know that the issuing of a catechism does not thereby raise its content to such a level of certitude that it becomes Catholic dogma, authentic church teachings whose central kernel have something to say to peoples of all ages and culture.

The catechism, by its very form, will tend to overstate the dogmatic certitude given to the theological opinions of the school of thought of those with the power to dictate the content of the catechism, but this is not the principal worry we have with the process.

Our principal concern is with the process itself, and with the position bishops have in it. Ratzinger has issued the draft catechism to the bishops under a stamp of secrecy. It is for bishops' eyes only. This stamp of secrecy says much about what the authors of the catechism mean by calling bishops "the teachers of the faith."

The bishops do not need to discern what their people believe; they are not even allowed to present the draft to them and ask them if it resonates with their experience of what it means to be Catholic. The bishops are seen as capable of deciding what the people should believe. They stand outside and above the "People of God" — a phrase the council issued as its central appellative for the church itself.

Gone is the notion of the *sensus fidelium*, gone is the notion that the bishop is teacher of his people insofar as he stands in their midst — so close to the local church that he can speak and pray in its name. That such central notions of our Catholic tradition are so cavalierly disregarded in the process whereby the church will be given a new catechism does not bode well that it will be a useful tool as the church attempts to inculturate the faith, that is, to make it part of every culture, in one of the fastest changing times in human history.

Runcie prepares for Rome visit   October 2, 1989

Archbishop Robert Runcie of Canterbury, head of the Anglican Communion, promises to create an ecumenical storm during his forthcoming visit to the Vatican. In a warm-up press conference for the visit, he told journalists, "Anglicans are beginning to recognize and welcome the possibility of a universal primacy to be exercised by a pope."

He made no effort to be subtle: it wasn't the theological theory that bothered him; it was the current Roman practice that frightened him. "We would want to stress the necessity for a real autonomy," he added, and gave as an example the appointment of the bishops.

Catholics should not be surprised that prominent church leaders are shooting straight from the hip about various Catholic institutions, including the papacy itself. Did not Pope Paul VI during his visit to the World Council of Churches in Geneva acknowledge that he (meaning his office) was the greatest difficulty to ecumenism? And, significantly, did he not at that time also ask the other churches to help Christians one and all in surmounting that difficulty?

Runcie is telling us that Anglicans have taken up Paul's request — with some dramatic results: Anglicans are "beginning to welcome" a universal primacy exercised by the pope. But he is also asking us if we Catholics have done anything to lessen the ecumenical stumbling block Paul referred to while in Geneva.

Runcie does not mince words; he goes for the jugular. He questions the current papal practice of appointing bishops — a practice that has become for many the symbol of what can go wrong with a ministry that does not have any effective counterbalances. Runcie wants nothing to do with a church that is centralized around an absolute monarchical papacy.

Runcie knows the Vatican is on dangerously shifting sands in proclaiming that the naming of bishops is a papal prerogative. Throughout church history virtually every method possible has been tried in naming bishops.

There is no divinely chosen way for choosing bishops. The fact that so many different ways have been tried indicates that each procedure is fraught with difficulties. If one way had proven the best, the church would have stayed with it.

It is disheartening to see our separated sisters and brothers struggling with the meaning of the Petrine ministry while Catholics have done precious little to tackle the ecumenical hurdle which is the papacy.

It is particularly painful to have Runcie confront the Catholic community with the current practice of episcopal appointments. The Second Vatican Council, 25 years ago, addressed this issue and called for a governance of the church that in its daily exercise included the college of bishops.

The council called for many changes in the church, and in the following years structures were put in place so that the called-for reforms might be implemented — except for one. No structures have been forthcoming to implement the council's call for collegiality.

And now Runcie reminds us of the cost of that omission. We are less than prepared to take hold of the Lord's high-priestly prayer before his passion and glorification: "That they all may be one."

Papal office
June 27, 2001

With the full blessing of the Vatican, Catholic and Orthodox Christians gathered at the Catholic University of America in Washington on the eve of the papal visit to Ukraine to discuss the papal office.

Orthodox Archbishop Vsevolod, with a candour not often forthcoming from our eastern brothers and sisters, spoke of the need for an office of primacy in the church. He did not hesitate to give examples of the difficulties that accompany its absence in their church life.

The archbishop believes, however, that Catholics have something to learn from Orthodox practice. He praised the sense of conciliarity — having ecumenical councils (pope and bishops together) as the supreme norm of government, in their own communion — while admitting it must be "balanced" by an exercise of primacy.

As would be expected, he was quite forthright in his assertion that he could not find this gift of balance in the Catholic community.

Archbishop John R. Quinn of San Francisco, a frequent critic of curial conduct in the Vatican, was given the honour of being the keynote speaker on the Catholic side. His argument was simple: a clear distinction must be made between official Catholic dogmatic teaching and the current exercise of papal primacy. Catholic dogma, he maintained, need not get in the way of Catholic and Orthodox Christians enriching one another in the thorny issue of authority in the church.

It is with a touch of irony that the Divine Liturgy celebrated in Ukraine by Cardinal Lubomyr Husar, with the pope seated to the right of the altar, may give us a glimpse of how a reunited church might look.

As a fourth-century Milanese Christian would never accept the Bishop of Rome coming to Milan and occupying St. Ambrose's chair, or as a Pope St. Leo the Great would never lead the liturgy in another bishop's cathedral, so the pope this past Sunday sat on the side on a faldstool as the cardinal (patriarch) led his people in worship.

As the meeting in Washington should fill us all with hope, so let us be open to new expressions of authority — well, maybe not all that new! Let us not be surprised if some of the practices of an Ambrose and a Leo better express the balance between primacy and conciliarity than does our current practice of having the pope travel the world and, without question, sitting on the chair historically reserved for the local bishop.

The Spirit given to all

May 8, 1989

When the Spirit descended in the desert camp on two men who were not part of the local power structure, confusion and downright hostility reigned. But Moses refused to feel threatened. "If only the whole People of God were prophets, and the Lord gave his Spirit to all of them," he said (Num 11:29). Most New Testament authors found this text fulfilled in the church's experience of the Spirit of Jesus. With Pentecost the Spirit is given to the whole People of God.

And so Bishop Michael H. Kenny of Juneau, Alaska, can proclaim that the church is denying the reality of Pentecost if it does not involve all the faithful in grappling with the major issues facing it.

And major issues he means. A Pentecost church, he proclaims, will not leave it to a hierarchy to decide on such issues as mandatory celibacy for the clergy, the role of women, the methods of family planning, the place of the church in the culture of the age.

At the time of Christ's birth, a temple messianism dominated Judaism. The temple, not one individual, would shine forth in the new age. The temple, used by the religious leaders to control the people, would on the last day come to have dominion over the whole world.

It was not surprising that Christians proclaimed there would be no temple at all in the New Jerusalem (Rev 21:22). The light of the Lamb would do much more than anyone of old thought possible, even for the temple. The light of the Lamb would make everyone rulers (Rev 22:5).

Today many in the church are more at home with a temple-type power ruling over the people than with a Pentecost Spirit which makes rulers of the People of God. It is time we take Kenny's advice seriously: "The college of bishops and the pope himself cannot function in a vacuum. To be faithful to the Spirit the hierarchy must be in touch with the lived experience of people of faith."

Post-Vatican II church

September 8, 1986

It should not surprise us that the Second Vatican Council continues to cause some tension in the church. The tension is a good sign that the council had the courage to go to the heart of issues and call the church to a profound re-evaluation of itself.

The issues before the church today remain basically the same as they were 20 years ago. The issue is not choosing between a too liberal or a too conservative theology. Thus the tension in the church will not be resolved with the church settling unanimously for this or that theological viewpoint on various concrete problems.

Two much more fundamental moves marked the council and continue to challenge the church.

First, as Father Dan Donovan from Toronto noted in his recent Saskatoon lecture, the council refused to characterize itself as anti this or that. It proclaimed that only an optimistic spirit will grasp the reality of life about us, will find the Lord's presence in the world.

In other words it saw pessimism as the first heresy. Pope John's trumpet call at the council's opening to disregard "prophets of doom" continued to ring forth throughout the council.

Optimism does strange things to people and even to huge institutions like the Catholic Church. Suddenly the church found great things in other confessions of Christianity and even in non-Christian religions. Not surprisingly the bishops rejected the centuries-old tenet that error has no rights and espoused instead a profoundly encompassing teaching on religious freedom.

The council's spirit of optimism was most clearly seen in its treatment of the church in the modern world. While not closing its eyes to various problems in the world, the council remained upbeat in listing the signs of the times. It found good news everywhere — and, incidentally, excited people the world over in the process.

The clearest sign that the courageous spirit of the council is being rejected is not, as was said above, in the formulation of liberal or conservative theological principles, but in the espousal of pessimism. An institutional church which spends more of its energy condemning evils than convincing its members and the world that Jesus Christ is Good News in every age and every situation has effectively rejected the council.

The second mark of the council was equally all encompassing. Choosing the concept of community as central, the church viewed itself as the

People of God. It surely did not deny its hierarchical structure, but it insisted that its priestly ministry must be seen in the context of the people, of the church community, not vice versa.

In doing this the church recovered the ancient notion of the *sensus fidelium*, that the community is the depository of the faith, that it has a deep sense of the fullness of tradition.

In this community-centred church, the priesthood was not something outside or over the church but a charism at its heart capable of harnessing the power and discerning the faith of God's people.

In this church vision one did not automatically become an official teacher simply by virtue of one's episcopal ordination. It came much more from the bishop's marriage to the local people (diocese). The bishop's power to teach, to heal, to consecrate is never his own; it is always — if it is to be truly effective — an expression of the church, the People of God.

At their deepest level these two marks of the council are really one. Only optimists will find the full catholicity of our tradition in the Christian community about them. It is not only bishops and other church leaders who at various times cannot resist the temptation to place themselves above the church (community) and attempt to lecture it on truth and virtue.

It is always an awesome moment, though, when the minister, lost in the midst of God's people, gathers their fears and difficulties, their hopes and dreams, and their faith in Jesus and proclaims the catholic tradition that they are the Body of Christ, a special presence of divinity in this present world.

There is nothing more optimistic than to celebrate the Eucharist, than to proclaim that the cross of Christ has become the tree of life, that this motley group of successors to the prostitutes and sinners whom Jesus so loved is the Body of Christ, the flesh for the life of the world.

A sinless church

April 8, 1998

Pope John Paul II has made the Year 2000 a jubilee. One of the central themes of jubilee years in the Hebrew Scriptures is reconciliation. This suits the papal agenda to a "T."

Italian writer Luigi Accattoli, in his latest book *When a Pope Asks For-*

giveness: The Mea Culpas *of John Paul II,* notes that he found the pope saying *mea culpa* 94 times. Canadians will remember his eloquent apology to our Native peoples, that the church did not reverence their culture in telling them the story of Jesus.

In 25 of these 94 instances, the pope expressly said: "I ask forgiveness." He certainly was not trying to say that he personally committed the faults he was talking about. He was speaking in the name of the whole church, begging the victims to begin "a process of healing of memories" so that they could forgive the church the wrongs done to them.

In planning the church's response to the Year 2000, the pope called a 1994 meeting of the cardinals. There the pope suggested that the church, in order to be credible to the men and women of the third millennium, should "rid itself of some historical baggage and own up to past mistakes."

According to many, the idea went over like a lead balloon. Cardinals from behind the old Iron Curtain said the church would be opening itself to a new wave of criticism. Third World cardinals did not want to dwell on "European sins." Curial cardinals noted that it would direct attention to the church and not to Christ.

The pope listened quietly — and then went his own way. He published his powerful apostolic letter, As the Third Millennium Draws Near, in which he calls upon the church to purify itself and to acknowledge its past sins.

Not everyone at the Vatican, however, fell into line. Especially this past year things began moving in a new direction — has the poor health of the pope anything to do with this?

The late October symposium in Rome on the Christians' historical treatment of Jews suddenly changed its focus. What had been billed as a study of Christian roots of anti-Semitism was narrowed to a study of anti-Judaism. Jews were no longer invited to the symposium, not even as observers.

Msgr. Rino Fisichella, the vice-president of the Historical-Theological Commission for the Jubilee, while responding to a reporter's question on the effects of Christian behaviour on the growth of anti-Semitism, dodged the question and declared that "as far as the sources of revelation are concerned, there is nothing that can lead to anti-Judaism."

We know now that this was preparing us for a document that would declare no Christian input into the development of the hatred of Jews that became part of the German Nazi platform.

Fisichella went on to lecture the media at the press conference. They should not, he said, expect any "*mea culpa* by the church as an institution."

The pope's call "to an examination of conscience" is not, he said, intended to move "toward a cataloguing of church errors."

"This is a wrong attitude, because there are no sins of the church, because the church cannot sin; the church by its nature is holy," he said.

He concluded by noting the dangers of "a *mea-culpa* debate. It can generate misunderstanding, giving the impression that these 2,000 years of the church have been only a history of sins and not of holiness."

Hence, the radical shift in the apology from the advance text given to Jews a mere three months ago. Instead of an emphasis on the "Catholic" teaching of contempt toward Jews (as in the text), the new text finds reasons to praise the German bishops and especially Pope Pius XII.

This shift, however, should not be viewed simply as a disappointment to Jews; it reveals a theological shift to fundamentalism that should worry every member of the church.

One would have thought that the great document of the Second Vatican Council on the church would have forestalled any attempt to see the church independently of its members, that the church cannot sin but only its members can.

As the apostles could not touch the divinity of Christ independently of his "lowly" humanity, so Christians cannot experience the holiness of the church independently of its human frailty.

There can be no church independent of its members, no magisterium independent of the *sensus fidelium* exercised by the people, no functioning priesthood above and beyond the priesthood of all believers, no act of holiness except that carried out by the sinners who by the sheer grace of God see themselves as the church of God.

This Easter paradox enables us to love our highly imperfect selves as true icons of the God of the highest heavens. At the same time, this greatest of mysteries opens the way for us to love a disfigured world as God's special sphere of influence and, not least of all, it empowers us to embrace a self-contained church, which far too often idolizes past glories and structures, as the very presence of God — and as our home.

The alternative to this paradox is fundamentalism. Of this we can be certain: if we part with paradox, if we give up the holy chaos of the cross, we end up with a church above and beyond the people; we have a hierarchy with more power than earthly monarchs; we have defined dogmas based not on the lived experience of the people but on the understanding of a privileged few; we have some people more sacred than the "temples of the Holy Spirit"; we end up with a church in the clouds — not exactly what St. Paul meant when he dreamed of the church of the final age as a bride without stain or wrinkle — no longer grounded in human history, no longer formed precisely of those seeking salvation.

We must do all we can to return to the mission our pope has given us for the Year 2000. It is only a church that can say with him again and again, "I ask forgiveness," that will become for this age a beacon of holiness. Only a church that knows its sinfulness can be a sign, a sacrament of hope to the world.

United in charity

July 5, 2000

For centuries the people of Israel had a vision of their messiah being perfect. They dreamed, too, of creating a perfect community which would so impress God that the Almighty would not be able to resist sending the messiah right away.

Orthodox Jews at the time of Jesus believed that if they formed a holy group rightly preparing for the Sabbath meal, a group which was not marked by any sin and was deeply studying the divine law, the messiah would rejoice and come to join them in their Sabbath celebration.

Jesus, alas, was not perfect enough for them. To use the words of St. Paul: rather than come in pristine purity, he came "in the likeness of our sinful flesh" (Rom 8:3). Jesus himself once said how fortunate were those who were not scandalized by him (Mt 11:6).

If God "for our sake made the sinless one into sin" (2 Cor 5:21), we should not be surprised that Jesus in forming the first apostolic college did not strive for that purity of form that would impress the self-righteous.

It was quite a motley bunch Jesus gathered. There was that cocky Peter who usually talked authoritatively first and thought second; there were James and John who had no time for the little children who naturally streamed to Jesus but had lots of time to argue about being first in rank and power in the kingdom; there was Simon the Zealot who could not have been further removed theologically from Matthew who made a living collecting taxes for the Romans; there was Judas who could not rise above the thought of worldly possessions; and, of course, there was

Thomas who doubted the central act Jesus underwent for our salvation.

If people were scandalized by Jesus, how much more likely were they to take offence at the foibles constantly perpetrated by the Twelve.

It would do us well as a church to reflect deeply on this, to ask ourselves why Jesus did not choose like-minded people who could easily come to an agreement as to how the church community should move into new situations.

Surely, we ask, would not the whole operation have gone so much more smoothly without a Simon arguing that they must keep themselves totally removed from the Romans while a Matthew kept countering that it was only by working with them that one could open the necessary lines of communication?

Obviously Jesus did not treasure that unity which comes from everyone thinking the same way. He realized that for such unity to continue on, two things had to happen. First of all, most people would have to stop thinking altogether and simply obey their elders; secondly, those who thought anything out of the ordinary would have to be ostracized from the community.

And that is exactly what was happening in the Pharisaic community which was so scandalized by Jesus.

Not a lot has changed over the last two millennia. The *Prairie Messenger* carries a story this week about "hair-splitting and fine-grained readings of the law" as a substitute for "charity, compassion, forbearance. and forgiveness."

In a companion story from Great Britain, "faithful Catholics" are ready to find fault with the whole hierarchy in their country and declare themselves the faithful remnant obedient to the pope.

Many of the letters to the editor that we receive maintain the same stance. Bishops and whole hierarchies are dismissed without so much as a backward glance, as people declare their own purity of doctrine, their obedience to a pope who — most conveniently — is more than 10,000 miles away.

When we notice how easily bishops are found wanting, we do not take it personally when hate letters — there is no other word to describe them — come our way. But we wonder how people can hate so easily — and all in the name of Jesus Christ.

All of us too highly value our own way of thinking. We must ask ourselves why we must pontificate so assuredly as did the young Peter. We must question ourselves repeatedly why we must be so much like James and John wanting to order others around. We must acknowledge, too, how similar we are to Judas, subtly believing that the more money we have, the more weighty are our opinions.

And ultimately all of us should thank Jesus for having the foresight to call poor Thomas. A little doubt now and then, a little less self-assurance would help all of us.

The church will become for us a saving experience not by its being more monolithic, but by each of us making room for a Peter, a James and John, a Simon and Matthew, a doubting Thomas — and, not least of all, a Judas.

Our unity will be salvific not by common understanding of all the dots and tittles of the law, but by our charity, our compassion, our forbearance, and, when needed ("seven times 70 times!"), our forgiveness.

Chapter 3

The People of God

World Synod on the Laity September 14, 1987

Few preliminary working papers of the synods (they are called *instrumenta laboris*) have had the difficult time the current one has received. Few people in the church — whether lay or clerical — who are out in the trenches have expressed much praise for the document.

A group of leading laypersons, gathered by the Vatican two years ago from around the world, were merciless in their criticism of the document. They refused to see as central the document's concern about "the clericalization of the laity and the laicization of the clergy."

One year ago, when the Canadian bishops gathered lay leaders in Ottawa from every diocese in the land, they heard very similar comments. The laity were not interested in being the non-clergy; instead they invited the bishops to join the ranks of "the baptized."

Baptism, and not participation in the work of the hierarchy, gives the laity their mission to sanctify the world. Pope John Paul II could not have put it any clearer in his 1985 talk to workers in Antwerp: "You share in the church's mission of salvation. You are called to the apostolate through your baptism and your confirmation."

All ministry, even that distinctive service asked of the clergy, finds its proper setting in the whole People of God. It is not a little disconcerting that this undeniably central image of Vatican II for the church is used but once in the working paper for this synod. (And that is exactly how often it was used in the document issued by the last synod. Few would have dreamed 20 years ago that in evaluating the council, bishops would be able to do so with only once mentioning "the People of God.")

Does this term, "People of God," bring the laity too close to the heart of the church? Is the problem that the expression presupposes that the baptismal unity of the community is a more central fact in the church's life than the distinctiveness inherent in the call to ordination?

The centrality of baptism is the issue at the coming synod. It is always a bit frightening for members of the clergy the first time they truly hear that their call to orders is the church's discernment that such service is to be their way of being faithful to their baptismal call.

Catholic piety has often hidden this fact. We forgot that priests in leading the community in its eucharistic service were celebrating exactly the same central truth as all the people — their baptism, that they are called to be the Body of Christ, the dwelling place of the Holy Spirit.

For an embarrassingly long period of our history official Catholic piety has stressed what is different. It is no accident that 170 out of the 173 saints explicitly mentioned in the Roman Missal are celibates. We have so exalted things that separate the principals from the masses of the laity that we have scarcely any official models of lay holiness.

If we cannot spontaneously see "the lay state" (about 99.8 percent of the church, but who wants to be caught dividing!) as the normal focus of holiness, we had better ask ourselves: Are we truly interested in assuring the laity their full dignity in the daily life of the church?

While it is true that the church is not a democracy, it is equally true that it is not a hierarchy according to the principles of the world. Jesus was somewhat definite about that (see Mk 10: 41-45). Only within the paradox of the cross in which death is life, the last are first, and the least are the greatest can the ordained proclaim themselves a hierarchy.

The working paper will stand or fall in the critical light of the Gospel by how power is understood.

If the synod sees this power as God's might to empower the People of God so they might have the confidence to believe they are indeed the sacrament of the world's salvation, the working paper will surely stand.

If this power is seen as God's gift to the hierarchy whereby they can control the church, it will fall. If the coming synod, which by its very nature does not have an official lay voice, sees power in these terms, it will weaken the church for generations.

The easiest way for the church leaders to avoid this all-too-possible pitfall is to go back to the genius of Vatican II and revitalize its central image — that of the People of God.

This image, more than any currently employed in the synod's working paper, will help us all to recognize the glorious mission of the baptized.

Secularity and the synod

October 19, 1987

Two issues dominated the bishops' eight-minute interventions at the synod: the role of women and the laity's central mission in the life of the church.

Bishop Francis Xavier Kaname Shimamoto of Urawa, Japan, summed up the issue succinctly. In calling for a true recognition of the laity's role as an integral part of the church — "not just as subordinate to the clergy" — he said: "Lay Catholics are not just the bridge between the church and the world. They are the church itself present in the world. Their secularity is the church's secularity."

Australian laywoman Marvis Pirola developed her intervention along a similar line. She called for "a spirituality appropriate for the married state" which stresses "the sexual nature of this sacrament." She minced no words with the bishops. At the centre of a couple's relationship, she said, "is their sexual responsiveness to each other, manifested especially in genital sex. Sexual intimacy is what distinguishes matrimony from all other Christian relationships."

In this regard she did not quote Genesis 1:27 which proclaims that it is as male and female that we are made in God's image. Interestingly, Bishop Jean-Guy Hamelin of Rouyn-Noranda, Quebec, alluded to this text at the end of his intervention calling for the full participation of women in the church.

Hamelin, the vice-president of Canada's bishops, reminded the synod that this full participation is not a new idea. It is, he said, as old as Genesis: "According to the heart of God, humanity is not humanity without the mutual presence of man and woman to each other, without the original covenant between them."

The author of Genesis was arguing for the secularity of human sexuality and against the pagan temptation to make it part of the sacred. The challenge before this synod is to follow Hamelin's lead and take hold of this teaching from Genesis. Bypassing it has led to many critical conclusions in the church — including that of the exclusive male priesthood.

A church that wants to be in the world will cherish this secularity proclaimed in Genesis. It will teach us how men and women, laity and clergy, are to relate to one another in today's world.

Gospel and the world

January 31, 2001

Perhaps the most noteworthy speech at the World Synod of Bishops was given by Bishop Francis Xavier Kaname Shimamoto of Urawa, Japan, near the beginning of the gathering. "Laypeople are not just subordinates of the clergy," he said. "They are the church itself present in the world. Their secularity is the church's secularity."

The Japanese bishop was quoted around the world — and most of the stories stressed the liberal interpretation of the Gospel that underpinned his remarks, hinting, none too subtly, that they did not go over very well at the Vatican.

Pope John Paul surprised many observers by incorporating Shimamoto's insight into his closing address to the synod. But really, should we have been surprised?

It is difficult to imagine a more secular statement than that given recently by the pope as part of his Wednesday papal audience to the pilgrims gathered from around the world: "Every act undertaken to create a better future, a more habitable earth and a more familial society participates, even if in an indirect way, in building the kingdom of God."

The pope notes that we can easily become "paralyzed by the destruction, ugliness and evil" around us. If anyone should know how difficult it is for the church to be truly in the real world, the pope should. He knows what it means to be bloodied by the world.

And so he reminds us that "we are called first of all to cancel fear of the future." It is fear, he tells us, that tempts us to believe that "war, violence, oppression, injustice and moral degradation dominate."

It takes courage, he implies, to work in the world confident that Jesus is the Lord, the most powerful (and most secular) force operative in this age.

Conversion does not challenge anyone to turn one's back on the world but, rather, to use one's skills as a member of the baptized to create a better world.

St. John once said that the bread, which the church uses to celebrate its very meaning, is the flesh of the Lord "given for the life of the world."

It is so much easier to break up reality into sacred and secular and, in the process, create a church holier than the world, a church which the world is called to worship and serve.

The pope in so closely tying the building up of the kingdom with the creating of a better world adroitly bypasses these temptations. It is wonderful to hear an old man, deeply scarred by years behind the Iron Curtain, gently remind us not to be paralyzed by fear but rather, from our very home in the world, "to reveal God's design of peace and love, of truth and justice."

Faith and culture November 2, 1987

Optimism was one of the key marks of the Second Vatican Council. The council believed it could enter the culture of the global village and impregnate it with the Gospel of Jesus Christ.

The council was not blind to the difficulties that beset the human family today. But the bishops refused to give up their faith that the Spirit of God can fill the world. Our world, here and now.

Such optimism has filled the Canadian bishops' interventions at the recent synod on the laity. Writing on faith and culture, Bishop John Sherlock of London, Ontario, quoting the pope, reminds us that a faith which does not become a culture is "a faith which has not been fully received, not thoroughly thought through, not faithfully lived out."

We have no choice. There is only one world in which we can discover, love, and serve our God. Any temptation to flee this world for a more spiritual dreamland of our own making is a temptation to forfeit the Gospel.

Sherlock acknowledges that fleeing the real world out of fear for our spiritual being is not the only way of despairing that the Gospel can fill today's world. We can also capitulate. "Catholic schools," he said, "are discovering that they need great vigilance and creativity to avoid being accomplices in promoting the same standards of successful living as the consumer society."

We believe Sherlock has wonderfully captured the optimism of the Vatican Council's constitution, The Church in the Modern World, in his solution to cultural capitulation.

He does not ask for blanket condemnations. In no way does he support church leaders who have only negative things to say about culture today. Sherlock gives us a far different tool whereby to discern the seeds of life and the seeds of death in the modern world.

The evils of society, he notes, are best unmasked in the suffering of the poor and powerless in our society.

The church is accountable not just to itself, to the members in whose name countless decisions are made. It is accountable to the world, especially to the people of no account. Such is the way the church must give account to its God, the God who through his covenant has made himself accountable to humanity.

Faith becomes culture, Sherlock tells us, by our identification with those denied justice. He spoke at the synod in glowing terms about John Paul's visit to aboriginal people in Fort Simpson in the Northwest Territories. The pope's listening, his concern, his willingness to learn, his courage to speak out on their behalf — this, Sherlock points out, is what the Canadian church needs to avoid the temptation of cultural capitulation.

Likely we are more comfortable with condemnations — or flights into religious fundamentalism which can so marvellously avoid the real world altogether.

Inculturating the faith   July 15, 1985

Pope John Paul II in his fourth encyclical praises the work of the apostles to the Slavs, Sts. Cyril and Methodius. He does more, however, than simply eulogize these missionaries from the East who 11 centuries ago brought Christianity to the Slavs. He presents them to the church as a model of inculturation.

He acknowledges that this is never easy work. Cyril and Methodius, he points out, had to fight steadfastly against powerful opponents in both church and state who could see only the glories of the Greek and Latin cultures and the power of the ascending Germanic kingdom.

In the face of this opposition, these saints immersed themselves in the Slavic world making their own the needs and aspirations of the Slavs. Only through this identification with the Slavs did these apostles become convinced that their language, considered barbaric by the establishment, was a fitting vehicle for Christianity's highest expression, the Eucharist.

While church leaders deemed that the Slavic tongue was too rudimentary to handle the highly refined dogmas of Christianity, civil leaders had no time to give weight to rustics. Their world vision could not extend beyond the new Romano-Germanic Empire. Through this empire the world would be given peace and made secure for Christianity.

The principles of inculturation the pope praises are important for the church today. If they are applied in Africa, where the church is growing by leaps and bounds, a very different church will emerge. The African church today is in many regions practically a non-eucharistic entity. The laws surrounding priesthood, based more on culture than on the New Testament, have prevented the priestly ministry from keeping pace with the growth of the community at large.

Theologians from Latin America have said repeatedly that the growing tension between them and Rome is more a cultural than theological difficulty. While Rome continues to view reality through the universal absolutes that are at the heart of classical philosophy and Roman law, the new theologians in Latin America centre their struggle with the challenge of Jesus on the experience of nobodies in the slums, on the by-products of the new world order created by our western leaders.

There are a lot of similarities with these struggling theologians and the great apostles Cyril and Methodius. In both cases the church leaders did not want to part with the noble classical — and obviously correct — expressions of the faith for some rudimentary embodiment tied to a people of no account. Likewise the civil leaders, in their grand designs for the universe, could find no time to identify with the needs and aspirations of those lost in the world's sewers.

The pope in praising the daring work of inculturation by Sts. Cyril and Methodius has given the church an important charter for incarnating the faith in this post-Vatican II church.

Recognizing holiness
March 23, 1992

The pope was forthright; he told the Roman clergy in an impromptu speech that it was his "great desire" to canonize a married couple, but none worthy of the honour has been found so far. And he went further; he admitted there were no candidates in the Vatican's saint-making pipeline.

The only couple of the recent past to receive any serious consideration were the parents of Ste. Thérèse-de-Lisieux. And they were chosen not in their own right, but rather because of their famous daughter.

The pope gave reasons for the embarrassing lack of such canonizations. Priests and religious are always there ready to promote their own causes. There is, however, no "tradition" to promote the causes of married couples and thus they never come to the Vatican's attention.

One must wonder if much is going to be achieved if Rome somehow does finally find a married couple to canonize as its symbolic model of married life. When no example can be found among the 99 percent, while countless examples are readily found among the less than 1 percent, no symbolic act is going to save the day.

Celibacy practised by clergy and religious is a great grace to the church, but serious reflection is surely needed when it becomes for all practical purposes an essential mark of holiness. We simply cannot deny it: we live in a church that does not recognize holiness as it expresses itself in married life — notwithstanding protestations to the contrary in several Vatican II documents.

This is not a minor flaw that can be easily corrected — certainly not by a canonization or two. To correct it the church must come to acknowledge the fundamental imbalance in its vision of holiness. Holiness is never to be viewed as something out of the ordinary, something for the less than 1 percent who have responded generously to particular calls in the kingdom.

The only areas in which moral theologians have been called to task since the Second Vatican Council have been sexual ones. Is that because these are the only areas in which theologians have made mistakes, or is it, at least in part, an indication that the church is hung up on sex?

It is sobering to remember: not only has the church not canonized a married couple lately, but for a very long time it has also omitted celebrating the holiness of any one member of a Christian marriage who throughout life found the sacrament of matrimony a key source of empowerment.

Ordinary time

January 15, 2003

In the Catholic Church, Ordinary Time is celebrated in two segments: from the Monday following the Baptism of Our Lord up to Ash Wednesday; and from Pentecost Monday to the First Sunday of Advent. This makes it the longest season of the liturgical year.

In the church prior to the Second Vatican Council, we had Sundays of Advent, Lent, and Easter, and Sundays after Epiphany and after Pentecost. Thus it sounded strange to Catholic ears to suddenly hear a commentator or the priest himself telling the assembly that "today we are celebrating the Second Sunday of Ordinary Time."

We might have been tempted to say that it was more than strange, that it was downright silly. It is indeed a temptation for Catholics to believe that our lives would be more worthwhile (and more divine) if we could rise above what is ordinary in them.

Yet the introduction of "ordinary time" and its celebration is basic to the understanding of the renewal of the liturgy called for in the Second Vatican Council.

Christmas is not at the heart of our liturgical cycle, nor is Easter with its great octave of octaves, Pentecost; but the Sundays of Ordinary Time are. The church existed fully for centuries without any feasts (Easter included) other than Sunday, the Lord's Day. The first feast days were the celebration of the memory of local martyrs at their burial sites.

In speaking of the liturgical cycle, we now tend to think in terms of the year, whereas historically the weekly cycle was much more important.

Within the rhythm of each week, with its Friday and Sunday, Christians celebrated their calling to follow the Lord. There was nothing pompous or spectacular about it; there was no need for special feasts to bring out particular aspects of the Christian calling. Indeed, this lack of special feasts is a key to understanding what the first Christians thought their liturgy was.

Christians were ordinary people — sociologically, the vast majority of them were from the lower classes. A great many were slaves; a great many were women. Liturgy, for them, was a celebration of their new meaning in the Lord.

Whereas the pagans needed festivals as excuses for celebrating, Christians saw no reason for special feast days. Not until the Peace of Constantine in AD 313, which made it profitable socially, economically, and politically for the upper classes to become Christian, did the church do anything to develop its own cycle of festivals and holy seasons.

The early church did not have the notion of sacred time necessary for the development of festivals and special seasons. Nor did it speak of a sacred space where only especially holy or consecrated people could enter. The vision John had of the New Jerusalem in the last chapters of the New Testament (Book of Revelation) dominated Christian thinking about life and liturgy. They gloried in their New Jerusalem having in it no temple at all (Rv 21:22).

The only thing the church held sacred was its people. The story of St.

Lawrence at his martyrdom, proclaiming that the poor were the true treasures of the church, does not stand out as an exceptional narrative. It reflects the thinking of the time.

The church, therefore, was not surprised to hear St. Augustine, in explaining the meaning of the Mass in one of his mystogogical sermons say it is the mystery of the people themselves that is placed on the altar of the Lord, it is their story that is celebrated, and, in turn, it is their own mystery they receive from the altar.

Christians did not celebrate festivals; they celebrated ordinary time. Their liturgy was based on a simple premise: Jesus Christ, the lay son of a poor unknown carpenter in the lacklustre town of Nazareth which no one had heard of before, had entered fully into the real lives of ordinary people.

Christians didn't need festivals as a reason for celebrating; they were the reason. The only sacredness they knew was their ordinary lives, lives that had been touched by the man from Galilee, whose lowly lay state was all the more treasured since it reflected their own experience.

Their story was placed on the altar of the Lord. No sacred time (even as a special commemoration of an event in the life of the Lord), no sacred space was necessary. This was true per annum, throughout the whole year. The only church the Christian knew was the living stones of the community itself.

New lay spiritual movements   October 26, 1987

It is estimated that 20 million laypeople belong to new lay spiritual movements. Members of these movements tend to be highly critical of the local churches and usually do not look to bishops for direction.

Many bishops at the synod on the laity have complained about these movements becoming "a church within the church." During the past decade Rome has tended to support them, and thus, not surprisingly, these lay movements have found their support at the synod from the papal appointees to the synod.

Throughout its history the church has balanced local and universal oversight with regard to many church movements. It has not always been easy. Let us not forget that the Fourth Lateran Council was called largely because many bishops wanted Francis of Assisi condemned.

A balance has been found for the religious orders. A new balance must be found for these lay organizations. Cardinal Aloisio Lorscheider of Fortaleza, Brazil, is right in demanding that "parallel pastoral activity must be avoided," that "sincere obedience to and communion with the pastor of the local church" is necessary (cf. page 1).

Lorscheider is not asking for full control. He is asking for balance. Bishop bashing is too easy today. Any group unhappy with something in the local church can now declare itself the faithful Catholic remnant and can entertain a reasonable hope that some encouragement will come from some quarter in the Curia.

New movements, new newspapers arise continually and proclaim themselves Catholic without any regard to local episcopal oversight. It is a strange legacy indeed for a council that promised to make collegiality a mark of the post-Vatican II church.

The synod on the laity closes   November 9, 1987

The Second Vatican Council, in first putting the People of God at the centre of the church and only then discussing the role and meaning of the hierarchy, turned inside out a process that had been in effect in the church for more than a millennium.

We should not be surprised that this created a crisis for many in the church. At this synod, a quarter century after the council, we still hear bishops begging that those exercising the central authority in the church in the name of the pope be ready for a definition of laity that goes beyond their being non-clergy.

It is far too early to judge the effectiveness of this synod. But its credibility was not enhanced by its failure to come to an agreement on girl servers at the altar. No matter what one thinks about this issue — whether one is for or against them — it is difficult to believe that a body that gets bogged down on such an issue can indeed be grappling with the major problems facing the church today.

The synod certainly gave the lie to the view that the alienation of women in the church is a North American problem. Bishops from every region of the world insisted that women's place in the church be reconsidered.

The closing "non-substantive" document issued by the synod notes that "sin has obscured the full meaning of God's plan. We condemn the discrimination which proceeds from sin and still continues to our own day in many countries."

The statement does not directly confess that this sin resides in the church, but it comes close when it rejoices at the advances which have "enabled women to fulfil their mission in the church" (cf. pages 10-11). While the progress at this synod has not been great — Archbishop Rembert Weakland rejoices "that we did not pedal backwards, which is very important" (cf. page 1) — it is important to hear our church admit that the dignity of women has been "seriously wounded" in the present age.

It is only a small, small step, but it is encouraging to note that the message issued by the synod is written in inclusive language. It is cumbersomely done, but it is the attempt that counts.

This synod has revealed to the world the deep disagreements present in the church. One cannot fault Catholics for hoping for more than girl servers and the use of inclusive language. If the legitimate concerns of the world's bishops so eloquently presented at the synod are not addressed within a reasonable time, the church will be called to a reconciliation process which will pale in comparison with the current one undertaken with Lefebvre.

Devotion to Mary July 17, 1983

Recently the bishops of Saskatchewan rededicated the province to Mary, echoing the action the hierarchy had taken 50 years ago during the heart of the Great Depression. At a time of human crisis the bishops had spontaneously turned to Mary. Our leaders today again point out many critical issues.

In the first years after the council this action of our hierarchy would not have been well received. That is understandable. Catholics needed some time to separate themselves from the excesses and poor taste that had crept into our Marian piety.

Catholics, however, inevitably return to Mary. As James E. Milord notes in his essay on Mary, she helps us keep a balance in our faith. She prevents us from enthroning masculinity and reason. In a word, devotion to her humanizes, in the deepest sense of that word, our faith and religion.

Throughout our long history, whenever the official liturgy of the church lost contact with the ordinary people — because of language, clericalization, imitation of royal courts, or whatever — shrines to Mary multiplied. These shrines always had a light-heartedness about them. People flocked to them to celebrate the simple and the ordinary in their lives, and to ask for the help they instinctively knew they had a right to expect from their faith.

Saskatchewan has many shrines to Mary. Quite naturally many of these shrines have July 16 as the focal point of their celebrations. That day is a minor feast of Mary, but it comes at the critical moment. The crops are planted and utterly beyond the control of the men and women who have based so much of their lives upon them.

The crops are in the hands of God — and the official liturgy seemed to have so little to say on the matter. The human thing for the farming community to do was to bring this critical issue to the attention of Mary.

Mount Carmel in the Abbacy of Muenster is a good example. It has long been a place where people have laid their crops in the hands of God. Not surprisingly, it has always been much more than just a day of profound prayer. It has also been a grand diocesan picnic.

Devotion to Mary does that to the Christian; it brings out laughter and good-hearted sharing along with the most serious of prayer. It leads a people to celebrate who they are on many levels.

It is not surprising either that the Métis in Saskatchewan return in such large numbers yearly to St. Laurent, to a shrine in the heart of their ancestral homeland. True devotion to Mary, in humanizing their religion, leads them spontaneously to celebrate what is deepest and truest in their Native heritage.

It is good to hear that the organizers of the St. Laurent pilgrimage are having a Native, Rev. John Hascal, an Ojibway from Northern Ontario, come and show the pilgrims how many Native traditions can be fruitfully incorporated into Catholicism.

Mary will like that since her first job is to show the humanness of our God. And she cannot do this without getting us to celebrate ours.

KC (Fourth Degree) February 16, 2000

A high proportion of 19th-century immigrants to America were Catholic. And, like virtually all the immigrants, they were poor and distrusted by many in the establishment. Their Catholicism did not help either.

There were few social safety nets to carry those who met an unexpected disaster. An early death by the breadwinner of the family was often catastrophic.

The young priest who founded the Catholic brotherhood of the Knights of Columbus, Rev. Michael J. McGivney, addressed the issue directly. The purpose of the life insurance component in the brotherhood was not originally intended to be a financial success story that could fund great charitable endeavours such as the recent cleaning of the façade of St. Peter's Basilica.

The phenomenal financial success of the knights is surely one of the great stories of the American church. But it should be remembered that it started as a support system for poor immigrant Catholic families.

McGivney intended to do much more than create a Catholic alternative to the Masonic Lodge. He realized that for his new organization to effectively provide a secure social safety net for its members, it would have to make the Catholic faith itself something truly celebrated.

The decline in Sunday Mass attendance over the last quarter century should teach us that what we do not celebrate, we do not for long value or treasure. McGivney made the active treasuring of the faith a key element in the brotherhood. One hundred years ago the Knights Fourth Degree was established. Its key role: to make a celebration of our Catholic faith.

Thus the Fourth Degree Knights do not usually involve themselves directly in the great charity works of the order. Their job is to celebrate, to celebrate a faith and a church that were often highly suspect in the United States.

Recent events such as the rejection of a Catholic priest from becoming chaplain of the U.S. House of Representatives simply because he was a Catholic reveal that much still remains to be done before Catholics can live in America without experiencing open bias and downright prejudice.

The original knights who structured the Fourth Degree rightly realized that an appreciation of the Catholic faith included a positive remembrance of its long history.

Thus the garb of the Fourth Degree will never speak loudly of immediate relevance. Much like the uniforms of the Swiss Guard, which

Michelangelo designed, the garb of the Fourth Degree speaks of the timelessness of the church, a timelessness that is its glory, not its burden.

Yet there are elements of the Fourth Degree garb, particularly the swords, that should concern the brotherhood. Their ceremonial garb, as must be the case, is highly symbolic. Symbols, however, are always larger than their authors. To work, symbols must speak independently to the soul of a culture. You cannot tell people what symbols should or should not mean.

Thus the knights, as much as they might desire, simply cannot determine what the symbolic garb of the Fourth Degree should say to the world or, for that matter, to the church.

Two problems are evident. Before the Second Vatican Council the church was unabashedly triumphalistic. A church that long experienced itself as being rejected by the powerful of this world did not fear triumphalism. It was in this world view and mindset that the garb of the Fourth Degree was created.

Surely one of the gifts of the council to the church has been its rejection of triumphalism as a legitimate way of life. Most Catholics in the post-council church have readily accepted this teaching and have come to realize that triumphalism ultimately breeds contempt.

Nothing the knights might do to "explain" their garb will be in any way effective if the people of today's world and church find in this symbolic garb an element of triumphalism.

So too with the sword. The image of the sword runs deep in the human psyche — and it speaks to our soul of war, not of the struggle for justice, not of the Pauline imagination which compared the sword with the power of God's Word (see Eph 6:17).

We do not want to imply that these problems define the Fourth Degree Knights of Columbus. Over the last 100 years these men have helped us to celebrate the faith of our ancestors — and for that we wish to say, without the slightest hesitancy, a hearty thank you.

Cookie monitor

October 15, 1997

Rev. Tom Ehrich, an Episcopal (Anglican) priest in the United States, is not currently working primarily as a cleric. His experience of church is now closer to that of a layperson than that of a priest. He has found the change a blessing in his life.

The clergy, he notes, have their own concerns, which are not necessarily those of the people in the pews. Priests worry excessively about the church as institution and take "the energetic few" who fuss about church structures far too seriously, Ehrich maintains. The clergy run the risk, he notes, of fashioning a god much like the cookie monitor in a food line whose solemn task it is to enforce the one-cookie-per-person rule.

But Jesus gave us a very different God — a God who proclaimed that grace is never in short supply. The only God the church is called to reflect is the gracious giver who relishes the opportunity of feeding the 5,000.

Ehrich reflects on his past. As an active priest he recruited and rewarded the cookie monitors who carefully maintained church structures at all costs. Now he finds them an annoyance, not because he wants two cookies, not because church structures are not important, but because he knows the worshippers in the pews with their amazing collection of needs (broken marriages, lost jobs, financial stress, troubled children, failing health, loneliness, etc., etc.) need a God much bigger than our ecclesial concerns.

We don't need the cookie monitor in every circumstance; we need a church that always knows, and truly cherishes knowing, that the reign of God extends far beyond its church doors.

One with the earth

April 23, 1997

A church based on sacraments should quite naturally be ecological.

Maybe that is why over the years we have tended to over-spiritualize the sacraments. By downplaying the matter in these expressions, we could more easily lessen our commitment to Earth.

And so the eucharistic meal was stripped of the cup. To drink wine quite naturally evokes a communal celebration, but that would hardly do, if our goal is "to spiritualize" the experience.

Real bread was also discarded; for long centuries even the most respected catechisms declared that chewing the bread was tantamount to biting Jesus. Wafers that melted in the mouth became the norm, the spiritual thing to do.

Similarly, the sexual aspect of marriage became quite secondary to the sacrament of marriage; indeed, in time "sex" needed to be justified to be acceptable. Procreation came in handy here.

So little oil was used in the sacraments — and what was used was immediately wiped off! — that all sense of bodily massage (as in the anointing of the sick) and of worldly beauty (such as the use of perfume in the chrism) was totally lost.

By "spiritualizing" the sacraments we destroyed their natural and critically important ability to bond us with the world.

We have, in considerable part, lost our sense of being part of the world. Thus our theology tended to go off in dangerous directions. We either reinterpreted Genesis and saw it as a licence to dominate creation so we could rightfully use it for our own pleasure or we downplayed our earthly pilgrimage altogether and declared that achieving heaven was all that counted.

Both these aberrations enabled us to destroy our world while believing all along that there would be no spiritual ramifications to this folly. To solidify this foolishness we declared all peoples and cultures that maintained a spiritual link with their environment primitive and uncivilized.

And so it strikes us as odd that highly educated First World citizens are consulting Ecuadoran Shuar shamans to re-establish their broken spiritual links with Earth.

Christianity will continue to fail to meet this First World need until it effectively re-establishes the material basis of its sacramental system. This will not be easy, since we have strayed so far off track. It might not be what we want to hear, but it would be wise if we ate a little crow and asked our Native Elders to aid us in this monumental task.

Chapter 4

Women and the Church

Women's voice needed
August 28, 1995

A great many women, though they love the church dearly and would never think of leaving it, are uncomfortable with their role in it.

They see their place changing in the secular world and wonder why their situation is not changing faster within the church. Did not Paul, in the very first generation of church life, proclaim that in Christ Jesus no distinctions between the sexes have validity as regards life in the church, that "in Christ Jesus there is neither male nor female" (Gal 3:28)?

They recognize that while they do not enjoy equality in the world, there at least the principle is affirmed. Though, for instance, they are earning only 72 cents for the same work men do for a dollar, the principle of equal pay for equal work is accepted as valid.

The pope is fully aware that dissatisfaction with their church is increasing rapidly among Catholic women and he is, in his own way, trying repeatedly to address the problem.

To be sure, there are issues about which he is unyielding. He refuses, for example, to see abortion as a women's issue. Abortion, he maintains, is not about the free choice of women; it is about the lives of precious little ones who are much more helpless.

He is equally adamant about international birth control plans. He sees them more as the continuation of the ongoing colonializing activities of the powerful nations of this world, rather than as effective programs to improve the lives of suppressed Third World women.

His letter to the women of the world, as part of his preparation for the United Nations' Beijing Conference on Women, has received wide acclaim — and not just from women in the church. The pope states that much of our previous history has been "a long and degrading history of sexual violence against women." He especially thanks women for all they have done for the church and directly apologizes that the church has often failed to recognize their contribution.

In several talks in recent weeks the pope has stated how one-sided our history books are. He has not hesitated to repeat himself: without the explicit voice of women in telling our history, that story will be misleading. When men write the history (and they have produced virtually all the critical documents of recorded history), "the results are almost exclusively about the things men have accomplished," the pope states.

The papal letter is indeed a great step forward for the church. And so the pope must be dismayed to hear that his letter is not without its harsh critics. They find its tone patronizing and paternalistic. And that is not because the pope holds firm to his position that women will never function as ministerial priests. They wonder more about the meaning of the pope's apology. Does he just mean the church of the past, or does he include the church of today? If he also includes the current church, then one should expect to see, they argue, some process of transformation whereby the church of tomorrow will be better than the church of today. These critics ask: Is there any concerted papal effort to make certain that the voice of women will be more effective in tomorrow's church?

The Second Vatican Council proclaimed that the church, even in its essence, is not a perfect society above the foibles of humanity. It is, rather, a pilgrim community, a people on the way struggling to rise above its imperfections.

In other words, the church has the same problems as the other social entities in the world that wish to overcome their limitations.

The pope gives an example. Human history, he claims, is simply doomed to its current imperfections if it refuses to be enriched by the voices of women adding their critical insights.

It is no different for the church. Without the effective voice of women, the church has not been able to keep its balance in many, many areas — not just in its understanding and appreciation of women.

The meaning of male sexuality is safeguarded, for instance, by the appreciation of female sexuality.

However, we live in a church which, through most of its history, has seen women as being inferior to men. Woman was viewed as the temptress: that justified men in seeking to dominate them — for their own good.

Not surprisingly, in such a church little was said either about marriage being a partnership or about the positive value of the wondrous pleasure God tied to genital activity.

It is embarrassing to read what the great bishops and theologians of age after age in the church had to say about women.

St. Clement of Alexandria said that "a woman should be covered with shame at the very thought that she is a woman." Pope St. Gregory the Great proclaims "that woman is slow in understanding and her unstable and naive mind renders her by way of natural weakness to the necessity of a strong hand in her husband. Her use is two-fold: animal sex and motherhood."

Tertullian, a North African theologian (AD 160-220), gives this theology its classical expression: "Woman, do you know that you are Eve? You are the devil's gateway. How easily you destroyed man, the image of God. Because of the death which you brought upon us, even the Son of God had to die."

St. Augustine, critically important for so many avenues of thought in the church, also played a key role in evaluating sexuality. "Women," he said, "are not made in the image of God. I feel that nothing so casts down the manly mind from its heights as the fondling of woman and those bodily contacts that belong to the married state."

St. John Chrysostom said it even more bluntly: "Among all savage beasts none is found so harmful as woman."

St. Thomas Aquinas, the mind behind much of the thinking in the medieval church, saw women as clearly second-class citizens: "As regard the individual nature, woman is defective and misbegotten." Though Thomas was undeniably one of the greatest minds the church has ever known, he could unabashedly proclaim: "It is unchallengeable that woman is destined to live under man's influence and has no authority from her Lord. Woman is something deficient or accidental. For the active power of the male intends to produce a perfect likeness of itself with male sex. If a female is conceived, this is due to lack of strength in the active power, to a defect in the mother."

These many quotes give some idea how pervasive such thinking became in the church. Is it any wonder that every sexual act had to be justified? Is it surprising that the church became an active participant in the burning of witches, and that virtually every woman who claimed to have had mystical experiences different from those described by men had much to fear from the Inquisition?

Surely Augustine and Thomas Aquinas, surely John Chrysostom and Gregory the Great would not have made such outrageous statements if the women of their day — even with their much inferior educational training — had had any significant influence on their thinking.

Men cannot write a comprehensive history without the explicit contribution of women. Why should the church feel that it can present the Gospel faithfully without having to rely on the equally authoritative experience of women?

Women's gifts essential

March 14, 2001

A recent sociological survey was not based on a random sample. Indeed, the very opposite was the case. Every single participant was personally chosen by one of 128 diocesan bishops in the United States.

Those conducting the survey asked the bishops to name as participants those women they thought were diocesan leaders.

The goal of the survey by the Life Cycle Institute of the Catholic University of America was to "examine how women's voices were heard in church decision-making."

This highly selected body of women, women who had already found their way into the diocesan church structures, were not complimentary in their responses. Nearly a third of those who responded were rather blunt. "Diocesan leadership structures," they said, "do not allow women's voices to be heard."

Many were even more condemnatory. "Diocesan leaders or priests," they added, "have sexist attitudes or do not understand women."

One-quarter of them also noted that women's voices are muted by women who are "overly militant, combative, single-minded or insubordinate."

Of course, that is true for everyone. None of these attitudes fosters communication. However, the real question to be asked is: Are women given the same latitude in manifesting these faults as are men (priests and bishops included)?

Even that question is badly phrased. Given the desperate state the church is in by its not being able to hear the voices of women, one would think that more rather than less latitude should be shown to women.

St. Paul once gave the church a checklist whereby it could discern whether or not it was truly manifesting a catholic spirit, on whether it could indeed present to the world a truly "catholic" God, in contradistinction to presenting a god who was patronizing, authoritarian, and patriarchal.

Paul acknowledged that this trinity of narrow-mindedness marked his own God for many years — even for years after his baptism. So it was at great personal cost that Paul, in his instruction to the Galatians, reminded them that at their baptism they were clothed in Christ and so were not to make any distinctions "between Jew and Greek, slave and free, male and female" (Gal 3:28).

As was noted in the recent discussions with Lutherans on justification by faith and not by law, the church still has some practical preferences for the "Jew" over the "Greek." (Jew here is understood as Jesus polemically used it; despite Jesus's criticism of the good-works position of the Pharisees, the church has had a most difficult time clearly preaching the absolutely free gifts of grace over a faithful following of law.) Similarly, the church's propensity throughout our history to side with the rich and the powerful over the needs of the poor also shows us that we are more at home with the "free" than with the "slaves."

This survey of women employees of the American church clearly indicates that as church we much prefer the masculine to the feminine viewpoint on ecclesial matters. No wonder the God the church so often projects is precisely patronizing, authoritarian, and patriarchal.

It is important for us to remember that in parable after parable Jesus teaches us that this god in actuality does not exist. Rather, "he" is a theological construct of men who have in truth never moved beyond the world of the scribes and Pharisees.

But the issue is even more fundamental than that of faithfully revealing the true God whom Jesus, not without scandalizing many, announced to the world. Throughout our history the warmth and tenderness of our faith was handed on, not by ecclesial structures and mighty theological treatises, but by mothers with their children on their laps.

The church limped its way through centuries of anticlericalism; whether it can survive several generations of turned-off mothers is an altogether different question. Studies showing that families are currently not fostering "vocations" should be a warning sign.

Two dioceses recently refused to send their Catholic teachers to hear Benedictine Sister Joan Chittister because she was "too critical of the church." Is this a case of women being much more restricted in what they can say to the church than are its men, especially its clergy?

Chittister states beautifully why she is a feminist — and it's not because she is "overly militant, combative, single-minded or insubordinate!"

"I am a feminist," she says, "precisely because I am a Catholic — not as a reaction to what is wrong about the church, but actually as a response to what is right about the church. My Christian feminist commitment to the equality, the dignity and the humanity of all persons and the need to change structures to make that so does not come as a result of my rejection of what I see as bad in the church. It comes as an inevitable recognition of what I see as the great, the magnetizing, the empowering, the energizing good that is inherent for women in the church, even when I cannot see it yet being brought to fullness, even in the church."

It is this feminist spirit that will in God's good time heal the church. It is the same good news which the diocesan respondents mentioned above have daily given to the church. The bishops saw them as among their best. Thus, despite their recognition that "diocesan leadership structures do not allow women's voices to be heard," despite their daily experience that "diocesan leaders or priests have sexist attitudes," these women are standing by the church, nurturing it with life.

It is love such as theirs that has made our church so beautiful. It is this love that keeps encouraging many a male believer to continue to trust in the power of grace within the church. It is this love that gives credibility to our church in the eyes of the world.

First witness to the Resurrection April 9, 2003

It is one thing to proclaim that the church has no authority or power to ordain women. It is quite another to come up with arguments that not only women, but men, too, find convincing. In this regard it is important to note that the church throughout its history has never tried to bind its faithful to believe in the arguments used to define and underpin a dogma.

A history of dogmatic theology constantly shows that the reasoning behind a dogma often changes.

The pope is about to issue an encyclical on the Eucharist, the central mystery of the Christian worship of God. Since the Eucharist is so important to the church, theologians over the last 500 years have often gone overboard and identified the teaching of the real presence of Christ with the philosophical reasoning that has accompanied it. The pope will have to proceed carefully in calling us to cherish the real presence, while giving us the traditional freedom regarding its explanation.

No matter what one's understanding of the ministerial priesthood may be, one must recognize that there is an intimate relationship between apostolic authority and being a witness to the Resurrection of Jesus. And to complicate this matter further, it is important for us not to superimpose a fifth-century idea of the priesthood on first-century disciples — both male and female.

It is one thing for the church over many centuries to meditate and pray over the Gospel accounts of the Last Supper and find these texts truly important for our understanding of the priesthood. It is quite another to think that Peter, James, and John came away from the table believing that they had been ordained, that they were now priests.

Further, it is something else entirely to believe that only Jesus and the Twelve were at the table. Both Jesus's normal conduct during his public ministry and the customs of his contemporary Jewish brothers and sisters would strongly suggest that the opposite was the case, that the key women present in Jesus's ministry and in his terrible ordeal on the cross were also gathered around that most famous table in history.

It is not at all improper to wonder what personal interpretation the women as well as the men would have given to the event. Nor is it inappropriate to ask all the first followers of the risen Christ what they found more significant for their apostolic community — what transpired between Jesus and the Twelve at the table, or what Mary Magdalene and the other women experienced in beholding their Lord glorified on Easter day.

It had to be something quite extraordinary, or else the Gospel accounts would not be so clear on two points: first, that the men did not believe the women and tried to find out for themselves, and second, that even the empty tomb did not totally bring the men around.

In time, the story of Mary Magdalene was expanded to include stories of prostitutes and sinners. This change in one of Christianity's foundational stories was certainly done in part to meet a challenge within the church community. The new story of the Magdalene now highlighted the absolute gratuity of grace, and the fact that this grace was sufficient even for the most hardened of sinners.

However true (and fundamental) this latter truth is, it must never take away the original thrust of the Resurrection story. It is not at all unlikely that the original story was changed because its key truths had become uncomfortable for leaders in the church.

Yes, central to the original story are some facts men would rather forget. First, that a society built only on male thinking can easily become unbalanced, cold, and narrow. God with wisdom divine made men and women different, not only in body parts but also in thought processes and in sensitivity to others.

It is ultimately not surprising that it was the women who loved Jesus so much that neither cross nor tomb could separate them from their Lord. When all is said and done, the Mary Magdalene story, if it were allowed to flourish in the church and on the mother's lap as she teaches the faith to the next generation, would constantly move the whole church beyond a cultural mindset of male superiority. For some men, this second truth is more painful than the first.

In this regard, it is important to see how the early Christian community developed its process of bringing new members into the church. It is not by accident that the first formal scrutiny whereby the neophytes were to discern their reasons for wanting to join in the church's Easter celebration of new life was none other than the story of the Samaritan woman at the well. In this story we come face-to-face with basic cultural prejudices — religious, geographical, racial, and, not least of all, those of gender.

From the first stages of their formal entry into the Easter community, catechumens were being prepared to hear that first great witness of the new age, Jesus's close friend Mary Magdalene.

The language of liturgy December 7, 1994

It is a messy situation. There is no simple way out.

Cardinal Joseph Ratzinger of the Congregation for the Doctrine of the Faith, in his rejection of the *New Revised Standard Version* of the Bible for use in the liturgy, expressly noted that its use of inclusive language with regard to the believer gave him difficulties.

The Canadian and American bishops have committed themselves repeatedly in recent years to using inclusive language in their liturgical and catechetical books. And, subsequent to the Vatican's ban of the *New Revised Standard Version* of the Bible for liturgical and catechetical use, spokespersons for both episcopal conferences have stressed in press releases their ongoing commitment to using inclusive language.

"Inclusive language is a necessity in our American idiom and culture today," said Bishop Donald W. Trautman, the chair of the U.S. Bishops' Committee on Liturgy.

Msgr. James Weisgerber, general secretary of the English sector of the Canadian Conference of Catholic Bishops, was equally straightforward: "As for inclusive language, the bishops are totally committed to it."

Right now the American bishops have before them a text on providing new forms of leadership for women in the church. In this text they say: "Inclusive language is a particular concern in North America.... Although the English translation of the new Catechism of the Catholic Church does not use inclusive language, the pope has indicated that materials that evolved from the catechism could reflect the culture, language and idiom of a given country. In the United States our culture more and more seeks to honour the principles of inclusive language. We urge that catechetical and religious materials, as well as our daily language and prayer, do so as well."

Many people — both men and women — have strongly held views on inclusive language, and thus no one should be surprised that comments on this issue become heated. In her typical confrontational style, Joanna Manning of the Coalition of Concerned Canadian Catholics declares that she "would issue a challenge to the Canadian bishops to stand up and confront this example of the sin of sexism within the church."

The executive board of the Catholic Biblical Association, while not usually noted for its biting language, is this time, however, equally blunt in giving its opinion on Ratzinger's ban of the *NRSV*. They call the action "demeaning" to episcopal conferences, so much so that the "church's credibility is involved."

The Scripture scholars complained that the Vatican action "suggests that the (U.S.) National Conference of Catholic Bishops and its resources are not able to determine what is doctrinally sound and pastorally appropriate."

This criticism must be taken seriously. Pope John Paul II, in marking the 25th anniversary of the Second Vatican Council's Constitution on the Liturgy, praised the great progress that had been accomplished in the past quarter century. "But there remains," he noted, "the considerable task of continuing to implant the liturgy in certain cultures, welcoming from them those expressions which are compatible with aspects of the true and authentic spirit of the liturgy."

The bishops of Canada and the United States certainly believe that inclusive language is one of those cultural expressions which they should welcome as being compatible with the true spirit of the liturgy.

Inculturation cannot be decreed from above. Germans and Italians are simply going to have to listen when North American bishops tell them that "man," no matter how inclusive its meaning was for centuries upon centuries of English usage, no longer is an inclusive term for an ever-increasing number of Catholic worshippers.

And this does not mean that the bishops are insensitive to doctrinal concerns. The Canadian lectionary, for instance, will at times use the word "man" to prevent a doctrinal misunderstanding (see, for example, its translation of Romans 5).

It is difficult, however, to see the doctrinal problems the church was facing in its opening sentences of the new catechism, which has even one more "man" than l'homme in the French original: "God, infinitely perfect and blessed in himself, in a plan of sheer goodness freely created man to make him share in his own blessed life. For this reason, at every time and in every place, God draws close to man. He calls man to seek him, to know him, to love him with all his strength. He calls together all men, scattered and divided by sin, into the unity of his family, the church."

Ratzinger says that there must be a unity between the catechetical and liturgical dimensions of church life. The bishops must insist that this translation of the catechism simply does not reflect the idiom and culture of what is best in North America. If they fail in this, it will indeed be a "demeaning" time for episcopal oversight in our church.

Powerful scrutiny

March 4, 1998

One of the great blessings of the Second Vatican Council certainly has been the restoration of the Rite of the Christian Initiation of Adults. The RCIA, a process whereby candidates are gradually incorporated into the church as a community, is much more than an alternative to a private, cerebral memorizing of the right answers of a catechism, which previously formed the basis of "convert instruction."

If the process of the RCIA is allowed to take its course, it becomes a powerful tool in the pastoral transformation of the parish itself. While the church provides three full cycles of Sunday Lenten readings, the rubrics

Women and the Church

carefully note that Cycle A is to be preferred if the parish is involved in the RCIA.

The Third Sunday of Lent has traditionally been the day to begin the special scrutinies. St. John's story of the woman at the well (4:5-42) becomes the two-edged sword of the Word of God (see Heb 4:12) revealing to each candidate — and to the whole assembly — the meaning Christ both has and should have in their daily lives.

Choosing the Lord revealed in this story will radically change both the catechumens and the church community they wish to join.

Jesus begs a favour of a Samaritan woman. She is doubly surprised. Jews never deigned to talk to Samaritans, let alone admit to them that they could provide a service for which the Jews would subsequently be indebted.

Jesus has no time for the theological squabbles between Jews and Samaritans — and let us not forget that the differences these people practically worshipped were significantly greater than those today between Catholics and Lutherans or between Anglicans and members of the United Church of Canada.

Jesus goes further, calling both Jew and Samaritan to a new understanding of God's dealing with humanity. Jesus accepted both while gently leading them beyond their destructive theology of breaking the world into the sacred and profane. In a call to hold all that is profane as precious in God's sight, he invites the Samaritan woman to see beyond their mountain shrine (or the Jews beyond their Jerusalem temple) as liturgical foci, as special sacred places. Instead, he calls her to worship "in spirit," a term the first Christians closely identified with "in the church community" (note: that is the sacred place).

"In truth" called them to this new understanding of God's world.

Jesus scandalizes his apostles. They could not believe that the one they had placed on their sacred pedestal would so lower himself by engaging a woman in public conversation.

The Lord of this story must certainly be perplexed that the churches have spent so much time and energy making theological distinctions between men and women. Certainly central to this story is a breaking down of the distinctions between them.

Jesus knows human nature well. Making distinctions usually begins with a noble aspiration — the special gifts of each are means to be highlighted. But Jesus knows, and 2,000 years of church history proves him right: highlighting distinctions inevitably leads to value judgments, in this case to judgments (by men) that they are superior to women — in the home and in the church.

Yes, Jesus knows human nature well. This story celebrates this. The Lord we now know in the church can read our inmost hearts and, like the Samaritan woman, we are not to be disturbed that he finds sin in our hearts. Indeed, it was the reading of her heart, which entailed the revelation of her scandalous sex life, that triggered her excitement in meeting her Lord.

Most extraordinary of all, Jesus tells her how completely God gives the grace of the kingdom. God's grace makes her heart fully her own. Her very heart will become, he promises her, the wellspring of the living water gushing up to eternal life (Jn 4:14). Liberation theologians in Latin America have opened this text for the poor slum dwellers and challenged them to embrace the unbelievable: to drink from their own wells.

What a scrutiny this story provides the candidate and the church! Belief in Jesus as our Christ and Lord will challenge virtually everything in our lives: what we think about men and women, about church unity, about people of different races and cultures, about God's holiness in the very secularity of the world, and, not least of all, about our sinful hearts as the special thrones of God's glory.

Pointing out sin — at home

April 18, 1988

It is not too likely that those who are constantly asking the church to point out and condemn sin will be happy with the first draft of the recent American bishops' pastoral on women's concerns for church and society. The problem: the bishops do not start with others' sin, with the sin of the world. They start with the sin of the church.

The bishops plead with the People of God to face "the sin of sexism." But they do a lot more than condemn individual church members of insensitivity toward women. They acknowledge that sexism is institutionalized in the church and thus the church is called upon to change not only attitudes but also its structures.

The clergy — bishops and priests alike — are entreated to confess their "patronizing, condescending attitudes" toward women. Perhaps the most frightening aspect of the pastoral is the bishops' concern for many of those currently in seminaries. But they do not allow the shortage of priests to colour their advice to those called upon to discern vocations. They mince no words; they tell their colleagues that an inability to deal with women as equals should be considered an indication that a seminarian is unfit for ordination to the priesthood.

Such discernment would require seminarians to be less segregated than they are at present. The bishops make an important point in this regard. They ask that church law be changed so they can encourage women to teach in their seminaries.

St. John tells us if we live our lives in the light, the blood of Jesus purifies us of our sin (1 Jn 1:7). The American bishops have given the whole church a wonderful example of exposing their sin to the light of Christ. Such Easter faith can make the church an altogether new creation.

Women's ordination
April 2, 1997

The Catholic Theological Society of America (CTSA), in its next plenary meeting in June, will be examining the reasons behind the Vatican decision that it is infallible teaching — according to the ordinary and universal magisterium — that women cannot be ordained priests in the Catholic Church. The CTSA is not directly addressing the teaching; they are simply looking at the reasons the Vatican has given in support of its teaching.

In a nutshell, they ask a very pointed question: Is the church's action the result of a teaching of Christ, or does it stem from a long, consistent pattern of thinking in the church based on the cultural and philosophical view that women are inferior to men?

It is such a painful question because throughout so much of our history we have — undeniably — treated women as second-class citizens. And we must acknowledge the following: even if the church were perfectly consistent in such a practice throughout its long history, it would have absolutely no theological bearing on the issue at hand.

In theory, it is easy to separate a command of the Lord from a custom of the church. In practice, however, it is far from simple.

To look at two little rules repeatedly stated in the post-conciliar church:

1) No woman was to read a lesson from the pulpit in which the Gospel was proclaimed. (It was no problem if a man were to read Isaiah or St. Paul from the pulpit.)

2) Even with the breakdown of the notion of sanctuary with the removal of communion rails, it remained the law of the church that only its

male members could carry the water cruet to the altar during the eucharistic service.

In making these laws, church officials would vehemently deny that they were treating women as second-class citizens. And, without a shadow of a doubt, these legislators would have been personally convinced that they were being faithful to the call of Jesus.

Yet, when we look back on it, the vast majority of Catholics have concluded that these laws reflected a prejudice against women rather than the will of the Saviour.

These two little examples are not isolated or arbitrary choices. Church historians can find similar examples in virtually every age of the church.

And so, the question the Catholic Theological Society is addressing is a necessary one — as unsettling as it is to so many. Without facing squarely our habitual practice of treating women as inferior models of humanity, we will never come to a peaceful resolution of what role the Lord Jesus actually wanted women to play in the church.

Women hearing confessions   September 10, 2003

An English bishop has suggested that Catholic women be commissioned to administer the sacrament of reconciliation. At the same time he acknowledges that, with the shortage of clergy, many of the faithful, in facing serious illness, do not have access to the sacrament of the anointing.

It is interesting to note that, in advocating women as confessors, Bishop Vincent Malone of Liverpool does not give the current shortage of priests as his primary reason. Rather, he compares the confessional with a medical practice where patients are routinely given the choice between a male and female doctor; Malone asks whether the time has come for the church to offer Catholic women a similar choice of confessor.

A historical study of the development of priestly ministry is critically important in this regard. Of late, many people — including some members of the church's central administration — believe it is time to re-examine the division of authority between the pope and the diocesan bishops.

The division of authority is not, however, a theological issue only at the top. The same sort of simplification of structures has taken place at the "other end" of the clerical world. With the Peace of Constantine (AD

313), there developed rather quickly a deep separation between the clergy and the laity: all sacramental ministry (with the exception of emergency baptism) was taken from the laity and centred in the ordained.

So, just as all authority came to be centred in the pope, with the bishops becoming his "delegates," in an analogous way all sacramental power came to be exercised only by those who led the eucharistic celebration. Both these developments need careful reassessment.

If one takes Jesus's words seriously, one would have to conclude that he was not interested in establishing a church principally noted for its hierarchical structure. When the disciples were jockeying for position, Jesus chided them: "You know that among the pagans their so-called rulers lord it over them, and their great ones make their authority felt. This must not happen among you. No, anyone who wants to be great among you must be your servant. The Son of Man did not come to be served but to serve and give his life as a ransom for many" (Mk 10:42-45).

In this regard, it is important to note that the early church, usually in the midst of persecution, could not have developed much hierarchical order in its underground existence even if it had wanted to.

If its priests had to carry out all sacramental actions (as was the case later in Elizabethan England), they would have been discovered and martyred: as it was, the early church hid its leaders of the Eucharist very well; few of those we came to call priests were ever caught by the Roman persecutors of the church.

The meaning of the priesthood changed rapidly with the Peace of Constantine. When the Roman state, as it had long done with pagan priests, began paying the Christian clergy (and thus freeing them from other work), Christians naturally expected these underemployed citizens to do most of the work in the church.

And, as one might suspect, it did not take the clergy long to develop a theology of authority to suit their new position. With little to support any model of authority in the New Testament — especially not in the words of Jesus himself — they turned to the Hebrew Scriptures and found there a wealth of material. Soon, according to the ordination rituals, the bishop (and, to a lesser extent, the priest) became the successor not only of Old Testament priests but also of prophets and kings.

All the charisms of authority and sacramental expression came to be centred in the sacrament of orders. A great divide between clergy and laity developed. The priest was not just ordained; to symbolize his complete mastery, he was ordained in a sevenfold manner. He was not simply ordained priest but also, among others, Mass server, deacon, and doorkeeper.

Authority for the clergy was now complete; the clergy not only claimed exclusive right to define dogma, they also claimed exclusive right to administer the sacraments.

One of the last areas of sacramental administration to fall under this clerical coup was the anointing of the sick. We have a vestigial remnant of this in the Holy Thursday Chrism Mass. While chrism and the oil of the catechumens are blessed together by the bishop, the ritual still suggests the oil of the sick be blessed as part of the eucharistic prayer.

The oil of the sick and the eucharistic food have always been closely identified in the church. We all know how we lose our appetite for food when we are sick — and how our desire for a massage increases at the same time. The church acknowledged this, and in its solicitude for the sick presented both — usually together — but in individual cases presented one or the other, depending on which was especially appreciated as Christ's presence by the sick person.

Already in the early third century, in the Apostolic Tradition of Hippolytus, the bishop was instructed to bless oil during the eucharistic prayer for the laity to take home to anoint their sick.

Pope Innocent I expressly resisted the move of the post-Constantinian clergy in Rome to make themselves the only ones who could anoint the sick. They had used the text from James (5:13-15) to back up their argument.

Pope Innocent said: "Now there is no doubt that these words of James are to be understood of the faithful who are sick, and who can be anointed with the holy oil which has been prepared by the bishop, and which not only priests but all Christians may use for anointing, when their own needs and those of their family demand."

While church history is clearer on the appropriateness of having the laity anoint the sick, a good case can also be made for the celebration of individual confession by "lay" men and women. It is crucial for the health of the church that we have the honesty and the courage to open fully the question of ministry. We will never arrive at satisfactory answers to the questions of priest shortages, priestly celibacy, and, yes, the ordination or non-ordination of women with our current practice of ministry.

Could it not be that the Spirit is calling us back to pre-Constantinian practices in which ministries were not centred in a class of people but widely shared among many? Need our confessors always be those who lead the Eucharist for us, or those who anoint our sick also be those who decide church policy?

Should we not commission those who are especially gifted in visiting the sick to anoint them "in the name of the church"? Likewise, should we not admit that many who are good at leading the Eucharist are less than adept at listening with the tenderness of God to the woes of the sick?

Thirty years ago a mother of two priests complained to me that it was not fair that she had to go to confession to a man. A simple, poorly educated woman, she was anything but a flaming feminist in her desire to have a feminine ear to hear her confession.

St. Paul often seems to indicate that some are called to be confessors, some administrators, some baptizers, some the visitors of the sick. It never occurred to the Apostle that someday the church would be so fortunate as to find all these charisms in the same person.

Both crises, that of the lack of clergy to take tender care of the sick and that of so many Catholic women not feeling that they are equal members in the church, should prompt us to make this move to break up the ministries. We will, no doubt, find that in struggling to solve these two problems, we will have gone a long way toward solving most of our problems with ministry and the priesthood.

Dysfunctional church

July 19, 1993

The pope used his address to a group of American bishops making their *ad limina* visit to Rome once each five years to warn them that in its extreme form feminism is undermining the Christian faith itself. "Sometimes forms of nature worship and the celebration of myths and symbols take the place of the worship of the God revealed in Jesus Christ," the pope told the bishops.

American nuns especially, he said, must be watched; a feminism which advocates a worship of the earth is promoted by some whose beliefs, attitudes, and behaviour no longer correspond to the Gospel.

This papal address was reported in the major international news services; it made it onto the pages of most Canadian daily newspapers; it was even covered on the CBC's national TV news.

Canadian Catholic women have just absorbed the insult of one of the country's leading archbishops calling someone in his archdiocese "a bitch." It must be very painful indeed for them now to hear the pope speaking so harshly about the problems feminists are causing in the church. Little is said about their contribution to the church's well-being, though the pope does remind the bishops that in the secular world "respect for women's rights is without doubt an essential step toward a more just and mature society, and the church cannot fail to make its own this worthy objective."

One cannot miss the sweeping general tone of the pope's words: American women who are pushing for changes in the church are harming it. The pope, it is obvious, is afraid of what is happening in the North American church. And it's not just a small fringe of extremists that is bothering him; he sees the problem as much more pervasive, and calls upon the bishops to challenge these groups in the church and in sincere and honest dialogue to tell them what are their proper expectations as women in the church.

At issue here is much more than the pope's own view of the role of women in the church. While that indeed may be troublesome to a great many women and men in the church and will itself need "honest and sincere" dialogue before the air in the church can be cleared, there is an immediate problem which must be addressed: Where is the pope getting his information about the activities of women in the church? Who is telling him about all these "women religious whose beliefs, attitudes and behaviour no longer correspond to what the Gospel and the church teach"?

We must ask: Who has the ear of the curial officials who daily brief the pope and write his speeches?

Historically, the *ad limina* visits of the world's bishops were instituted to make certain that communication between bishops and the pope would be maintained at the highest level possible.

Yet there are many indications that the world's bishops are not the primary source the Vatican curial officials rely upon for information — not even for the critically important function of naming new bishops. It is common knowledge that the Canadian archbishop who made headlines throughout the country for his disparaging remarks about women was on no bishops' lists of suggestions for such an appointment.

The pope must be made aware of the resultant fallout from a talk such as the one he gave to the American bishops. He must be told forcefully that it does not, in any substantive way, represent life in the North American church.

And who can tell him? Few beside our bishops ever get to talk to him.

This fall it is the turn of the bishops of western Canada to go to Rome for their *ad limina* visit. They each get 10 to 15 minutes for a private meeting with the pope.

It is not a time for piety. It is not a time for basking in the personal privilege of meeting with the pope.

It is time to be a bishop, to be, as the Second Vatican Council reminds them, responsible for the whole church. They must tell the pope of the pain women needlessly experience today in our church — and the harm this is doing to the church's mission of being an agent of salvation for everyone.

They must tell him, too, how much good is being done in their local church by strong, self-reliant women and how desperately they need such women in the forefront of church life for the effective operation of their church.

The pope has called for honest and sincere dialogue with women about their expectations in the church. That is not at all possible, the pope must be told, until the church at its highest levels stops appearing as afraid of, if not hostile to, the aspirations of strong, self-reliant Christian women.

Neither male nor female   September 30, 1985

The Gospel of Mark (10:2-12) deals with the issue of divorce. In its original context Jesus was being asked whether he followed the Shammai or Hillel school of thought.

Shammai was a rigorist and allowed a man to divorce his wife only for adultery. Hillel was a much gentler sort. Being a poor cook was reason enough for him. Indeed, he was most understanding of male weakness: a wandering eye discovering new beauty was sufficient reason.

Jesus simply ignored both schools of thought as irrelevant. Both schools, for all their differences in interpretation, were based on the same premise — that man was superior to woman.

Jesus based his teaching on the equality of the sexes. He bypassed all the legal quibbling in divorce, both inside and outside the Bible, and quoted Genesis on the creation of man and woman.

Jesus's teaching on equality was obviously far too much for his audience, which was not ready to part with its prejudices and propensities for legal gymnastics.

Nor has this teaching sat well in the Christian community. The church down through the ages has been far more prone to quote the young and highly opinionated Paul who was all too ready to mouth the prejudices of his time (see 1 Cor 11), than to teach the later Paul who had suffered a painful conversion at the hand of the unruly Corinthians (2 Cor 12:7ff.).

It is not the old authoritarian Paul who tells the Galatians that in Christ there are no significant distinctions between male and female (Gal 3:28). We have not only maintained that the distinctions between the sexes are important for church life; we have concretized these even in our God. While we know that God cannot be male or female, that the fullness and beauty of all masculinity and femininity subsist in God, we have insisted on viewing God within a patriarchal mindset that only solidifies the prejudices that Jesus undermined in the Gospel story on divorce.

Someone once said that nothing is more powerful than an idea that has reached its time. The equality of man and woman is such an idea, and no theologizing over 2,000 years of prejudiced history is going to make a particle of difference.

It is simply a question of whether the premise of the Lord will be accepted by the churches. And let there be no doubt about what such acceptance will entail — it will mean a conversion every bit as painful as Paul's.

Women and the faith

November 3, 1999

Twelve years ago a sociological survey in the United States found that 68 percent of women and 62 percent of men said they could not imagine circumstances that would cause them to leave the Catholic Church.

The same questions were asked this year. Fifty-six percent of women and 57 percent of men now hold this position. One wonders if there was ever a time previous to this when women would outnumber men in questioning their very membership in the church.

The church has survived long periods of anticlericalism. The role of the clergy, though of great central importance, can be deeply resented and yet, as we have seen, the church can survive.

But it is another question as to how well the church will survive if the primary teachers of the faith (and they are mothers, not clerics) do not hand on the Catholic ethos in their homes.

In the first period of church history, the overwhelming proportion of converts was women. They saw in the church a wondrous, and totally unexpected, pledge to dignity and respect. How painful it is to realize today that it is young women, more than young men, who question their very membership in a church community, which they see as anything but a pledge to personal dignity and respect.

Chapter 5

Religious, Priestly Vocations

Specialized vocations
April 25, 2001

The Second Vatican Council changed our way of thinking about vocations. In truth, there is only one Christian vocation: the baptismal call to follow Jesus Christ.

Specialized vocations, such as to the religious life or to the priesthood, are in fact concrete ways in which we are called to express our baptismal commitment. All vocations are fulfilled around the table of the Eucharist, a table which helps us realize our true worth as the Body of Christ.

So, in one sense, we cannot have a "vocations crisis." Everything pales in comparison to our being a Christian. When, after our death, we stand together to celebrate the great act of thanksgiving around the heavenly throne, we will not marvel at so-and-so being a nun, at so-and-so being a priest or bishop; the great gift of God making us in the very image of Jesus, transforming us as daughters and sons with the dignity of the Lord Jesus, "levels" out all specialized callings — and not to the lowest common denominator but to the highest: We shall all as kings and queens reign for ever and ever (Rv 22:5).

The church celebrates this sheer gift of grace from the Father of the Lord Jesus by insisting that there be no special seats around the eucharistic table. One of the most important reforms of Vatican II was the unheralded removal of communion rails. Their removal destroyed the notion of a sanctuary; now all the people as equals gather around the table in one space.

At first sight, this eucharistic theology appears to downplay specialized vocations, especially to ministry and religious life. But nothing could be further from the truth. Each of us is called to do our part in making the church community a whole. Yet "the eye cannot say to the hand, 'I do not need you,' nor can the head say to the feet, 'I do not need you'" (1 Cor 12:21).

Yes, glorying in one vocation as greater than another is a thing of the past. But each of us has the supreme opportunity to hear God's special call to us.

The church is ill prepared to preach this notion of vocation. Since the current expression of the institutional church is in such dire need of priests and religious, it has an extremely difficult time in not succumbing to the temptation of seeing priesthood and religious life as special (in the sense of higher) callings.

As with all temptations, the rosy future they envision soon evaporates into thin air. The dishonesty of the whole process quickly backfires. A study about 10 years ago in the United States had less than 25 percent of practising Catholic parents expressing a hope that one of their sons would enter the priesthood. Less than 18 percent would have been happy if one of their daughters entered religious life.

These are indeed sobering statistics, but they need not be frightening. They simply tell us something we know in our heart of hearts: that we cannot shore up the old church by preaching the special place in God's kingdom for these vocations.

There is much out there that appears to contradict this. The religious communities that most carefully imitate the religious life of the pre-Vatican II era are getting the most "vocations." Those seminaries that promise to restore the ancient glories of the clerical state and put priests back on pedestals have more candidates than those that emphasize the sheer grace of God given us in baptism.

We should not be surprised by this. We are at the end of an era, called by the council to enter a new age. Sociologists and church historians tell us, however, that a sense of great insecurity is quite naturally present at the end of each era, and thus people will cling in a more desperate way to the old and tried. Before the breakthrough to each new age there is one last fallback to the old, one last desperate effort to make the old ways work. In this regard we must be extremely careful in evaluating the apparent success of those religious communities and seminaries that are adopting with a vengeance pre-Vatican II forms.

The religious vows are not signs of greater holiness, nor are they principally ascetic tools to perfect the soul. Their aim is to free the religious from bondage to the status quo so that the religious has the freedom to envision a new church in a new age.

If history is to teach us anything, it is that ultimately there is only one way to foster vocations to the religious life today: we must allow religious to be at the cutting edge. We must let them be prophetic.

Being prophets is never first-place-in-the-kingdom stuff. It usually is standing with the poor and marginalized. The poor would never come to trust religious if they were specialized people in the church community.

In an analogous way, so, too, the priesthood. Gone is the day that the priest stands between God and the people as a mediator over and above the People of God. Gone is the special status in the kingdom for priests.

Celibacy has been a great blessing for most priests. We always smile, though we be over 60 years old, when people ask us if we would marry should the pope allow it tomorrow. As much as we cherish our celibacy, we recognize a difficulty. In proclaiming celibacy as a holier way of life than celebrating the sacrament of marriage, we set the priesthood apart and use this moral superiority to solidify the sociological foundations for a clerical state.

Rather than see the priest as an intermediary above and beyond the people, the council recaptured the patristic meaning whereby the priest is called to be spokesperson for the People of God. The priest is to gather the faith of the community and mould it into a new song of praise.

Countless priests have discovered that the satisfaction derived from enabling a community to celebrate its very meaning as the Body of Christ far outstrips the glories of their pedestal existence of former days when they stood over and above the church community. In this they also experience the great joy of acting in Christ's name insofar as they gather the community together and pray in its name.

As the church community comes to terms with the world-shattering changes of the council, there will be turmoil. The old reasons for becoming a priest or religious no longer hold water. But just as the current groups of veteran priests and religious had to fundamentally re-examine the reasons for sticking with their calling, so the Holy Spirit will find ways to inspire today's Christians to the prophetic life of religious and to the servanthood of the priesthood.

The greatest disservice we can make to the church and to "vocations" is to insist that choosing the old forms of the priesthood and religious life is the best way to be faithful to the Good News of Jesus Christ.

A prophetic call

April 9, 1997

Benedictine Sister Joan Chittister did not mince words in her talk to Saskatchewan religious April 5. "Old answers to old questions," she said, "will not form the foundation for a new generation of religious."

"Religious," she added, "are being called out of isolation into the world, out of piety and personal perfection to deep prayer, and out of a clerical (special) status into Christian commitment."

In giving a new twist to poverty, chastity, and obedience, Chittister noted that "it's precisely our security that is killing us, our isolation that's insulating us from the Gospel, and our obedience that's making us useless lackeys of oppressive and unjust systems."

One might be tempted to dismiss ideas such as these as the agenda of a radical whose spirit had not yet been tempered by the realism of everyday life. But that is certainly not what her audience thought. This gathering of Saskatchewan religious rose as one person at the end of her presentation with a long-standing ovation.

And, not for a moment did they think she was calling them to something easy. Yet they identified with Chittister, who had no time to justify religious life. The Pennsylvania Benedictine called out, not for people who think their way of life is better or higher than that of the rest of the People of God, but for Christians who know that religious life is the only way for them to become fully alive to the will and Spirit of God.

Saskatchewan's religious, especially women religious, have come upon hard times, very hard times. The dreams they had upon entering religious life have cruelly evaporated. Many communities have gone decades without professing new members.

It would not be surprising, therefore, if they would circle their wagons and, with all the security they could muster, find some comfortable space to gently lick their wounds before they die.

Instead, they heard and responded enthusiastically to Chittister's wake-up call. She told them not to wait for some new unfolding of religious life but rather to see themselves — though they possessed nary a black hair among them! — precisely as the future of religious life.

Chittister's call to see religious life principally as a call to prophecy is certainly not a signal of a reprieve from the pains of the past; rather, it is an invitation to share more deeply in the cross of Christ.

Prophets are never the most popular people in town, and the church as a whole is never going to get excited about its religious communities setting new corporate agendas centred, not on the church's institutional needs, but rather on the great issues of justice in today's world.

One has only to remember the Word and Life process developed a decade ago by the religious of Latin America. Curial offices in Rome and in the great dioceses of the region vied with one another to destroy it.

The religious of Saskatchewan have gone through a great fire and have been purified. They are ready to hear the call; they are ready to see themselves as the future of religious life or, to use Chittister's words, "to be the fire in the ashes."

It is not, however, simply a question of what these religious will do. Equally important is that other side of the coin: Is the Saskatchewan church ready to welcome prophetic communities in its midst, or will it find a thousand ways of reminding them — for all the wrong reasons — how wonderful were the moulds of the past?

One of the great challenges of religious throughout the ages has always been their vocation to be a wake-up call to the church itself.

Vocations to the religious life   May 4, 1992

Religious life is prophetic. Religious, by their vows of detachment from the status quo, are called to envision for us a new church in a new age.

That we are going through a period of very few religious vocations is nothing new to the church. Periods of social disintegration such as our own have usually begun with a drying up of religious vocations.

Religious communities of women are suffering much more today than are communities of men. It would not take any sociologist long to document the following: women communities have taken the Second Vatican Council much more seriously than have the men, and have done much more work on a full community level discerning what the Spirit is asking of them in a new age.

This work has reaped rich benefits for individual religious, but it has not taken place without a terrible price. Religious communities feel deep tensions with a church that does not want them to be prophets. And young women, filled with the Spirit, do not trust the institutional church enough to throw in their lot with these religious.

Bishops seek married priests
September 27, 1993

Celebrating the Eucharist on the Lord's Day is not just a long-standing practice in the Catholic Church. It is a mark of its very essence, of its deepest self-expression; one really cannot talk about a Catholic Church where the faithful do not regularly gather and celebrate their calling to be the members of the Body of Christ.

The bishops of western Canada, and even more especially those of the northern regions, have been hard pressed to enable the baptized to express this basic right. They have found this very painful for they know it is not just a privilege the faithful have; it is a fundamental right of theirs.

In this regard our bishops have had to make decisions they are no more comfortable with than are the laity in their dioceses. They have accepted as seminarians men rejected by other dioceses. They have gone to other countries, notably Poland, looking for priests.

Often this has not worked out well. Cultural differences, among other things, have hindered these priests from being effective in their ministry. One bishop, answering to his priests concerning the difficulties the importing of foreign priests had caused among the faithful, publicly promised them he would not bring any more into his diocese.

If we think some foreign priests have caused difficulties in our dioceses, one should remember for a moment the situation in the North.

None — not one single one — of the priests in the northwest is indigenous to the region or culture. Few of the priests serving our northern dioceses are even from Canada. Most are imports from Europe. No one wants to discredit in any way the heroic value of these missionaries; they have given their all to the Gospel. But missionaries they have remained.

Without a process of inculturation, the churches there have remained missions. And now, as the supply of priests from Europe (and southern Canada) has completely dried up, the Native peoples' regular access to the Eucharist — a fundamental right — is not just endangered but virtually certain to disappear, given the current legislation in the Roman Rite.

Our bishops, meeting last winter in Edmonton, made an important decision. Unanimously they decided to plead the case of the northern dioceses with the pope and the various curial departments of the Vatican during their forthcoming *ad limina* visit to Rome. Next they took this proposal to the whole plenary of Canadian bishops, asking for their backing as they pleaded their case in Rome. One thing is certain: they did not make their decision lightly.

Another decision had to be made. How were they to plead their case? The bishops could have used the central theological argument of the right of all the baptized to regular access to the Eucharist on the Lord's Day. And that must have been tempting since virtually every diocese in the West is fast approaching a disastrous shortage of priests. And every diocese has a pool of early retired professional married men who are willing to be ordained and who would be warmly welcomed as priests by the laity.

The bishops limited their argument, however, to the core situation of the northern church. They argued from an inculturation perspective. They indicated why, after so many years of heroic missionary work by foreigners, virtually no Native men have come forward to be priests or elders in the church community. (The New Testament word for a leader at the Eucharist, *presbyteros*, means elder.)

Bishop Denis Croteau, the bishop in Yellowknife, explained the situation while in Rome. "The idea," he said, "is that these peoples have a family value in their culture where, unless you are married, you're not a leader (elder) and people will not listen to you. If you have married and raised a family, then you're an elder, a man of experience. Then you can talk and people will respect your position." With such cultural values, Bishop James Mahoney of Saskatoon noted, many northern dioceses have not had a priestly vocation in more than a century.

Pope John Paul II has made inculturation one of the key themes of his pontificate. Already in 1982, he noted "that the synthesis between faith and culture is not just a demand of culture, but also of faith.... A faith which does not become culture is a faith which has not been fully received, not thoroughly thought through, not faithfully lived out."

The pope insisted during his Canadian pastoral visit in 1984 on spending much quality time with our Native peoples. When fog prevented him from going to the Dene in the Northwest Territories, he promptly — to the great surprise of our country's civil and episcopal leaders — invited himself back to Canada. And back he came three years later.

The pope must have liked what he said in 1984 at the Canadian Martyrs shrine in Ontario, for he repeated it in 1987. It is not enough to declare, he said, "that Christianity is relevant to the Indian peoples."

John Paul went on to say why he was repeating himself. "Today I repeat those words to you and to all the aboriginal peoples of Canada and of the world. The church extols the equal human dignity of all peoples and defends their right to uphold their own cultural character with its distinct traditions and customs.

"What," he asked, "would become of the 'life' (Mt 16:26) of the Indian, Inuit and Métis peoples if they cease to promote the values of the human spirit which have sustained them for generations? If they no longer see the earth and its benefits as given to them by the Creator? If the bonds of family life are weakened, and instability undermines their societies? If they were to adopt an alien way of thinking in which people are considered according to what they have and not according to what they are?"

The pope spent much time in Canada with the marginalized in society. His doing so was not just to give an example of charity. It is part of his theory of inculturation. To prevent a false interpretation of capitulation to the world as inculturation, the church must be accountable to the poor. The evils of society, the pope often reminds us, are best unmasked in the suffering of the poor and powerless in society. In Canada, the pope told us in word and deed during both visits, our aboriginal people have become the prime expression of the marginalized.

The pope, in marking the 25th anniversary of the promulgation of the Second Vatican Council document on the liturgy, noted that much had been done during this quarter century. But the big task, he noted, still lies ahead. "The liturgy is not disincarnate," he said. "There remains the considerable task of continuing to implant the liturgy in the various cultures."

Inculturation cannot forever be a theory of evangelization. Sooner or later it must either be put into practice — or abandoned.

The pope has come and given his word to our northern peoples. He has praised them for their cultural values, explicitly mentioning their dedication to family life. This very culture, roundly praised by the pope, cannot, however, at this present time appreciate in practice the great evangelical value of celibacy. We all must remember, though, that some things are simply more important, more central to the faith. It is in the Eucharist, first of all, that our northern peoples are called to celebrate that "Christ, in the members of his body, is himself Indian."

Priests for the North   October 22, 1997

The seven northern bishops have reported to the Canadian bishops' plenary that they are continuing to present to the Vatican "respected individual married men" as candidates for ordination in areas where there are no priests.

This practice was formally begun in 1993 when, with the unanimous support of the western Canadian bishops, the northern bishops first made a united request during their *ad limina* visit.

They used principally two theological arguments in presenting their case. First of all, they insisted that celebrating the Eucharist on the Lord's Day was in no way accidental to Christianity. Rather, it was the most profound way whereby the church expressed its meaning. These northern bishops reminded the Roman Curia that, according to the Ancients, the church effectively sacrificed its salvific presence in this age whenever it ceased to call the People of God together to celebrate in sacrament its living today, with its risen Lord, the newness and holiness of the End Times.

Their second argument took up a theme common in the talks Pope John Paul II made while in Canada. The pope stressed the essential value of inculturation. Though missionaries have been in the North more than 150 years and have deeply touched the lives of Native peoples, not one single man has chosen to be a celibate priest. With no new missionaries to take the place of the current priests who are, for the most part, old and long past the ordinary time of retirement, countless Native communities in the North no longer have access to the Sunday Eucharist.

And so the northern bishops continue to plead their case. And the Vatican continues to give the same answer: No.

Rome does not want its answer to appear cold or uncaring. But a dominating fear has gripped the Curia. To give in to Canada's northern peoples, curial officials believe, is to create that proverbial leak in the dike. They are afraid they will no longer be able to withstand "attacks" on the celibacy rule for priests of the Roman Rite from bishops in every corner of the globe.

They are likely correct in this.

But being correct in this regard is not enough. They must remember the example of Jesus. Never once in the Gospels do we see the Lord choosing the institution, as important as it might be, over the needs and rights of the individual.

We as church must face it: there is little doubt what Jesus would do if he were in Paulatuk or Kuujjaq and the people in these communities asked him for an elder who could lead them in a sacramental expression of their faith.

Regularizing the Czech church   April 27, 1992

Communist rule was particularly harsh in Czechoslovakia. The church there knew the full brunt of persecution. At times Czech Christians surely despaired that their church institution would survive.

They did what they thought they had to do; they clandestinely ordained priests and bishops. They ordained married men; they ordained men who later married to escape drawing attention to themselves; they even, it would appear, ordained women.

While these clandestinely ordained constantly faced persecution, prison, and often death, there were many priests who collaborated with the communists and had a better life than most Czechs and Slovaks.

To regularize all this is no mean feat. The clandestine clergy have worked only in small groups, in home liturgies; understandably they have had, from the day of their ordination onwards, little respect for many of the clergy who functioned publicly in the churches.

Misgivings about the institutional church ran deep.

That is unlikely to improve, now that Cardinal Joseph Ratzinger, to regularize institutional life, has asked the local church to judge each case according to some very simple, straightforward thumb rules.

First, the ordinations of the women are invalid. The women do not have the right stuff, and the bishops, it was concluded, must have been mentally ill from harsh prison life. (Nothing is said about the sacramental invalidity of men ordained by these bishops.)

Second, priests who were married before they were ordained, can now, if they wish, function in the eastern rites; the celibacy rule in the western church is to be re-established, and thus they have no place in their home rite.

Third, priests who married after ordination will not be allowed to continue functioning as priests.

Fourth, the *Pacem in Terris*, a regime-sponsored organization of priests who collaborated with the communists and now repent of their actions, are to be forgiven.

(It must be difficult for the clandestine ones not to be a bit cynical about this: one can be certain that these men who knew how to seize an opportunity with the communists will now see "conversion" as the appropriate response.)

These rules of thumb are certainly slanted toward the current view of the institutional church espoused in Rome. The actions of the Czech church during the persecution, we are told, were not based on Catholic principles but rather on the necessity of the moment.

There certainly is truth in that. But still, an intriguing phenomenon remains. Jesus repeatedly told his disciples that they were in the end times, and that they should make decisions not as if they had a great many years to live but as people facing the absolute.

Jesus had little time for compromise; "Let the dead bury the dead," he said, "and come, follow me" (Mt 8:22).

No one should be surprised that the Czech church, in its life-and-death situation, would be ordaining without ultimate regard for married or unmarried, or even for male or female. Churches, in life-and-death situations, stick with essentials.

Ironically, the Czech church under the communists just might have been closer to deciding things as Jesus would have done than we are inclined to do, we who love our church institution so dearly and want it properly regularized.

Crisis in priestly vocations

January 23, 1993

We tend to speak of the crisis in priestly vocations in bald numbers: we used to have almost twice as many priests; we used to have three instead of one serving in our larger parishes; the majority of our priests are now getting the old-age pension; our nearly empty seminaries used to be full of young men preparing for ordination.

The numbers crunch certainly has much to tell us, but these numbers, painful as they are, do not in any way indicate the full extent of the crisis unfolding in our midst.

If numbers, or the lack thereof, were at the heart of the crisis, the church could take at least a little comfort in the statistics of the last several years. There has been a slight increase throughout the world, though not in Canada, the United States, and Europe, of seminarians in their final years of study.

The crisis is much deeper, as a recent study of Canadian and American seminaries indicates. This study, funded by the Lilly Endowment, reports on what seminary instructors think of the current seminarians and of their readiness to take on pastoral work in the church.

In several areas they give seminarians positive marks: they have a spirit of service, an ethnic diversity, sensitivity to others, a concern for spirituality, a love for the church.

But when one reads what the instructors say negatively about these same seminarians, one soon senses that they were really trying hard to find some good things to say about them. Much of the criticism negates these positive statements. The list of negatives is scary.

Frequently the seminarians come from dysfunctional families. They tend to be sexually immature, have a low self-esteem, and have many unresolved psychological hang-ups. As a result, they tend to be rigid and individualistic, and are wont to accept fundamentalism as the correct way of life.

They lack a shared "Catholic culture." They lack a common experience of the faith as it is lived. This becomes all the more dangerous since they tend to be academically weak.

This lack of an adequate academic background is "exacerbated by a lack of intellectual curiosity." The church is ordaining men, the study noted, with a strong anti-intellectual attitude.

Today's seminarians are more conservative than are their predecessors. This, however, is not of much consolation even to the truly conservative among us once we note how they express their "conservativeness."

They are both politically and theologically conservative. Politically, they have little time for the social teachings of the church. Theologically, they want to re-establish the old clerical order, whereby they have the right and obligation to run the church without undue lay interference.

Few, if any, in the church take consolation in today's seminary faculty's description of "the typical seminarian." Yet it is important to note that the heart of the crisis facing us is not that so many of our current seminarians think and act the way they do. It is not a matter of "converting" them. And the last thing many of these seminarians need is a full-blown criticism of their being on the fringes of modern church life. The study shows that they are zealous, that they wish to be generous in their commitment to the priesthood.

The questions we must ask are much more problematic. Why is it that the church is doing so much better at attracting those youth who are on the fringes in their society? Why is the church not attracting the de facto leaders among today's Catholic youth?

Priesthood plays such a critical role in the Catholic ethos. We simply need the best, the leaders. The skills priests need in our church today with its great diversity of dreams are perhaps greater than in most other ages of the church's life.

We do not have the luxury of staying with the status quo. The canonical requirements for ordination, as wonderful and helpful as they have been for the church in past times, must be subject to re-evaluation. Studies in a seminary setting have been helpful for many; the call to celibacy has ever so richly graced countless priests in their work; the limitation of the priesthood to one-half of the human family has not been without its benefits throughout various periods in our history.

But we do not need a male, celibate clergy educated in a secluded seminary. We need the best priests we can get. All else is secondary.

Is the crisis that we do not have in the church enough priests-in-the-making with the right faith, or is the crisis that our church leaders are not reaching the natural leaders among our Catholic youth (and many who are not so young!) who perceive them, rightly or wrongly, as having no faith in a Spirit who just might be calling for new wine in new wineskins?

It is a painful question, but we as church must in conscience ask it — with humility and deep respect.

Receiving disgruntled Anglicans   May 3, 1993

It is rumoured that several hundred, perhaps even a thousand, Anglican priests and several bishops, unhappy with the Church of England's decision to ordain women, will be seeking admission to the Roman Catholic Church.

Their leader, retired Bishop of London Graham Leonard, had been hoping for a "personal prelature" which would in effect create a new rite in the Catholic Church. They had hoped to be able to use the *Book of Common Prayer* — all modern liturgical books within Anglicanism were a bit too much for most of these disgruntled Anglicans.

The situation has become an embarrassment to both churches, and the British Catholic hierarchy did what it had to do. It stated it wanted to keep close ecumenical relations with the Church of England and that it would not allow "a church within a church."

Significantly, the bishops said they would not require Anglican priests to disavow the validity of their years in the Anglican priesthood. Yet, in a move that defies all historical reality and the 1,500-year traditional "pipeline" teaching on priestly orders, the bishops note that each Anglican priest entering the Catholic Church will have to be ordained again "in an absolute manner."

But the real question is not being asked: Why should these Anglicans entering the Catholic Church presume that they have a right to exercise the priestly ministry in the Catholic Church?

British Catholics worry about this influx of priests. "We do not relish," one has stated, "a thousand priests coming over who are misogynist in their views." They have a point — a very important point — even if they express it in such a narrow way.

Priesthood is never a right a person has. It is a service in the community, and normally communities have some say as to who should be their servants and as to how they ought to be served.

Most likely very few of these Anglican men would be readily chosen by Catholic congregations to lead them in prayer and work — or to help them become a more vibrant parish community according to the image of church proclaimed in the Second Vatican Council.

The Roman congregations are worried about what will happen to their legislation concerning the celibacy of the western clergy when such a large number of married Anglican priests come knocking at their door. That surely is a problem. But it is not the only problem they are facing. Their view of the priesthood itself, as something that has its own rights and existence over and above the church community, suddenly appears woefully inadequate.

It will take a whole new approach to priesthood before the Roman authorities will be able to see what is already painfully evident to the British Catholic laity, that most of these men have no calling to exercise the priestly ministry (service) in a Catholic Church of flesh-and-blood people.

Roman fever revived

November 30, 1992

The retired Bishop of London, England's third-ranking Anglican See, Graham Leonard, is already talking of leading a large flock of traditionalists toward unity with Rome. In doing so, however, he wants "to preserve our Anglican identity while being in communion with the Holy See."

"I would want to stress," the bishop adds, "that we are not asking for recognition to continue an Anglican ministry, but as those who have accepted the magisterium and are in communion with the Holy See."

Leonard already has a plan for such a merger. He is asking for the establishment of a personal prelature, similar to the one the pope has established for Opus Dei.

In other words, these ex-Anglicans would not be full members of any territorial church under a local bishop. They would have their own bishop who has no local church to lead, but who instead, directly under the pope, would have direction over them, no matter where they lived.

This is indeed a strange request from one who claims to be a traditionalist! It is the very destruction of the episcopal nature of the church, of the church seen as a community of churches each united around its local bishop.

Seeing this request, it is hard not to conclude that these traditionalists are not, as they proclaim, interested in maintaining the purity of the Christian priesthood. Could it be that Archbishop Rembert Weakland is right and the real issue is maintaining that all-sacred teaching that women are inferior to men?

The establishment of a second personal prelature would be a tragedy for Anglicans and Catholics — and for the integrity of our theology of the priesthood.

And that, after all, is what this issue is supposed to be about.

Priests for the community

February 4, 1985

Last week we carried a news story on Cardinal Joseph Ratzinger's communication to Rev. Edward Schillebeeckx asking him for a public acknowledgment that he accepted the teaching of *Sacerdotium Ministeriale* (On the minister of the Eucharist), a letter the cardinal published last summer on the need for the presence of a priest for a valid eucharist.

The cardinal informed Schillebeeckx that "the Congregation for the Doctrine of the Faith pronounced in an authorized manner in its letter *Sacerdotium Ministeriale*." In fact, the cardinal declared, "The 'last word' has been said."

Nothing is said in all this about a eucharistic truth that is more fundamental than any question about the role or importance of the priest. The

Eucharist is the celebration of the church, the grace whereby the People of God express their meaning in Jesus Christ.

The right of the People of God to the Eucharist is absolute. Catholics have always held that the right to the Eucharist on the Lord's Day is a fundamental canon which is not to be superseded by any human structures.

It was in dealing with this question of fulfilling the Christian community's right to the Sunday Eucharist that Schillebeeckx went back to and studied the earliest traditions of the church concerning the minister for the Eucharist.

Since Cardinal Ratzinger has cut off all speculation on extraordinary ways in which the People of God might have access to their eucharist, it is right for us to expect that he initiate immediately a serious study of all the human traditions that now surround the priestly office in the church.

Today we have a serious shortage of priests. Sociologists tell us it cannot but get worse, even if all the church's seminaries became overcrowded tomorrow.

The problem is 10 times worse in Latin America. In Africa, conversions are far outstripping ordinations — so much so that many people have only one chance a year to celebrate their faith at the eucharistic table.

For the ancient church a shortage of priests was inconceivable. In exactly the same way we today always have the right number of bishops — we ordain a bishop every time a cathedral chair becomes vacant — so the church of old chose priests as the need arose.

They believed that the number of priests should be determined by the number of congregations that needed one. The congregation was the determining factor.

Today we have reversed the order and have made the priest the determining factor. We have as many parishes — or as is all too often the case, pastoral regions — as we have priests.

In allowing this reversal we have undermined that fundamental canon of our faith which proclaimed that the Sunday Eucharist belongs to the people, that it is the norm for their weekly song of praise in Christ Jesus.

Cardinal Ratzinger has been afraid that the church, in following some present-day theological expressions, was in danger of losing something essential concerning one of its greatest treasures, the priesthood. Yet it must also be noted that it will not be of great consequence to many Christians if the priesthood is saved while they themselves lose the Eucharist.

Corpus Christi

June 7, 1993

The Eucharist is the centre of our church life, the symbol that signifies the fullness of Christian life. In celebrating the Eucharist the church is expressing itself at its deepest level. The Eucharist makes present to a celebrating community the full benefits of the Lord's passover from death to the newness of life.

These three modern expressions, which could easily be expanded, indicate how important the Eucharist is to Christian life. The "old" theology, which nurtured most of us pre-Vatican II Catholics, in its own way also highlighted the Eucharist's centrality: the Mass is the unbloody sacrifice of Calvary; bread and wine lose their fundamental natural meaning and are transubstantiated into the real presence of Christ; one cuts oneself off from the Christian community and from God (commits a mortal sin) if one intentionally misses Sunday Mass.

One might have a personal preference for the old or the new, but in neither school of expression can one avoid an important truth: the Mass or Eucharist is central to church life, and what we express in that liturgy has monumental ramifications for the communal life of the church and for the self-understanding of each individual Christian.

One would expect, in such circumstances, that the church would struggle mightily in every age and culture to give the Eucharist its broadest and fullest expression so that everyone might be personally flabbergasted at the meaning Christ gave them when they became part of his body in baptism. Yet a study of church history shows that the exact opposite is the case. In most of our history the Eucharist was given narrower and narrower expressions.

Rather than highlighting the communal nature of Christian worship, the liturgy became more and more the domain of the clergy and an expression of clerical power. It became something the clergy did for the people. For a priest to celebrate Mass became the greatest privilege in the world.

This had great ramifications for lay life and work. Gone was any notion that the bread and wine celebrated the many hands and hours that went into producing the basic foods of life. Gone to a very large extent was any notion of a meal at all. The wine became the sole preserve of the clergy; the bread lost any resemblance to bread. Indeed, eating became highly secondary — communicating once a year practically became the norm for the laity who were more often told that they were unworthy sinners than that they were the Body of Christ — and adoring the host from outside the sanctuary was all that was left to them.

But what happens when the wine is taken from the People of God and the bread is reduced to a dried flour paste which is presented as so angelic a food that it is indeed right and proper that a priest should give it to the laity in exactly the same manner as a parent feeds a helpless babe — right and proper too that it should melt on one's tongue and make the natural food-consumption processes of chewing and swallowing unnecessary?

Rather than addressing the communicants as full adults marked with a grace that aids them along a road of self-acceptance which becomes ever more glorious, the Eucharist reminded them that the clergy alone had the significant power and that the obedience of babes unable to feed themselves was their proper response.

The disappearance of the wine taught the community to forget that Jesus called his disciples to a party, to the marriage feast of God's reign. Self-sacrifice, so important to the Lord, takes on a totally different meaning when the fun in life can no longer be symbolized — only the unbloody sacrifice of the cross is remembered.

Once the bread (and that's all that is left) is an angelic wafer calling us out of everyday existence, the stuffings of life are gone. No wonder Christianity became, in practice, the world religion most harmful to the environment.

What a surprise that must be for Jesus Christ who gave us a religion he so carefully grounded in reality through such everyday sacramental signs as breaking bread together, drinking wine among friends, indulging the body with the best perfumes, massaging the sick lovingly with oil, making love with uncontrollable climaxes of pure sexuality!

Once the clergy had full control of the liturgy they quite naturally, over many centuries, reshaped it to fit their own image of the perfect church. The everyday work and workplace of the vast majority of the church members no longer rated. And once the clergy had become a totally celibate lot, family life in general and sexuality in particular lost their symbolic relationship to the Eucharist.

All the laity lost meaning as the liturgy became more and more the domain of the clergy. But it is not an overstatement to say that the male members of the 99 percent have suffered little in this transformation of the liturgy when compared with the women. For women to even come near the liturgical action was to desecrate it. Reading an Old Testament lesson, even carrying a cruet of water to the altar was anathema.

In his life Jesus broke all the taboos he could against women. He repeatedly destroyed his respectability among the spiritual elite by associating with women of ill repute. After his resurrection he even appeared first to a woman and told her to tell the disciples he was alive.

Yet in the church which, after the persecutions, came above ground and confidently built basilicas in which the men and women intermingled equally as the one living Body of Christ, the clergy came in time to insert sanctuaries into the community's worship space — sanctuaries which it was sinful for women to enter. They even built choir lofts behind the congregation so no one would have to see it was women (and not young boys and castrati) who were singing the soprano and alto parts of their sacred music.

In the world of politics we often speak about the need of checks and balances. Without checks on power and authority, those holding these trusts of the community are all too prone to use them for their own ends. Should we be surprised that a male clergy with no earthly checks and balances would in the course of many centuries create a church in which the laity and especially the women would feel like second- and third-class citizens — even though many of those clerics prayed daily for the grace to be faithful to the Lord?

We can speak only for the western world in which we live: we live in a church in which a strong majority of women, especially those professionally trained, experience the church as a community biased against them. We get excited by the divisions the ordination of women is causing in the Church of England, and yet remain blind to the much deeper divisions that continue being enacted in our liturgy and in the exercise of authority in our church.

But it is not principally a problem of our communities of religious women. It is a church problem. Bright young women cannot come to trust a church which they see preferring men to women. They are not about to enter religious life.

We must address fully and honestly the place of women in the church. We must acknowledge as wrong all that has made them feel they are not called to celebrate as full citizens of God's reign. If women cannot celebrate *Corpus Christi* (being the Body of Christ) with joyful abandon, it is a sign that we have not been faithful to the Lord.

Chapter 6

Pope John Paul II

Pope is *PM* churchperson of the year
January 2, 1989

This past year Pope John Paul II issued his second social encyclical, *Sollicitudo Rei Socialis* (Concern for Social Things). With pointed precision, it deals with global social issues and is a most fitting addition to the great social encyclicals that date back to Pope Leo XIII.

According to the pope the great powers of this world, especially the two superpowers, are to a large extent responsible for the growing inhuman impoverishment of one-fifth of humanity: 1 billion people without proper shelter or food.

The time has passed, the pope declares, for vagueness about social issues freeing peoples and nations of moral responsibility. The pope believes today's social issues are not so fuzzy as to be open to radically different interpretations. He wrote his encyclical as pointedly as any statement he has given on church order, sexuality, or the ethical dimensions of science and technology.

Using Paul VI's encyclical *Progressio Populorum* (On the development of peoples) as his springboard, the pope notes that the poor nations of the world have "become parts of a machine, cogs on a gigantic wheel." Both superpowers are indicted for cleverly crafted "ideological conflicts which inevitably create internal divisions in poorer nations."

Totally rejecting the current world doctrine which states that ideological differences between the superpowers are the greatest obstacle to peace, the pope finds their very similarity as the great threat.

The pope is thoroughgoing in this. He does not simply condemn "the neo-colonialism" of the superpowers; he also condemns much of the activity of NATO and the Warsaw Pact. He sees them as little more than pressure groups to aid the superpowers in their work of colonization.

In his encyclical he praises the work of the International Movement of Non-Aligned Nations — a group Canadian and American politicians have spent much energy maligning.

Subsequent to issuing the encyclical, the pope has gone even further in this regard. In his trip to Latin America, he showed how he wanted his encyclical interpreted. In Bolivia he outlined many of the defects of capitalism and showed how these defects had hurt that nation. Then, dealing with Bolivia's foreign debt, he suggested exactly what the World Bank had long been dreading: John Paul called upon Latin American nations to unite in a bloc so they could "dialogue on a level of equality with the industrialized nations."

In every section of the encyclical the pope worked carefully to avoid appearing to be making theoretical judgments. He wanted everything to be seen from a solid, down-to-earth base. Everything is to be judged from the practical angle of development.

He judges both capitalism and socialism and finds them seriously wanting. In this he has set the agenda for the church for years to come. All church organizations (and publications, too!) will have to do a lot of violence to themselves before they are sufficiently "left" in a worldly political sense to be able to actualize the pope's dream of justice, development, and peace.

If the Canadian church wishes to remain faithful to the pope it will have to struggle to make Canada re-examine its foreign policy within NATO and its rationale for building a trading bloc with the United States — a nation which at the recent GATT talks in Montreal put up endless roadblocks against fairer trade for Third World nations.

Following this papal encyclical will also push Canadians into re-examining their own propensity toward neo-colonialism. Canada's role with the World Bank and the International Monetary Fund clearly stands condemned by John Paul.

The pope sees the Cold War primarily in economic terms. He sees it as a camouflage "legitimating" this neo-colonialism that has impoverished so many millions of people.

For this fearless condemnation of the Cold War and its awesome price on the poor, we proclaim John Paul II as our churchperson for 1988.

John Paul and the papacy

January 30, 2002

Early in his pontificate Pope John Paul II, while here in Canada, voiced something that would be often repeated during the many years he has occupied the Chair of Peter; he acknowledged that the exercise of his special ministry is an ecumenical problem.

Speaking in the royal plural more about the papal office than about himself personally, he told a group of Protestants in Toronto that he knows "it is ourselves who are the problem."

The pope has often spoken about "this problem," especially in his dealings with the Orthodox. So it should have surprised no one that when John Paul II wished to write an encyclical on ecumenism he should turn to the author of the monumental ecumenical book, *The Bishop of Rome*. The late Canadian Dominican Jean-Marie Tillard was called to Rome to ghostwrite the section on the papal office. In its final form the encyclical, *Ut Unum Sint* (That they may be one), called for a patient dialogue to find new and better ways of exercising papal primacy for the good of the whole church.

During the recent formal consistorial meeting of the cardinals in which the pope elevated 44 men to the cardinalate, he mentioned once again "the obstacle" his own office is to church unity.

It is well and good for us to take the pope at his word and look again at the papal office. But let us not do it only from a negative perspective, seeing it as an ecumenical obstacle. The meeting in Assisi earlier in January reveals the other side of the issue. This pope has given the office a power unparalleled in church history — a power we must never weaken, for the sake of the world as well as for the churches.

In a world mesmerized by the war in Afghanistan, John Paul called religious leaders to Assisi both to name war as it really is and to call the religions of the world to their task of creating a peaceful space in the hearts of their members and in the lives of the citizens of the world.

Who but Karol Wojtyla could have done this? He has already done much to transform the Chair of Peter. When before in church history has the Bishop of Rome called together Catholics, Orthodox, Anglicans, and Protestants, and they were honoured to hear his call?

But not only Christians have heard his beckoning; Jews and Muslims, Hindus and Buddhists, among many others, have come to join the pope in issuing the message the world must hear: peace begins in the sacred interior of each heart, and this peace is not possible without forgiveness.

Rabbi Israel Singer, touched by the power of the Assisi assembly, put aside his prepared text and spoke directly to John Paul: "Only you can make this happen, only you can lead us to elicit from our own faith communions the potential for peacemaking."

The day after the Assisi meeting the pope invited "his friends" to lunch. It all seemed so ordinary, so much what one would have expected of John Paul.

But, on second thought, we remember how extraordinary it all is, that the papal office today has a power that Leo and Gregory never dreamed of — or, for that matter, Popes Boniface VIII or Pius IX.

In both positive and negative ways, this pope has surely opened the papal office to new, life-giving possibilities.

Pope as ecumenist

May 23, 2001

The lead story in this week's *Prairie Messenger* speaks of a coalition of one of the main political parties in Russia with the Russian Orthodox Church. The patriarch and Vladimir Zhirinovsky, leader of the ultranationalist Liberal Democratic Party, have become strange bedfellows.

And what has brought them together? The impending papal visit to Ukraine. Zhirinovsky, a vice-speaker of the Duma, has for the last two months been complaining of Catholic proselytizing in Russia and continues to call for laws against Catholic expansion in Mother Russia, the home of Russian Orthodoxy.

Patriarch Alexei II has bitterly reminded the pope that no one from the patriarchate has invited him to visit Ukraine, a protocol the pope has always followed in the past.

Pope John Paul II is aging rapidly and his great desire for unity has led him to cut corners. This has not always sat well with the Orthodox — nor with his own Curia.

In an earlier visit to Greece, the Greek Orthodox had been backed into a corner and reluctantly invited the pope as a "private pilgrim." That, however, meant explicitly that no head of the Vatican's Congregation for the Oriental Churches would accompany him on the trip. It also meant no presence of the Catholic hierarchy of Greece at any of the official functions.

To the Curia, these were unacceptable snubs. Add to this the long list of apologies the pope gave in Athens, and one soon realizes that the pope does not have the support of a significant part of his Curia.

The Curia has never been enthusiastic about church apologies. When John Paul first proposed, at the 1994 extraordinary consistory of cardinals, to apologize in the name of the church for past sins, he found little support anywhere.

The curial cardinals were against it in principle. They quickly resurrected the pre-conciliar theology of the church as the "perfect society," which had been replaced at the council by the presentation of the church as a pilgrim. The church being perfect, they noted, technically cannot sin and therefore should not be apologizing. (These same men were against apologizing in the East for the AD 1204 Crusaders' sack of Constantinople and its churches; Pope Innocent III had excommunicated these Crusaders and that should have been enough, they said.)

But it was not only the curial cardinals who opposed the pope's jubilee apologies. Cardinals from behind the former Iron Curtain said the church would be opening itself to a new wave of criticism. The Latin American bishops did not want to dwell on "European sins."

The pope did not listen to the cardinals. The church's "process of healing of memories" was, in the pope's mind, much more than a "ridding itself of some historical baggage and owning up to past mistakes."

The pope was looking for credibility — credibility in asking the rich nations of the world to forgive the unjust debts which were crippling the poorest nations of the world. John Paul knew that the church's failures were not that far removed from those of the world of big business. Authoritarianism, patriarchism, pretexts of spiritual superiority, reliance on unwarranted secrecy, claims of being the innocent bystander, triumphalism, dogmatism, legalism — whatever sins the pope confesses, ultimately all of them reflect one common moral defect: power is used to abuse the weaker, all in the name of strengthening the institution.

And so it was a humble pope who went to Greece. And he did not worry that the Greeks, in laying down some stringent restrictions, were forcing him into a position of weakness.

His call to the business community and to national governments to forgive debts and to pledge to stop abusing their power was never made in isolation. He knew that call, to be credible, would carry a high price tag, one the church as institution would be hesitant to pay.

The pope, however, is willing to pay it. He knows his days are limited. Almost as a dying man, he has set his priorities. And like Paul VI near the end of his life, he is ready to kiss the feet of the Orthodox.

Of course, it is a concern of the whole church when an aging pope loses control of his Curia. But it should be remembered that curias throughout history have, at the end of each papal reign, dug in their heels and used their window of opportunity to solidify their own agendas. (The new laws for translating liturgical texts appear to be in that category.)

It would seem that John Paul is not afraid to reveal his weakness. He is using his frail body to further his cause. He went to Greece as a humble pilgrim asking for forgiveness. He will certainly do the same in Ukraine.

To be a forgiving church, to be a church seeking the forgiveness of all, is the overriding, and possibly final, agenda of a pope who has done much for the church. In this regard he needs the explicit support of the bishops and of the People of God.

Unity with the East
May 15, 1995

The pope minced no words in the opening chapter of his apostolic letter The Light of the East. The church in its present stage, he says, cannot manifest the true catholic spirit given it by the Lord. He goes further: catholicity will never again be a full mark of the church so long as it tries to express itself "by means of a single tradition."

The church must seek purification. The division in the church between East and West stems from a jealous attachment to things human in our past. This attachment makes it difficult for the church to set its heart, in the words of the pope's letter, "on the great things God has done for us."

We as church, the pope notes, have made ourselves prisoners of our present understanding. This narrowness of vision has meant the loss of a "perception of belonging to a history." Rather than choose a "heritage which preserves an original, living kerygmatic proclamation," we have tried to find security in "an unchanging repetition of formulas."

This is hardly language many have identified with the pope. Few, if any, will be able to read this apostolic letter without a new understanding and assessment of the pontificate of John Paul II.

He acknowledges that the Latin Rite simply needs the traditions of the East to express its catholic character. And it is within this need that he theologizes on the very meaning of his own papal office.

He recognizes that the Latin Rite with its patriarch, the pope, has been part of the problem. But, he insists, it was not "a mere question of pre-eminence that tore the fabric of unity." There was, rather, "a progressive estrangement, so that the other's diversity was perceived no longer as a common treasure, but as incompatibility."

The Office of Peter, he stresses, must be one of service. And he does not leave this in the abstract. The pope, he observes, must insist that churches are given "full respect for the traditions of each and for necessary autonomy."

"Peter's task," the pope notes, "is to search constantly for ways that will help preserve unity. There he must not create obstacles, but must open up paths."

Then the pope puts words in the mouth of Christ: "It is as if the Master himself wanted to tell Peter: 'Remember that you are weak, that you, too, need endless conversion. You are able to strengthen others only insofar as you are aware of your own weakness.'"

The pope sees only two options for the church today. It can either "proclaim the kingdom" or "become the upholder of new divisions." Seeing the current situation of the church in such stark terms leaves everyone with a "most serious responsibility." It is obvious which option the pope wishes to take. He says he longs "to write at last a history of our unity."

Observers at the Vatican note that the pope, with the lessening of vigour that comes with age, is centring his output of energy on his favourite projects. As a Slav he wants more than anything else to reunite the churches of East and West.

This apostolic letter shows a very flexible occupant on the Chair of Peter, one ready to admit the shortcomings of the Latin tradition, one ready to do all in his power to rewrite a theology of the papal office so that it can be seen by his brothers and sisters of the East as a grace for them.

If the churches take this letter seriously — if the Vatican itself takes this letter seriously — the institutional church will never be the same. The pessimism and cynicism that mark so much of church life today will vanish and be replaced with the joy that comes when "one's gaze turns to the rising Sun."

That they may be one   June 12, 1995

In the first ever encyclical addressed to all Christians, Pope John Paul struggles to put ecumenism on the front burner of all the churches.

Ut Unum Sint is only the second encyclical that deals specifically with ecumenism. The first, by Pope Pius XI in 1928, forbade any Catholic participation in "pan-Christian" movements. Such movements, he noted, were infected with modernism in theology, relativism in doctrine, indifferentism in ecclesiology.

Catholics could not participate, the pope concluded, since these ecumenical movements "failed to recognize the Catholic Church as the only true church of Christ."

The current encyclical illustrates how drastically papal teaching can change. This encyclical places a serious obligation on Catholics to reach out to others — and John Paul calls upon all Christians to do so with confidence and optimism.

The pope speaks about saints in all the churches, saints we should imitate. If we, like the saints, he notes, "are truly able to be converted to the quest for full and visible communion, God will do for us what he did for the saints. God will overcome the obstacles inherited from the past and will lead communities along his paths to where he wills."

The pope notes that the papal office is a problem for the ecumenical world. He states, as Catholics know he must, the need for the Office of Peter to sustain the churches in unity. But he also invites the leaders and theologians of the other churches and ecclesial communities to join him "in a patient and familial dialogue" to find new and better ways for the exercising of papal primacy.

By hinting strongly that this study should centre on the first 1,000 years of church history when the churches remained united, the pope has left the door wide open to a critical evaluation of the developments concerning expansion of the papal office in more recent times.

The developments in travel and communications that have enabled the world to become a global village have also enabled the church to centralize its exercise of authority in ways that were utterly impossible even one-half century ago. Now the pope is taking the very courageous step of asking the other churches to help him in an evaluation of that development.

As the contrast between the two encyclicals on ecumenism could hardly be greater, so also Catholics should not be surprised if some day in the not-too-distant future — the pope is optimistic — the accepted description of the Petrine function in the church is closer to that of a St. Leo or Gregory than to the formulations we have grown up with.

John Paul has called us to embrace the Spirit of ecumenism — one which, the pope knows, could transform quite radically the church structures we have come to know and cherish.

Pope an Orthodox Christian   January 16, 1995

It is a small story, but it is pregnant with meaning. The pope has been named an honorary member of a new Russian Orthodox parish.

In Ulyanovsk, the birthplace of Vladimir Lenin, the poor Russian Orthodox Christians were struggling to build a modest cathedral. The pope heard about their plight and sent them $14,000 for their new Cathedral of the Resurrection.

At a time when Christians set aside a week for special prayers for unity, this story should be an encouragement to all. To be sure, it's not about high theology. Rather, it is a simple story of an Orthodox parish in the backwaters of the Volga doing the inconceivable — welcoming the pope as a member of their community.

The issues between the Orthodox and the Catholics have little to do with theology — and a lot to do with blind hatred and unbelievably stupid politics. All efforts by theologians to justify the divisions between East and West have at best stumbled forward badly. And the West, in recent years, has gone a long way in addressing the difficulties between the two communions.

The western church has acknowledged that the Nicene Creed is a full and proper proclamation of the faith without proclaiming that the Holy Spirit also proceeded from the Son (the filioque controversy, as it is known) and it has formally stated that all the developments in faith and juridical practice originating since the split between East and West may not be pressed upon the Orthodox in any reunion of the churches.

This acknowledges that all the dogmas proclaimed in the last 1,000 years of church history are not central enough to our faith to be considered church-dividing. It also acknowledges that the pope, while he plays a key role in maintaining the unity of faith in the church, has virtually no claim to any jurisdiction in the patriarchal territories of the East.

The Vatican has also accepted the work of a joint Catholic/Orthodox commission that has decried the uniate model of church governance in which at least in theory local churches in eastern Europe or the Middle East acknowledge papal authority but maintain their own governance.

It was not theology that separated East and West but politics — and downright prejudice at its worst. It was one thing for Crusaders from the West to sack the greatest church in the East, Hagia Sophia in Constantinople (Istanbul), while on their way to Jerusalem. They had a terribly simplistic mindset in which they saw themselves as God's army called to free the Holy Land from the Muslims whom they saw as the devil's henchmen. It was quite another thing, however, for the West (which the eastern Christians saw more in ecclesiastical rather than political terms) to allow most of the eastern churches to come under Muslim domination with nary a helping hand. Their desperate cries to western European Christian princes went unheeded. It should surprise no one that before long the East decided that the Christianity of the West was devoid of substance. And it never takes long for bitterness to turn into anger and hatred.

And so, the importance of the little story from Ulyanovsk. This town just might go down in history, not as the birthplace of Lenin but as the community of faith that welcomed the Slavic pope into its very community.

It may be a modest little cathedral — nothing comparable to the $64-million marvel being planned in Los Angeles — but as a sign of bridging a millennium of distrust and hatred, it may indeed become for all the churches truly a Cathedral of the Resurrection.

Prophetic journey
May 9, 2001

Pope John Paul II is a charismatic leader. He has a way of rising above local controversies, above dogmatic differences in the church. Even those who disagree strongly with his views on birth control and mandatory celibacy for the western clergy and on his centralization of power in Rome at the expense of local bishops — the three things for which he is most often criticized — will come out in great numbers to cheer his presence among them. His prophetic stature simply rises above the difficulties of his pontificate.

His recent visit to Greece and his coming visit to Ukraine — an area technically under the oversight *(episcopé)* of the Patriarch of Moscow — show an important aspect of this pope. He is aging at an accelerated rate and knows he does not have much time to further his dreams of church unity — especially with the eastern church. And so he is gambling.

He quite literally backed the Greek Orthodox hierarchy into a corner, practically forcing them to invite him "as a humble pilgrim" to their land. He is going to Ukraine without an invitation from the Orthodox patriarch.

His first gamble, to Greece, seems to have worked out well. He celebrated the Eucharist in Athens with precious little fanfare. The venue: an undisguised basketball court.

His official church and state activities centred largely on apologies. He touched on most of the long-standing grievances; he admitted western guilt and begged for a forgiving heart.

And his apologies rang true. None of his Orthodox hosts questioned his sincerity. John Paul did what no theologian could do. He rose above the hatred and controversy of a millennium and, quite literally, charmed his hosts.

Considering the predominance in the world of the Latin church, it is right and proper for the pope to apologize without any hope of a reciprocal move. Given the numerical superiority of the western patriarchate, there is no need for the West to remind its eastern brothers and sisters of their foibles in the Great Schism (AD 1054).

While it is right and proper for the pope to apologize, it is not right and proper for the East to continue to nurse a bitterness and hatred as if the rift happened yesterday.

Yes, the western powers abandoned Constantinople when the Muslims were at its door. Yes, the Crusaders looted its sanctuaries and razed the city. But, as the pilgrim pope noted, all of us — easterners as well as westerners — must find a way to that reconciliation which lies at the heart of the Gospel.

Yes, we believe Orthodox Christians must find it in their hearts to forgive the Latin church. But we must also change as a church, if the pope's apology is to continue ringing true.

Orthodox Archbishop Christodoulos of Athens was quick to point out one area not covered in the long list of papal apologies. He pointed out bluntly that the pope made no mention of Uniatism, the system despised by the Orthodox whereby eastern churches came under the shepherding surveillance of the Bishop of Rome.

Currently curial Cardinals Joseph Ratzinger and Walter Kasper are strongly debating the proper role of bishops in the church. The Orthodox will never even discuss the possibility of unity so long as western bishops are treated, to use Kasper's language, "as delegates of the pope."

The whole question surrounding Uniatism will come to a head in the papal visit to Ukraine. The pope deeply wishes to visit the eastern Christians who, over the last 100 years, have paid dearly for their unity with the Bishop of Rome.

The Latinization of their eastern traditions, which progressed steadily right up to the Second Vatican Council, does not sit well with the East. And rightly so. The continuing practice of making their leaders cardinals (honorary clergy of the Diocese of Rome) does not help matters either.

To be sure, Orthodox Christians must find it in their hearts to forgive; the Roman church, however, must clearly show its readiness to change, to faithfully return to the episcopal model of ordinary church governance.

This will mean significant changes to the uniate system — Curia members have already acknowledged the absolute shortcomings of this practice for full church unity.

It will also mean significant developments in our relationships with the mainline churches in the West. The Anglicans have recently pointed out the inconsistencies and backward movements, ecumenically speaking, of Catholic practices surrounding eucharistic hospitality.

In the West, full unity with the pope is fast becoming the new law for intercommunion; in the East, this is not necessary. In the West, only the scholastic philosophic explanation of the real presence suffices; in the East, the obvious shortcomings of this explanation are lampooned. The Curia does not like this but accepts it begrudgingly.

However much the situation is loaded in its favour, the East will have nothing to do with such machinations of the Curia — all in the name of the pope. Yes, more than apologies are needed.

The Orthodox Archbishop of Athens did not even wait for the pope to leave Greece before flying to Moscow to report on the pope's visit. John Paul's visit to Ukraine will be more closely watched than was his visit to Greece. But let us not sell our pope short. His charism carried the day in Greece. He will do all in his power to meet the challenges the visit to Ukraine will bring.

All of us, however, must recognize that the pope must put his body where his heart is. His dream of unity will not only affect the papal office; it will have major ramifications for the whole western church.

Pope on the attack   June 4, 1990

During much of John Paul II's time as pope a strong warning against certain forms of liberation theology were repeated again and again — so often that many began to wonder if indeed he wholeheartedly accepted the guiding principle of the Latin American bishops' teaching at Medellin and Puebla.

After his recent visits to Czechoslovakia and Mexico there is no longer a shadow of doubt. He has explicitly preached God's preferential option for the poor with an enthusiasm unparalleled in the church since the heady days when Archbishop Helder Camara led the Latin American church.

To be sure, the pope still warned against a liberation theology based on Marxist principles. "God's preferential option for the poor is not an ideological option," he told Mexican priests. "Nor does it mean to become trapped by the deceitful theory of class struggle as the motor of historical change," he added.

But little of the pope's time was spent attacking aberrant theologians. His attack was directed against the economic community as it actually practised capitalism. Many of the statements which in former times branded liberation theologians as out-and-out communists now pale to a constrained harmlessness beside the bold assertions the pope has been making lately.

And the papal attacks against capitalism are no longer couched in vague generalities. He makes sure those whom he is attacking know it. The Secretariat of State, the highest ranking curial office in the Vatican, has taken notice. It approved for publication an 11-page editorial in *La Civilta Cattolica*, the official publication of the Jesuits, which explicitly attacked "the economic and military imperialism of the United States." Japan did not fare any better.

Liberal capitalism, according to the current papal viewpoint, cannot be trusted. It is not to be chosen as the model for socio-economic development.

What has led the pope to join the ranks of liberation theologians and sound like one of the more radical among them? He sees what lies ahead for Poland, his homeland, and for the other emerging nations in eastern Europe.

He sees that the liberal capitalist community is intensely interested in turning that region into another Third World colony. And he knows the danger of that taking place is high indeed.

No longer is he viewing with cold intellectualization the problems liberation theologians have long struggled with. He is involved in the issue with his own flesh and blood. And he realizes that one does not always have the luxury of nice clean distinctions. Theology is about people, people struggling for self-realization and dignity.

And for theology to be authentic, it is about people the theologian knows and loves well enough to be able to identify with them.

One should not expect the current theological thrust of the pope to be a passing whim. He is passionately involved. And so, liberal capitalists, beware! — and that includes virtually all of us, for Canada operates almost exclusively by the liberal capitalist standard.

Does the pope have Parkinson's? January 10, 2001

Precious few 80-year-olds in the very best of health can match the hectic schedule Pope John Paul II maintains. This was particularly true during the jubilee year in which the pope attended public functions almost daily. Indeed most octogenarians would be justly proud of themselves if they could tackle half the workload the pope daily imposes on himself.

Yet Catholics, through the merciless eye of modern communication, see him look more and more tired; they know that over the years he has fallen several times; they see his left side constantly getting weaker — he can no longer walk the length of St. Peter's Basilica in an opening liturgical procession; they notice him shake uncontrollably and have come to realize that when he is tired he cannot enunciate his words clearly enough to be understood.

And his flock worries, for John Paul is in a most special way their father. While few are happy with everything he has done during his long reign as pope, love and respect for him and for the office he holds run deep throughout the church.

People want to know about the pope's health, not because they want to lay down early bets on who will come out of the next conclave as his successor. Rather, they have come to love and respect him as a generous servant struggling mightily with the most difficult task in the church. They want to pray for him — in truth.

A saying circulating around Rome is as cynical as it is ancient: "Every pope dies in good health." In other words, curial officials throughout the centuries have lied about the health of the popes. The "justification" for this is easy to see; they do not want to set off a beehive of political scheming and manoeuvring about the next papal conclave.

But, of course, the more they issue official statements that run contrary to the people's observations, the more they increase rather than reduce meaningless speculation about the imminent demise of the pope. And, in every such case, the pope is ultimately the loser.

It appeared for a day that things were changing. The pope's doctor and close personal friend Gianfranco Fineschi was quoted in an Italian journal as saying that the pope had Parkinson's disease, that his rapidly decreasing ability to walk was "neurological and not orthopedic" in nature.

But this illusion of openness did not last long. The very next day the doctor was forced to deny that he ever said it. The Curia was not about to admit to the obvious.

In his powerful encyclical *Veritatis Splendor* (Splendour of truth), the pope fought more than anything else against moral relativism, which he believes is one of the great evils of modern culture. In countless different ways, he said, a lie is a lie is a lie. Extenuating circumstances can influence but never change the ultimate moral value of a human act. Relativism, John Paul insisted, only cheapens human nature.

It will always be a fine juggling act. The pope has a right to some privacy about his person but, at the same time, the People of God have a right to know about the well-being of their father. There can never be, however, any moral justification for misleading the people.

Throughout his pontificate John Paul has made masterful use of the television camera. There is no reason to suspect that he will be any less skilful in using it as the ravages of the papal office and of time itself take their toll on his astounding vitality. The pope will be all the more successful if the People of God feel they are getting an honest assessment about their father in Christ.

Should popes retire? November 5, 2003

Not many have retired, and fewer still for personal reasons. None, it would appear, because of old age. The tradition of popes hanging in there "to the bitter end" — as part of God's personal calling for them, as part of their acceptance of the cross of Christ — is certainly long and intact.

As Catholics, we always hesitate to break with tradition, especially with one so firmly rooted in our history.

We think of having two popes at the same time and shudder. There were times when there were two (and even three) popes; and these were bad times, confusing times. Having one man, one infallible man on the

Chair of Peter, keeps things simple. The lines of authority clear; the power structures intact.

Yet the present pope is seen to be aging rapidly. Being a man of the theatre, his person has been more observable than that of any previous pope. We know he cannot stand up alone. We know he can no longer speak publicly; it's not simply that he cannot enunciate his words; he runs out of breath after two or three lines and has to stop for air. And as older people are wont to do, he falls asleep at the most inappropriate times, even during high liturgies over which he is presiding. And, as was evident during his last foreign trip to Slovakia, knowing the location of the nearest private washroom was indeed critically important knowledge.

None of this is secret. The pope has hidden none of this from our sight. He has no desire to be seen as an aged pope shuffling along the inner corridors of the apostolic palace; for him the Chair of Peter is of necessity part of the world stage. His frailty has become part of the package. And, being a consummate actor (in the very best sense of that word), he has turned his weakness into the strength of the Gospel of the Cross of Christ.

That has not, however, kept the world's media from speculating on when he would — or, for that matter with their glaring lack of subtlety, when he should — retire. The more media members tended toward a negative evaluation of his 25 years in office, the more likely they were to proclaim the wisdom of a papal resignation.

The Vatican Curia has been strong in its defence of no papal resignation. *L'Osservatore Romano*, revealing that a raw nerve had been touched, called all such talk "shaky and indelicate discourses of a pseudo-canonical nature."

But do all suggestions of a papal resignation need to be "indelicate"? Cannot some Catholics, who stand in awe of this pope and what he has accomplished these past 25 years, see this as the time for beginning an important new tradition? As once it was unheard of that diocesan bishops would retire according to a timetable, a timetable with some flexibility, is it that inconceivable to foresee a day when popes would no longer see it as their cross to remain in office to the bitter end?

We must admit it: there are problems with the current system, especially since modern medicine has greatly lengthened the declining years of senior citizens. It is not a matter of having all one's marbles; it's about having the creative energy to move forward, to explore new vistas, to lead the People of God into the newness of the Gospel of Resurrection.

Church history professors always insist that, in studying historical events, their students remain cognizant of the state of the pope's health, that it is always in the interest of the Curia that their pope have a lingering old age during which time they can consolidate their own grip on power. And, without fail, the best way to achieve this is to develop a personality cult around the pope.

Few things authoritarian are more obviously contrary to the thinking of Christ than the promotion of a personality cult around pope or bishop. This fact alone makes the resignation of popes such a powerful tool for promoting the Gospel.

The suggestion that popes might normally resign from office, as do the other bishops in the church, is not made because John Paul has not been a great pope. Let us see it rather as the grand capping to a most extraordinary ministry. For him to resign from office would go down in church history as one of his greatest acts.

Cheering the pope   September 3, 1997

It certainly is a help, indeed it is a great blessing to the church, if the pope is revered and loved — not as some idealized abstraction but as a flesh-and-blood person.

To be sure, it is primarily the office the pope fulfills that makes his presence at an event important. But until that office is incarnated in a human person like all of us, it is a cold, ineffective administrative function.

John Paul has charisma. He, as few popes before him, knows how to unite a crowd and transform it into a celebration of church. This is a great gift; but it is also a dangerous gift which can easily be misdirected, even abused, by those planning papal events. They may be tempted to centre their success on getting people excited about meeting the pope.

The church treads a fine line between loving the pope and adulating him, making a cult of his person. Rhetoric gets the best of all of us at one time or another, but still it's a bit scary to hear a young Catholic, on making eye contact with the pope, say it felt like she "was in the presence of God."

Yes, that fine line is critically important — as it certainly was for Jesus.

Virtually every page of the Gospels records Jesus's fear of popularity. He did not want to be the centre of attention. He was always afraid people would get excited about him and miss the kingdom, the gracious reign of God. Jesus constantly told those for whom he worked a miracle to shut up about it.

The Lord certainly included himself when he taught that under God's reign the first will be last and the last first. Parables and paradoxes fit the teaching style of Jesus so well precisely because they diverted attention away from his person. It mattered little what one thought about Jesus when confronted with a parable about the prodigal son or the tax collector and the pharisee. One is judged by the story, not by the storyteller.

After the death and resurrection of Jesus, the church proclaimed Jesus its Lord and brought him to the very centre of its faith expression. Jesus became the perfect sign of God's presence and the sacramental symbol making the church alive and present.

This is our Easter faith and it is our greatest joy to proclaim it. Yet even here we must be careful. We Catholics know how easy it was for us to make our religion a Jesus-and-church affair. For centuries the reign of God was barely present in our preaching. And, to make matters worse, we didn't worry about this absence because we tended either to equate church and God's reign or to see the church as replacing that reign.

Few things are as important to the current pope as the ecumenical vocation calling the churches to be one voice on behalf of God's reign. The pope knows this dream challenges Catholics to rethink the role of the papal office and even of the church itself in relationship to the reign of God.

It is a great blessing that we have a pope we can easily love and revere, but, should we cross that line and adulate him, we certainly place obstacles in the path of God's reign.

It is good for us to remember a story about the first pope. Peter wanted to adulate the historical Jesus and so would hear nothing about him suffering and dying. Jesus, in some of the strongest rhetoric in the New Testament, calls Peter a devil: "Get behind me, Satan! You are an obstacle in my path, because the way you think is not divine but human" (Mt 16:23).

Chapter 7

That They May Be One

Proclaiming the kingdom June 20, 2001

In the days before Pope John XXIII opened the windows and allowed the Spirit to renew the church, Catholics tended to believe that God's ultimate concern was the health of their Catholic institution. The church, they believed, built on the rock of Peter, would never lose its perfection and, as the perfect society, had rights over all other institutions — religious or lay — in the world.

In order to safeguard this perfection, it was out of the question to actively attend an Anglican or Lutheran church service. Ecumenism was simply a non-starter. Any Catholic who attended a World Council of Churches' General Assembly in the '40s or '50s was excommunicated. If members of the United Church, for instance, wished to become Catholic, they were baptized "again" (we, of course, used the word "conditionally," but to Christians of another confession it certainly appeared as rebaptism, as a sign that Catholics did not know — and highly doubted — whether the Spirit was active in the other Christian churches).

Other churches were treated in much the same way as secular governments. Only the Catholic Church was perfect; all other societies were in error, and error had no rights.

It was a tremendous step forward for the mainline Canadian churches, after the Second Vatican Council, to get together and officially recognize one another's baptism. Catholic priests were told by their bishops that henceforth they were not to conditionally baptize "converts" to Catholicism.

The ramifications of that decision were far reaching. Catholics in particular had to acknowledge that the Spirit was alive in the other churches. And if the Spirit was at work, say in the Presbyterian Church since the days of John Calvin, surely that same Spirit of God had poured abundant blessings on that church during the past four and one-half centuries.

Acknowledging the presence and action of the Spirit in the churches changed the face of ecumenism. Christian unity no longer meant wayward denominations coming back to the one perfect church. Ecumenism was seen as enrichment for all the partners.

This was the topic of Paulist Father Tom Ryan's lecture on ecumenism given recently in Saskatoon. He outlined five special gifts the Protestant, Pentecostal, Orthodox, and Roman Catholic communities have to share with and enrich one another. Thus, he said, it was surely to every Christian's advantage to hear, understand, and appreciate the songs of the Lamb sung in all the churches.

Not all Catholics are ready to be enriched by other Christian traditions. It is difficult for them to part with the notion of perfection, to believe that Catholics could possibly receive anything from their sister churches.

While the Vatican council's paradigm shift — from being a perfect society to being a pilgrim church seeking to find the kingdom in God's (secular) world — has been difficult for many Catholics to swallow, it is only the beginning. Asian theologians, especially the Jesuits in India, are calling us to move beyond the Christian church(es) and find the Spirit of God in the major religions of the world.

Of course, as Christians we must do this without lessening the centrality and all-sufficiency of Jesus as Saviour. But we must not do it at the expense of radically reshaping the reality of the historical Jesus, of significantly changing his message. Who Jesus was and what he believed must remain normative for all Christians.

There is no doubt that Jesus always saw the kingdom as something greater than himself; he would never have accepted the notion that he in his person would come someday to replace the kingdom, or that his person should become the central announcement of the Good News. For Jesus, and we have no reason to believe he would think differently of the first Christians, the Good News is and will always be that "the kingdom of God is here" (Mk 1:15).

The last thing one can imagine about Jesus is that he would ever wish to dominate or to have exclusive claim to God's power. It is difficult for the church to remember that it is not the kingdom, that the kingdom will always be bigger and more important than the church.

As a church community we must soberly and with a good dose of humility always remember the day the disciples complained that others who were not with them were casting out devils. Jesus's simple answer sprang spontaneously from his soul: "You must not stop them; anyone who is not against us is for us" (Mk 9:39-40).

We as a church community do not know at this time how we can fully value non-Christian religions and still treasure Jesus as our one and only Saviour. But we do know — or at least we should know — that we cannot do it at the expense of losing sight of the historical Jesus.

We must learn from our mistakes. We have destroyed, at least in our day-by-day spirituality, the humanity of Christ in a one-sided effort to emphasize his divinity. We have also lessened the kingdom of God by equating it with a church supposedly so perfect that it lost its mooring in human history.

In the process we held our noses far above not only our separated brothers and sisters but also above the Hindu mystics and Buddhist monks — all in the name of him "who came not to be served but to serve and give his life as a ransom for many (all)" (Mk 10:45).

Catholics today need ecumenism   January 23, 1989

Religion deepens to the extent that people are called to faith, to levels of existence unknown to human understanding or feeling. The disintegration of religion manifests itself in the growth of legalism and dogmatism, and in the acceptance of magic.

Jesus, throughout his ministry, had trouble teaching the people the meaning of his miracles. Instead of receiving these signs of healing as calls to repentance, they found them wonderful marvels, the work of one with a divine wand (Mt 11:20-21).

Jesus was always in difficulty with those who thought God's will could be expressed in law. At every turn he confounded those who believed that by law they could know how they stood with God.

Those inclined to dogmatism fared no better. Always, but always, Jesus refused the straight, simple answer. Rather than allow for simple answers — which invariably dehumanize — Jesus answered his critics with parables and paradoxes.

Today we see within Catholicism a weariness with the call to faith. The temptation to choose these options which Jesus struggled so hard against has become quite appealing. Many Catholics are leaving the church for fundamentalistic religions which can assure them they are saved. (Not surprisingly the growth of fundamentalism has led to the birth of Fundamentalists Anonymous to counteract the imprisoning nature of all simple answers.)

Many in the church have found much to praise in Archbishop Marcel Lefebvre's movement to rid the church of ideas about religious freedom, about a servant church open to the modern world, about the need for ecumenism to free the church from a triumphalism that hinders the work of the Gospel.

Fundamentalism has become very appealing. Rather than parables and paradoxes (good enough to carry the message Jesus meant to leave us), we want simple dogmas that can be written in stone. Rather than preach the cross of Christ, we want moral answers in black and white. Rather than find the kingdom in the necessarily ambiguous signs in our midst, we are prepared to run halfway around the globe to witness miracles that do not challenge our basic value systems.

Before the Second Vatican Council the Catholic Church largely scorned ecumenism. Church leaders reminded Catholics they had not strayed from the truth and thus had nothing to gain from ecumenism.

Lefebvre does not stand alone in this position. It is easy to assume that the truth we have is still salvific — even though we have often stripped it of paradox, of its ability to call us to conversion.

Ecumenism often confronts the churches today in much the same way Jesus challenged his people with parables and paradoxes. Ecumenism does not call churches to part with the truth they possess, but challenges them to place this truth in a creative tension with another (usually paradoxical) truth.

If Catholics see the Eucharist as a sign of unity achieved, other churches will be called upon to remind them that this same eucharist is God's principal means of effecting that unity.

Both are truths, but neither is salvific without the other. A church which does not struggle to hold on to and put into practice both truths will never know the full meaning of the Eucharist.

Catholics have been told again and again that birth control by artificial means is wrong. Much of the argument for this position is based on a study of natural law. In a world of black-and-white answers Catholics feel they have only two options: to accept it fully even though they have no knowledge of or confidence in natural law, or to reject it.

As we know from study after sociological study, a majority of young

Canadian families have rejected this teaching — with an inevitable weakening of their tie with the institutional church.

Jesus went out of his way to prevent such black-and-white choosing. (He was not out to make things difficult, but to force choices that led to deeper experiences of life.) He would not only tell a couple of the evils of a contraceptive mentality; he would also remind them that achieving a healthy life-inducing Christian marriage was an obligatory task as well.

The ecumenical movement has repeatedly reminded us that both truths must be adhered to. We must ask young couples to accept both truths and must try to give them confidence in the paradox of Christ, that in this difficulty they can discover that the cross of Christ is always new life and joy.

The ecumenical movement is not straightforward and clean. It always messes things up a bit. But that is exactly what is needed by a Catholic Church which is, almost by its very nature, tempted to find its salvation in a legalism and dogmatism that is seasoned with a dash of divine magic which wondrously raises it above a sinful world.

The faith of Peter

August 10, 1984

We grew up in a strong and glorious church, one in which we felt much pride and great security. We were the true church and we knew it.

For most of us there was a wee bit of arrogance about it all. It was usually in polemics or self-righteousness that we quoted Matthew's Gospel: "You are Peter and on this rock I will build my church."

If anyone — just 20 years ago — would have tried to tell us about the weakness and seeming vulnerability of today's church, we would not have believed it. We knew better.

But here we are in quite a different church than we had hoped for. How differently we now hear those famous words of Jesus to Peter — likely we are beginning to hear them in the spirit in which they were written.

Matthew's intent certainly was not to give us some first-class polemical artillery to be used against rival churches. They were words of confidence, of service. They were to assure the church it could change, that despite its fears and stubbornness it could break out of its Jewish mould and serve the whole world.

Matthew's hearers were anything but bold. As a result of repeated persecution they lacked the confidence even to live in small ghettos, to say nothing of breaking out into a world they tended to see only in the darkest of colours.

To help them fulfill their vocation Matthew gave his people not one but two special stories about Peter and the Lord.

We usually remember only one, the one about the rock foundation of the church. We forget Matthew's first story of a somewhat cocky apostle trying to walk on the water and sinking with fright on feeling the first gale.

The early church liked to compare itself to the ark. As the ark saved Noah from the waters of the flood, so in the church Christians found their salvation. They pictured themselves as an ark on tumultuous waters, for they sensed that the waves of persecution so often appeared ready to capsize them.

In their honesty they added another element to their story. Jesus, they noted, was often asleep on the boat. The Lord so often seemed absent from their lives, they confessed, and just at the times when they needed him the most.

This image tells us much about how the church looked at itself. We see a weak church, a church desperately in need of its Lord.

To be sure, Matthew tells his people to hold fast, to stick with that creaky boat. Changing the image, he noted that nothing, not even death, could crack their faith in Jesus. This foundation is solid rock. So, stick with the church, believe with the faith of Peter.

But all this must be seen in the light of the first faith story which was built upon more familiar imagery. We are told how frail and fragile the faith of Peter really is. One puff of wind and down he goes.

Any self-reliance in the church, even in its head, is sheer impotence. Only in the risen Lord can the church find the strength to walk on the waters of persecution and weakness.

Today we are called in a special way to join in a celebration of the faith of Peter. It is a humble calling. It is a calling to follow in total confidence one who cannot walk on the waters and knows it.

It is a calling to be a little church, a community in which the weak and helpless can feel perfectly at home.

Twenty years ago we were so strong. Now we know how illusory that was. These 20 years have been painful ones — and blessed ones. Now we are more ready to share the rock of our salvation.

We seem to be a lot weaker, but this weakness has made us more open to see ourselves as an ark on the tumultuous waters with a Lord who seems to sleep far too much.

We are more likely to see the rock of our strength, not in some narrow, self-serving Catholic polemics, but as an ecumenical call to serve everyone as a brother or sister of the Lord.

Unity of Christians
January 22, 2003

In one of his most passionate speeches while touring Canada in 1984, Pope John Paul called for a greater effort by all the churches toward Christian unity. He told the various Christian communities gathered at St. Paul's Anglican Church in Toronto that he was "very pleased that they had seized this opportunity to affirm the necessity of the ecumenical movement."

The pope continued: "The restoration of the complete unity of Christians, for which we so greatly yearn and pray, is of crucial importance for the evangelization of the world....

The proclamation of the Good News of our Lord Jesus Christ is greatly obstructed by doctrinal division among the followers of the Saviour. On the other hand, the work of evangelization bears fruit when Christians of different communions, though not yet fully one, collaborate as brothers and sisters in Christ to the degree possible and with respect for their particular traditions."

The pope went on to speak of the many things Christians should always be doing together. He spoke of judging technological developments by the moral light of the Gospels. "For instance," he noted, "the needs of the poor must take priority over the desires of the rich; the rights of workers over the maximizing of profits; the preservation of the environment over uncontrolled industrial expansion; production to meet social needs over production for military purposes.

"These challenges present us with important areas of ecumenical collaboration and form a vital part of our mission of proclaiming the Gospel of Christ."

The pope indeed makes many important points. But what is particularly important to note is that he makes them without fanfare, makes them in a matter-of-fact manner, as if we now simply take them for granted.

He does not talk about churches coming back to the one true church.

Rather, he speaks of the restoration of the unity of Christians. In calling for joint evangelization efforts, he reminds the churches that they must respect their own traditions.

He accuses no one of leaving the fold. Rather, he speaks of all breaking the bond of unity. But perhaps most importantly, he assumes that the Holy Spirit has abandoned none of the churches since their separation one from the other. Thus, all the churches must respect their own traditions — and the traditions of each other. All this is required if the role of the Holy Spirit is to be respected.

The pope calls on the churches to serve one common social gospel. Not only will this help overcome the obstacles to unity within the churches, it will also lessen the scandal of division so clearly noted by a world profoundly in need of hearing the message of Jesus.

The pope highlights the necessity of Christian unity for the effective evangelization of the world. But he also notes the necessity of ecumenism for the renewal of the churches. Doing social gospel projects together will do much to break down the hatred created by centuries of bitter polemics.

But it will do more. It will look again at those very polemical arguments — not in a competitive spirit, but in one of mutual concern — and come, in the Holy Spirit, to a new appreciation for the arguments themselves.

Christianity is based on the paradox of the cross of Jesus Christ, a paradox that cuts to the heart of every human being. Every one of us must learn that in seeking to preserve our life we will lose it, and in losing it for the sake of the Gospel we will keep it safe.

The paradox of the paschal mystery of Christ, in touching every human heart, fills every human act with meaning. This, of course, includes our religious observance. Thus, every dogmatic statement of the churches, if it is to contain the healing grace of our crucified Lord, must of necessity be a paradoxical expression — in other words, a call to faith.

But from the days of Adam and Eve in the garden we have preferred knowledge to faith. Not without reason was the tree in paradise called the tree of knowledge.

Indeed, we prefer knowing to believing. Since paradoxes demand a creative balancing in faith of two seemingly opposite positions, the church tended to choose one horn of the paradox to the virtual exclusion of the other. Jesus's divinity was highlighted to the detriment of his humanity; the sacrificial nature of the Eucharist was emphasized to the exclusion of it being a communal celebration of table fellowship; the priesthood of the laity was forgotten to the benefit of the ministerial priesthood; the importance of the Bible as the living Word of God was sacrificed so that the sacraments could be absolute expressions of faith; papal primacy was so stressed that bishops became subordinates of the pope; celibacy was chosen as the expression of the kingdom to the downplaying of sexual intercourse. This list could be extended almost endlessly.

A dispassionate study of the Reformation reveals an honest zeal by the Reformers to heal the corruptions in the church. In actual fact, in the majority of cases this meant choosing the horn of the paradox that the medieval church had conveniently forgotten. If Rome highlighted papal primacy, the reformers spoke of local authority; if Rome saw the ministerial priesthood as the be-all-and-end-all, the reformers gave weight to the priesthood of all believers.

It is always necessary to keep both sides of the paradox. Each is necessary for the health of the other. Remembering the sacrificial nature of the Eucharist will bring dignity to the table celebration. Treasuring Christian marriage as a sign of the kingdom will bring a healthy balance to the practice of celibacy. Not holding on to the Bible as the Word of Life in people's daily lives and worship leaves the sacraments open to being reduced to magical rites. Not without reason did the reformers refer to the Catholic Mass as "hocus-pocus."

Ecumenism is essential to the churches today; it is the road to renewal. Each "side" needs the other to restore the balance of the paradox. Catholics need look no further than the restoration of the Word as an essential part of our Sunday worship to realize the benefits arising from the ecumenical spirit.

In this regard, it will serve all the churches well to study the practices of the desert monks with regard to spiritual direction. They always told the person seeking direction to choose the horn of the paradox they wished to avoid. For instance, a priest ready to overturn every apple cart in sight was told to meditate on the Lord's saying, "Blessed are the peacemakers." But the timid one, afraid to offend anyone, was told by the monk to remember that the Lord said, "I have come not to bring peace but the sword."

Herein lies the tremendous challenge of ecumenism: each church is called upon to treasure the gifts of the other, believing that the Holy Spirit is calling all faithful people to value the other's tradition. In the process, they will not lose the horn that they long had nursed to their own comfort; rather it will, as part once more of God's eternal paradox, spring to new life with a saving power they never previously imagined.

Healing the churches

January 16, 2002

Churches have suffered gravely because of their lopsided polemics. Protestants have lost the power of seeing their daily life in sacramental terms. With their emphasis on sacraments, Catholics developed a great reverence for the ministerial priesthood, seeing it as the highest expression of the Christian faith.

And, of course, the more we stressed this priestly expression, the more reformers stressed the baptismal priesthood of the laity. So totally did Catholics buy into a priest-centred church that we could develop structural forms of governance that completely — yes, completely! — excluded any hint of lay authority. The priest became the sole authority in the local parish.

Despite all the goodwill in the world, over long centuries priests, on their pedestals, saw everything more and more through clerical eyes. The values that lay members of the church would naturally treasure always came second to priestly concerns. And with a celibate clergy, marital values took second place to celibate ones. It was not by accident that the church knew more about every sin in the bedroom than it did about sins in the boardroom.

And with an all-male clergy, who can be surprised that a male perspective was preferred to a feminine viewpoint. "Preferred" — is that not radically understating the problem? It is not that the church prefers a male way of looking at reality; it has decreed that it is godly to give authoritative voice to men only.

A great divide was created between the laity and the clergy. Ordination came to be totally separated from 99.9 percent of the church community. The sacramental character of holy orders was something over and above the (lay) church community. The validity of the sacrament came to be judged solely on a mechanistic "pipeline" theory of apostolic succession through an unbroken line of ordinations stretching back to one of the apostles.

The validity or, more specifically, the invalidity of Protestant eucharists was determined by this pipeline theory. Though Paul VI had once asked the Archbishop of Canterbury (dressed in full episcopal garments) to bless the people of Rome gathered at St. Paul Outside the Walls, curial members a few years later were referring to him as a layperson.

While the pope has personally pulled out the keystone in our "papal fortress," little progress has been made in admitting the shortcomings of the pipeline theory of priesthood — that is, until Cardinal Walter Kasper came to head the Pontifical Council for Promoting Christian Unity.

In *Ecclesiology: A Second Revolution*, a *Festschrift*, a multi-authored work, honouring the Jesuit liturgist Joseph Jungmann, Kasper calls upon the church to look beyond a pipeline that operates independently of the lived faith of the community at large. He insists that we must look to the "worldwide communion of the church catholic."

He calls all churches to see their hold on holy orders not in terms of validity/invalidity but in terms of fullness/defectus, in terms of "lack but not complete absence."

Kasper's ecclesiology stresses that full ecclesial reality comes from being part of the catholic communio. "The individual local church is the true church of Jesus Christ," Kasper teaches, "to the extent that it is in communion with all other local churches."

This ecclesiology indeed has the makings for "a second revolution." It breaks down the absolute distinction between lay and clerical worlds, bringing the ordination ritual into a true celebration of the apostolic faith of the whole (catholic) community. Catholics should rejoice in this, for they know through bitter experience the consequences of a practically idolatrous acceptance of a very narrow view of the ministerial priesthood.

Ecumenism may call us to places we would rather not go. But let us follow the lead of the pope. He does not know where a reassessment of the Petrine office will lead, but still he insists that "we cannot turn back on this difficult but vital task."

Ecumenism calls us to believe that the Spirit is alive in all the churches, that all the churches are called upon to enrich one another. So let us rejoice: what is true about our understanding of the priesthood and of the papal office is only a foretaste of the joyous catholicity to come.

Pope serious about ecumenism   January 21, 1998

Catholics who are not fond of ecumenism tend to stress the importance of following the pope rather than the theological fads of the moment. Ironically, there is no other area in which papal teaching has changed more this century than ecumenism.

In the first papal encyclical on ecumenism, by Pope Pius XI in 1928, Catholics were forbidden from participating in any "pan-Christian" movement.

Pope Pius XII, while not as strident as his predecessor, often equated the Catholic Church and the mystical Body of Christ as "one and the same."

Ecumenism in this theological world meant wayward Protestants and Orthodox were to find their way back to the Catholic Church where the fullness of that apostolic mark of oneness was maintained.

Catholics simply were not ready to admit that their church too had been impoverished by the bitter religious strife of the past. They had always told themselves that they had won the battles and had remained faithful to the Lord.

Even after the Second Vatican Council passed its epoch-making Decree on Ecumenism, many Catholics were not inclined to see their tradition in any way truncated. These Catholics were ill prepared for Pope John Paul II's declaration in May 1995 that the Latin Rite simply needs the traditions of the East in order to express its catholic character.

In this apostolic letter, The Light of the East, the pope bemoans the "progressive estrangement" that led both sides to perceive the other's diversity "no longer as a common treasure but as incompatibility."

One month after this apostolic letter, the pope issued his encyclical on ecumenism, *Ut Unum Sint*. The contrast between his encyclical and that of Pius XI could hardly be greater.

The first said we had nothing to learn from the wayward; the second humbly asked other Christians to help the pope better understand the role his own Petrine office should play in the church of the new millennium. He asked for "a patient and familial dialogue" to find new and better ways for the exercising of papal primacy for the good of the whole church.

The pope had already prepared the way for this. In the May apostolic letter he began talking about the Petrine ministry in ways unheard of for more than a thousand years.

"Peter's task," he noted, "is to search constantly for ways that will bring about unity. There he must not create obstacles, but must open up paths." Then the pope puts words into the mouth of Christ: "It is as if the Master himself wanted to tell Peter: 'Remember that you are weak, that you, too, need endless conversion. You are able to strengthen others only insofar as you are aware of your own weakness.'"

We need the ecumenical spirit to bring us back to the riches of the whole Christian tradition. Yes, we have much to offer other churches; but let us never forget that our blind spots need the gracious attention of other Christians opening them to the healing light of Christ.

And the world needs this ecumenical spirit. The pope, building on the teaching of the council, told our separated sisters and brothers in Toronto: "We cannot turn back on this difficult but vital task, for it is essentially linked with our mission of proclaiming to all humanity the message of salvation. The restoration of the complete unity of Christians is of crucial importance for the evangelization of the world."

The ecumenical spirit is as much about our feet as it is about our head. To be true to this spirit, we must take up the principle formulated at the World Council of Churches conference held at Lund, Sweden: "What our consciences tell us we can do together should be done together."

But it is also about the head. We Catholics have been strong on dogma, often insisting that other Christians express their faith in our terms, in our theological language. We often come close to believing that our dogmatic expressions of a theological truth capture the full meaning of that truth.

We know in our heart of hearts that that is not so, but still we hold on to old ways of expressing our faith as if they were the definitive way of doing so.

Such dogmatism should frighten us. It is healthy for Catholics to explicitly remember that Jesus did not formulate his faith in dogmatic expressions but rather in paradoxes and parables. Remembering how Jesus lived, it is hard to imagine the Lord being comfortable with a church armed against an evil age with a long list of dogmas which are seen as full expressions of his truth.

The true function of dogma is a negative one. It cuts off speculation in ways that take us away from a deeper understanding of the man of parables. Remembering this should free us from insisting, as the Vatican recently did with the Anglicans on the meaning of the Eucharist, on the use of our own theological language.

In the end it comes down to two views of ecumenism: Pope Pius XI's in which we have the truth as the only true church of God, or Pope John Paul II's in which we seek to restore our catholic spirit by listening to and praying with our brothers and sisters.

Christian unity revisited

January 21, 2004

It's not enough to be open-minded. Each Christian is called to the full unity of the Body of Christ. Pope John Paul, while in Canada, acknowledged that our separation was a scandal, that it essentially interfered with our witnessing to the presence of Christ in the world.

If we do not feel a deep desire for Christian unity as we brush shoulders daily with other Christians, then we are not ecumenists but ghetto-lovers content to live in the confining but comfortable world of our own truncated tradition.

As Catholics, we love to see ourselves as universalists, open to the best in every tradition. But let us be honest. We should be ready to admit that the bitter polemics of former times have destroyed the catholicity of every Christian tradition — including our own.

Polemics are always destructive. In its desire to defeat "the opposition," each Christian group at the time of the Reformation solidified its position and stressed those aspects which it felt the other side had denied or could not handle well in the theological battle. In this sense, we let our opponents to a large extent write our catechisms for us.

We need to become ecumenists not only to restore full Christian unity but also to find balance in our own tradition. In his 1995 apostolic letter, The Light of the East, John Paul II acknowledged that the Roman Catholic Church — the pope spoke in terms of the Latin Rite — needed the traditions of the East "in order to express its catholic character."

Gone — forever we hope! — is the day in which we can boast that the Catholic Church alone has the whole truth. To be sure, full reconciliation can still be obtained in the Roman church. Yet it is painful to say it: but we must acknowledge that much of our boasting about being the only church that remained faithful to its Lord has been little more than wallowing in a tradition that has lost its wide catholic sweep, narrowed as it is by past sins and polemics. Only an ecumenical spirit can bring us back to the riches of the whole Christian tradition.

Despite the fact that many leaders in the churches have lost their enthusiasm for ecumenism, this past decade has witnessed great progress. The burning issue of the Protestant Reformation, justification by faith alone, has been positively addressed by Catholics and Lutherans. Martin Luther once said, "If the pope would only grant that we are justified in Christ, I would not only carry him on my shoulders, I would kiss his feet."

The mainline churches of the Reformation are advancing speedily toward unity. Soon most Lutherans and Anglicans in Canada will be sharing full intercommunion and will mutually recognize one another's ministries.

Two problem areas stand out for Catholics — one long-standing, one of rather recent origin.

Not surprisingly, the one of more recent vintage appears right now to be the more difficult. The ordination of women to full ecclesial ministry has become a great stumbling block for Catholics. Church leadership declares it is impossible but has not been able to come up with reasons that the people in the pew find convincing. Add to this problem a review of our church history which, after apostolic times, is consistent in its treatment of women as second-class citizens at best, and one is left with a church full of people who think our hesitation to ordain women is based more on prejudice than on solid theological argument.

Certainly not everyone in the Catholic Church agrees with this analysis. But, at least one must admit that this issue is as much an internal Catholic problem as it is an ecumenical one. The lack of consensus within the church has made it doubly difficult to deal with its ecumenical ramifications. As a first step, we Catholics must face the issue straight on; we must admit that there are deep divisions within our church around this issue. A church leadership that does not acknowledge two millennia of putting down women is not going to have credibility concerning its theological reasons limiting the ministerial priesthood to men alone.

Nor will the issues around the ordination of homosexuals be laid to rest in our church until we develop a language truly based on pastoral care rather than on cultural bias. In this regard, it was encouraging to hear Cardinal Francis E. George of Chicago admit that the church's "exact" language "does not help us in welcoming men and women of homosexual orientation. Our language can seem lacking in respect. This is a pastoral problem and a source of anxiety for me."

The second issue, the exercise of papal primacy, periodically gives signs that it need not be the thorny issue it traditionally has been. Just before going to Jerusalem for the last meeting of the major Orthodox leaders (January 2000), Ecumenical Patriarch Bartholomew, likely more for his colleagues than for his western sisters and brothers, warned that John Paul's exercise of papal primacy is "still unacceptable to Orthodox churches." The papacy, he said, "expresses a spirit far removed from the spirit of the Orthodox churches."

Those are painful words for the pope to hear — even if they were primarily meant for Orthodox ears. John Paul knows he has a problem —

or, to put it more bluntly, that he is the problem. While in Canada in 1984 John Paul told leaders of the other churches that he was an optimist about unity but hoped the pope wasn't the biggest impediment to it. The pope, however, has not been a fatalist regarding this second problem. He has humbly asked the church communities to help him redefine the Petrine ministry for the good of the whole church.

But not everyone in the church is happy about that. There is a growing hard core who sees no need for any change at all.

In this regard, it is interesting to recall *Enthusiasm*, a book Msgr. Ronald Knox wrote in 1950. Heresies, Knox wrote, are never the work of prophets, never the result of people who are thinking new thoughts for a new age. Rather, he continued, heresies are the "gift" to the church of reactionaries who lose sight of the whole and, in their enthusiasm for the faith, centre on a few choice principles and make them the only true signs of orthodoxy.

All ecumenists must take reactionaries seriously, but they must not see them as the final witness to any tradition in the church. Rev. Konrad Raiser, recently retired as the leader of the World Council of Churches, calls on the clergy of the churches to see beyond the narrow clerical mindset that conveniently sees all those pet clerical theological dictums as "church dividing," and instead turn and notice how the laity view the church. "Lay ecumenism," he maintains, "will bring the churches to the unity Jesus calls for."

While serious book theology is always essential for the full life of the Christian church, it is well both for the professional theologian and for the authoritative teacher to realize how the 99.9 percent of the faithful experience the living presence of Christ. There is no doubt that if they did indeed so experience the Saviour, the whole Christian church would, for one thing, have an altogether different approach to ecumenical marriages.

We would also practise the Lund Principle with greater fidelity: what we can do together, we should do together. Maybe ecumenism's finest gift is that it frees us from ourselves and our truncated traditions, and thus gives us hope that someday soon we will be able to drink more deeply of the catholic spirit.

Christian unity sought

January 22, 1997

Before the Second Vatican Council, Roman theologians tended to view the church as "a perfect society." All other societies, civil or religious, were imperfect.

The *Syllabus of Errors* (1864) found fundamental flaws in every society save that of the church. The church did not have to change. The leading Catholic treatise on the church, the Spanish Summa of Joachim Salaverri, declared that "the church is a perfect and absolutely independent society with full legislative, judicial and coercive power."

Salaverri went further. He declared that only the Roman Catholic Church had the marks or notes of unity, holiness, catholicity, and apostolicity. All other churches were "false churches."

The Second Vatican Council took a radically different approach. It emphasized that the church, just like all its members, is on pilgrimage toward the fullness of the kingdom. Like all things human, the church is called to grow, to change, to develop as it travels on toward that glorious day when Christ will transform all things.

Surely the council did not deny that the church bore the four classical marks of unity, holiness, catholicity, and apostolicity. But it did not have them perfectly; rather these marks were radical calls to greater unity, to more perfect love, to a truer catholicity, to a clearer witnessing to its apostolic vocation.

Just as the author of Hebrews noted that Jesus the man had to grow by means of the trials of his life, although he was Son (Heb 5:9), so the church, though it be the very Body of Christ, has to grow. God, in creating human beings, made them such that they must either grow or wither in death.

As long as the church saw itself as "a perfect society" that had nothing to learn or receive from anyone, ecumenism made no sense. To imply that one could gain from others was tantamount to denying the true nature (perfection) of the church. But with the shift to the pilgrim image, all that suddenly changed.

In human society, individuals can meet others with two basic approaches: either they struggle to see what is wrong with the other, or they see their neighbour as an opportunity, as an enrichment in their lives. With the espousal of the pilgrim image, the church was able to part with its *Syllabus-of-Errors* attitude and recognize other churches as an opportunity to grow.

As it is deadly for individuals to seek first to discover the weaknesses of others, so it is for the church. How freeing it has been for the church to discover that it is not so perfect that it cannot benefit from its association with other Christians, with other believers!

The modern ecumenical movement for Catholics had its first spring in the Nazi prisons of Germany. Catholic and Lutheran intellectuals had to hold on to one another for strength. They prayed together, sang together, and, all too often, died together.

After the war there was no going back. Lutherans took another look at the sacramental base of the church, while Catholics came to realize that Luther's special treatment of the paradox of the Cross was a powerful tool in opening the Scriptures to modern society.

Ecumenism, as we know it in the church today, took hold. And Catholics have gained so much.

Anglicans were no longer regarded as hedonistic followers of Henry VIII. We learned how they had meditated deeply on the parables of Luke and used them in their catechetics in ways we never considered.

We studied again the Orthodox's love of mystery. We learned that St. John's Gospel, though not strong on institution, could powerfully shape a church community in ways unimagined by clerics dominated by law.

We looked again at our Mennonite sisters and brothers and rediscovered a Christ who based his life on pacifist principles. It was not by chance that so many Catholics on the Prairies learned the principles of social justice, not from reading the great social encyclicals but from seeing them in action — in the lives of their Mennonite neighbours.

The council, however, did not limit its ecumenical thrust to Christians. It took the unprecedented step of telling us we had much to learn from our Jewish forebears and from non-Christian religions. Soon monks like Thomas Merton were sitting at the feet of Buddhist monks trying to understand their prayer.

The truth we learned in all our ecumenical endeavours was precisely the opposite of what we had feared. We were afraid that their understanding of the faith would undermine or relativize our own. We learned, however, that any knowledge that has a truly human face can only deepen our faith, our love of the Lord, as we continue our pilgrimage toward the marriage feast of the Lamb in the kingdom of the one and only God.

Catholic/Lutheran healing

November 22, 1995

Martin Luther, certainly in the beginnings of his reforms, had no intention of breaking with the Catholic Church. Most Europeans knew only one church and could not even imagine the one church of Christ breaking up.

Catholics cannot quibble with most of Luther's reforms; no one in their right mind can argue against the need for a strong prophet in the early 16th-century church. Nor can anyone deny that many of the great Catholic reforms wrought by the Council of Trent (AD 1545-63) would not have happened then but for the brilliance and zeal of Martin Luther.

That issues got out of control is the responsibility of both sides. It was no more the result of Luther's growing messianic complex than it was the stubbornness and at times dishonesty of the Catholic leaders — popes included.

However, we should never forget — not to lessen the guilt of church leaders on both sides but simply to better understand the historical moment — that politics had as much, if not more, to do with the disastrous dividing of the church than did theology. The rise of German nationalism enabled petty princes to seize the moment and further their own monetary position at the expense of church unity.

Luther, as much as he believed in the reforms he wrought, was never fully comfortable with the divisions they created in the church. He repeatedly told his followers that only one teaching justified the division of the church. If the Catholic Church would acknowledge the correctness of his interpretation of St. Paul's teaching on justification by faith alone and not by good works, he said, he would be ready to move on all other matters.

We must ask again today: What issues do Catholics and Lutherans understand in so radically a different manner that these issues continue to justify our divisions? (There are deep divisions in the Catholic Church today, yet we do not see them as church-dividing.)

Are our differences with Lutherans today truly church-dividing? Years ago the most prestigious Catholic theologian in the second half of this century, Jesuit Father Karl Rahner, said they were not.

A commission of Catholic and Lutheran scholars has in the years following the council studied together the critical theological issues and proclaimed that there was substantial agreement on the issues important enough to be considered church-dividing.

One would think that would have led to dancing in our streets. Yet, as Assumptionist Father George Tavard bemoans, nothing, but nothing, happened. Their ecumenical work has become "dead letters."

Historians of the 16th century have had a difficult time discerning the root cause of the church divisions. Was it fundamentally theological or political? Will historians some day have to do the same gruelling work about our time? Are our continuing divisions theological or are they in fact political? Are our vested interests in the current church structure so powerful that the work of ecumenical theologians is not even given serious consideration?

One might justifiably argue that the work of Catholic/Lutheran dialogue groups has been done poorly or inconclusively. But surely there can be no justification whatsoever for allowing their work to become "dead letters," ignored by the leaders of the churches.

Diversity in the church   October 7, 1998

Canadian Oblate theologian Rev. Richard Coté said it succinctly at a recent conference at St. Paul's in Ottawa: "We have now come to realize that a church with only one theology is a dangerous church."

Historically, the church was structured to prevent this; it had many different faces in many different rites. Cardinal Achille Silvestrini, the prefect of the Congregation for Eastern Churches, noted at a recent church plenary in Rome that "the Eastern Catholic churches are living witnesses to the fact that the Catholic Church is a symphony in which the voice and witness of a variety of churches resound."

The cardinal went on to stress that these churches are not "branches" of the one true church. If they are not received as full churches in their own name, "the universal church risks losing one of the clearest signs of its catholicity."

The early church did not plan on developing different rites. They were the natural product of Christians who realized, to use the words of Pope John Paul II, that a faith that does not become a culture "is a faith which has not been fully received, not thoroughly thought through, not faithfully lived out." The various rites in the church correspond to the major cultures into which Christian missionaries inserted the Gospel.

This natural process met its most pronounced rejection in the Vatican rejection of "the Chinese rites" being developed by the 16th-century Jesuits led by Matteo Ricci. Since then the Catholic Church became officially more and more identified with the Latin Rite and, as eastern churches reunited with Rome as Uniate churches, they faced ever increasing pressure to adopt the "superior" Latin way of doing things.

Rome has now acknowledged the weaknesses of the uniate model. It realizes that only strong, independent eastern churches can dispel Orthodox fears of the Roman Catholic understanding of papal primacy.

The pope has called upon the eastern churches "to proceed courageously and resolutely in the ecumenical commitment." This challenge, however, would appear more workable if the Vatican would officially return to the ancient custom of a major rite for each major world culture. Until Rome is comfortable with a church with truly African and Asian faces, with a Latin American face formed in the ghetto slums, with an aboriginal face etched in Canada's North, there is little reason to hope that our separated brothers and sisters in either East or West will enter into a serious dialogue with us on the central ecumenical obstacle, the meaning of papal primacy.

Eucharist in ancient "Iraq"   October 31, 2001

The Anaphora of Addai and Mari is an ancient eucharistic prayer that dates back to the third century, the oldest eucharistic prayer that has survived intact in the church. The liturgy and doctrinal congregations at the Vatican have given it their full endorsement as a valid eucharistic prayer. What, we ask, can be the significance of that, other than the fact that it took the Roman church a mere 1,750 years to come to this conclusion?

The reason for doing so now is clear enough. The recent Gulf War delivered the final push. Chaldean Christians, both Orthodox and Uniate, have been spread thinly throughout the world. Very few places outside Iraq have the resources to build both Orthodox and Uniate churches. Because of necessity, authorities in both churches have encouraged joint worship.

But there was a problem for the Catholics. This most ancient eucharistic prayer did not have a narrative of institution (the Last Supper story) and thus did not contain those words which medieval theologians deemed essential to the sacrament, the "words of consecration" — this is my body, this is my blood.

The approval of Addai and Mari should encourage us all to accept the post-Vatican II teaching of the church that the whole eucharistic prayer is consecratory — a prayer that speaks more of consecrating a people one with pope and bishop, one with Mary, the apostles and all the saints, one with the living and the dead (of our own families) than it does about changing the ontological meaning of the elements.

Let us thank the Chaldean Church for forcing us to the essentials. The very presence of Jesus in the sacrament is a great and wondrous mystery. But this mystery is greatly enhanced when we celebrate it as part of the communion of saints of Mary, Peter and Paul, Francis and Benedict, Hildegarde and Teresa, John XXIII and the newly beatified men and women from our own country.

Once we truly celebrate the Eucharist as the communion of saints, we will no longer accept a world of Catholic, Lutheran, or Anglican eucharists. A special thank you to the Chaldeans (whom we have put through hell) scattered throughout the world for treasuring the Eucharist at its deepest levels.

A 1,500-year misunderstanding   November 28, 1994

It is a joyful little story. The small Assyrian Orthodox Church of the East and the Roman Catholic Church have declared that for 1,500 years they had misunderstood one another, but now can formally acknowledge that both their churches held the same orthodox view of Jesus Christ "as true God and true man, perfect in his divinity and perfect in his humanity."

For a millennium and a half we in the West have condemned this Assyrian church for its Nestorianism (the positing of two persons in Christ). Ever since the Council of Ephesus (AD 431), a council filled with as much political intrigue as with theology, whole churches lost the ability to understand one another. Each church decided it alone had the correct language, which it tried to impose on the other.

Even this reconciliation between Pope John Paul II and Patriarch Dinkha IV was long in coming. It was more than a quarter-century ago that church historians and theologians reached a strong consensus that the two churches, though talking past one another, were both upholding the same doctrine.

In this age, in which all the mainline churches officially espouse ecumenism as the call of the Lord, this little story has much to tell us. It should remind us that imposing our language on others is always fraught with danger. The Anglicans, for instance, have much to complain about when the Vatican, in giving its assessment of the work of the Anglican/Roman Catholic International Commission, demanded that the Eucharist be defined as a sacrifice in traditional Catholic terminology.

We are heading for trouble, too, if German and Italian authority figures in our church not only declare their right to safeguard the orthodoxy of the liturgy in English-speaking churches, but also see it as their prerogative to determine the meaning and practice of the English language itself.

Let us not pretend that language is not a powerful tool. Two churches remained in schism no fewer that 1,500 years because each tried to impose its language on the other.

The exclusive language found in the new catechism of the Catholic Church appears to many to have been employed precisely as a tool, as a sign to "radical feminists" that the church is not about to bend to their spurious demands.

Any language that makes dedicated women feel like second-class citizens in our church is unworthy of our liturgy. The English language is changing, and changing quickly, precisely because a growing number of people everywhere are espousing new cultural values — not the least of which is the conviction that our language should reflect the utter equality of men and women.

For our church to use any other language in its worship of the Lord Jesus Christ is to disgrace itself — and its Lord who in his day scandalized many a religious authority by his closeness to women.

Ukrainian Catholic Church June 9, 1984

Cardinal Myroslav Lubachivsky, major archbishop of the Ukrainian Catholic Church, is visiting Canada. He is ready to admit that his church has many problems as it lives in Canada as a small minority. He comes, he says, to confirm Ukrainians in their faith, to convince them that theirs is a noble and powerful tradition.

Often during their history they have in various ways been taught the opposite. Through most of their history they have been caught between two powerful patriarchates — Constantinople, an uncaring mother, and Moscow, ever ready to adopt them for decidedly political ends.

When the Mongols decimated Ukraine, both looked the other way. The bishops then turned to the See of Rome for help and encouragement. With the Union of Brest (AD 1596), Rome acknowledged the Ukrainians as a sister church and promised to respect their tradition.

It has not always been a happy story — especially after Ukrainians for painful economic and political reasons emigrated from the homeland into territory where the Roman Rite reigned supreme.

Ukrainian clergy were often barely tolerated; they were explicitly forbidden to be missionaries in Roman Rite territory. In 1929 Rome, under pressure from American bishops, forbade any Ukrainian eparchy from ordaining married men in the Americas.

How such a ruling could be squared with the Union of Brest was beyond the skills of even the most gifted canon lawyers. Brest was significantly forgotten.

A large proportion of the Orthodox in the United States today came to the New World as Uniate immigrants. They separated from Rome on experiencing that this See could be as uncaring as Constantinople had so often been of old.

The majority who tenaciously held on and treasured their union with Rome were not always capable of preserving their tradition intact. Scorned by their eastern brothers and sisters for their union with Rome, they could not look to them for aid in understanding their tradition. Western seminaries, where so many of the Ukrainian clergy studied, could not but give a Latin bias.

Many Latinizations crept into the Ukrainian Rite. Often they were warmly received by the people. These accretions made the Ukrainians feel less like second-class citizens and more at home in a church in which the majority identified totally with the Roman Rite. The Second Vatican Council declared unequivocally that these developments were tragic for the whole church. It called upon the eastern churches to fully restore their own traditions and thus enrich the true catholicity of the People of God.

The Decree on the Catholic Eastern Churches called for the restoration of the traditions of each particular church "whole and entire," and then from within that renewed tradition "adapt its own way of life to the needs of different times and places."

In the next paragraph the council proclaimed that all "these churches are of equal rank, so that none of them is superior to the others because of its rite." Then undoing the unbelievable restrictions to eastern missionary activity, the bishops in council continued: "These churches have the same rights and obligations — even with regard to the preaching of the Gospel in the whole world."

To ensure the independence of each rite in the church the council went on to call for the restoration of the ancient method of church government — the patriarchal office.

This, the Ukrainians have not been given. Once again their needs were not given priority. The Vatican's *ostpolitik* (looking to the East) has come first.

The acknowledged need of the Ukrainians for a patriarchate remains unfulfilled. It must be difficult for most Ukrainians, who see their brothers and sisters in Ukraine facing outright persecution, not to fall victim in their heart of hearts to a self-pity that cries out: Must we forever have an uncaring mother?

A strong, vibrant Ukrainian Church deeply rooted and in love with its ancient traditions should be a concern of all North American Catholics. There are many days Roman Catholics need to be reminded that unity does not mean uniformity, that subsidiarity is a principle which should touch every aspect of church life, and that religion has no lasting force unless it is inculturated in the ordinary lives of people.

As few other churches in either East or West have done, the Ukrainian Church has touched the soul of its people. The church fearlessly entered the culture. It has taken the warmth of the Ukrainian home, the exuberance of Ukrainians in their celebrations, and their love for ritual and pageantry and turned them into God's praise.

We pray for Cardinal Lubachivsky as he travels among his people confirming them in their tradition. We need a strong Ukrainian Church in our midst. In this age of multiculturalism a self-confident Ukrainian Church will have much to teach us as we diversify our Roman Rite in order to be a living word in the new age before us.

Vocation of Ukrainian Catholics   May 2, 1988

It is hard to fault Ukrainian Catholics for not getting excited about all the talk of *glasnost* and *perestroika* in the Soviet Union. This church has strengthened us all through its heroic example. No other church this century has been called to witness to the faith even unto martyrdom as have our Ukrainian sisters and brothers. With a faith reminiscent of the Roman church in the first centuries, Ukraine has blessed the whole church with countless martyrs.

Yet it must seem to many who are called to heroic faith that the church does not sufficiently treasure their witness. Like the martyrs in Latin America they do not seem to fit the establishment's agenda.

No martyrs are proclaimed from Central and South America. And many in the base communities ask: Is this because their witness always has a hint of politics in it and thus would be offensive to the United States since it contradicts that country's plans for the southern hemisphere?

No martyrs are proclaimed in Lithuania or in Ukraine either. And these catacomb communities wonder if their steadfastness in faith is not recognized since it happens to run contrary to the Vatican grand plan of *ostpolitik* and of ecumenical union first with the Orthodox.

The Ukrainian Catholic Church is in a most discouraging position. They who since 1596 have paid dearly for their love for the Chair of Peter are now viewed by so many as an obstacle to the reunion of East and West.

Perhaps the best news to come out of the Vatican as it prepares to celebrate a millennium of faith in the land of Prince Vladimir is the recent papal acknowledgment that all was not right with the AD 1596 Union of Brest. "New paths," the pope said, must be found that will link eastern churches to the Bishop of Rome.

No church, East or West, will want to form a true bond of unity with Rome so long as it sees the Patriarch of the West entering into the day-by-day activities and decisions of an eastern church. If the Uniate churches would have enjoyed the traditional independence of sister churches consistent with the first millennium of Christianity, they would not be so despised in the East.

While not openly admitting past failures by the Vatican, the pope hints strongly in this regard in his latest letter to his Ukrainian co-believers. In *Magnum Baptismi Donum* (The great gift of baptism), released in Rome in April, the pope centres our unity in baptism and promises the East that he will show the whole Christian family that the Uniate churches are "no obstacle to full communion," no hindrance to complete church unity.

It is a pledge the Ukrainian Church should take at face value. It makes for an altogether new understanding of the papal urging *Euntes in Mundum* (Go out into all the world), whereby the pope called the Ukrainian Church to enter into full ecumenical dialogue with the Russian Orthodox Church.

This will be no mean task. But surely the 20th-century martyrs in the Soviet Union can empower a Uniate church patterned on the Second Vatican Council for the great Easter work of reconciliation.

It will require humility and courage, a sense of tradition and a willingness to forget and forgive the wrong done to the Ukrainian Church by both Rome and Moscow. The greatness of this past period of faith (from the Second World War to the present) may be only a foretaste of the nobility of spirit now asked of this church.

We do believe that, if Rome gives them the full authority to be true to their tradition, they can indeed accomplish this work. They have the backing; the blood of martyrs is the seed of the church.

Salvation of non-Christians   October 30, 1995

Jesus loved paradoxes. Simple answers, he knew, never urged people to travel the way of salvation.

He did not just proclaim that those who seek to save their life lose it, and those who lose it save it. He saw this paradox as the underpinning of all life. In other words, salvation is always paradoxical; and vice versa, what is not paradoxical is not salvific.

To choose only one truth of a paradoxical pair turns that truth, no matter how true it may be, into a destructive force.

To give a simple example. We are taught that we must lay down our lives for others. Wise spiritual masters, however, also remind us that we must, first of all, take care of ourselves. Either one of these truths, without the corrective counterweight of the other, leads to destruction. The first alone will surely lead to burnout and depression. The second alone, just as surely, will end in narcissism.

How the two meld into a salvific peace is as varied as the very variety God planted in each and every special work of creation.

There are two truths the church has strongly resisted seeing together. It loved to proclaim that all salvation is in Christ Jesus and that thus outside the church there is no salvation.

But the Second Vatican Council, in its ground-breaking document on relations with non-Christian religions, also noted that God acts beyond the visible boundaries of the church, that the other classical religions of the world are helpful to their practitioners and — in a moment of sheer inspiration — declared that Catholics had much to learn from these other religions.

With the first truth alone to guide us, we send missionaries out to destroy other religions and conquer lost souls for Christ. With the second truth alone, Christ loses his meaning for us. As Christians we must ever sing in our hearts: "Nothing can outweigh the supreme advantage of knowing Christ Jesus as my Lord" (Phil 3:8).

What is so refreshing in the Vatican document dealing with these two truths is its ready admission that we will never know how the two of them are ideally to interlock. The Vatican writers say with humility — and with a healthy touch of humour — "It is a mystery!"

This is no hollow conclusion. It is a church humbly proclaiming that Catholics' attitude toward other religions must forever be "one of respect and dialogue, not annexation or conquest."

It is a beautiful example of the Lord's promise. Struggle honestly with the paradox and in the midst of that struggle you will notice joyfully that God has showered down the gift of salvation.

Jewish brothers and sisters   July 13, 1987

Nothing has so blighted the history of the Christian church as its treatment of its Jewish brothers and sisters. Blatant acts of prejudice, even outright sins of hatred, were often easily justified by a simplistic recalling that the Jewish people were deicides, murderers of the Lord Jesus.

Such questionable thinking was used to underpin most of our theology about Judaism. The Jewish people and their faith had no enduring value for this world. In rejecting Jesus as their messiah the Jews lost all relevance; they were completely superseded by Christianity. The only good thing that could happen to Jews was for them to admit to the sins of their ancestors and to convert to Christianity.

With such a theology it was a lot easier to overlook the racist thinking of Aryan purists. It is hard to imagine that Hitler would have been able to carry out his genocide policy had it not been for the inbred prejudice against Jews which the churches had quietly fostered over the centuries.

It must come as a shock to many Christians to notice that major mainline churches are now issuing theological documents contradicting the basic premises of traditional Christian thought. The Presbyterian Church and the United Church of Christ have published documents proclaiming both the abiding value of Judaism and the timeless validity of God's promises to the Jewish people.

It is important for all followers of Jesus to recall that the first Christians did not feel they had to part with their Jewish faith in order to be Christians. They remembered that the Lord had told them he did not intend to "abolish the law and the prophets" (Mt 5:17).

It is important, too, to remember that not all first-century Christians were comfortable with the split between themselves and their Jewish brothers and sisters. They refused to see the split as theologically based; thus they dismissed as misguided the fast-developing theology which proclaimed that God had rejected Israel and that now Christians — and they alone — were the true Israel of God.

To the author of Revelation, the last book of the New Testament, such thinking made a mockery of Jesus's struggle and death. So he gave Christians a new dream.

True Christians, he prophesied, never dream of themselves alone; they dream of a New Jerusalem with 12 gates that never close, each gate bearing the name of a tribe of Israel.

No Jew will ever have to crawl to enter the city of God. Each tribe will always have its own gate through which its members can enter with heads held high (Rev 21:13).

The author tells the Christian churches that if they have a vision of God's dwelling with the human family in which Jews — as Jews — are not at home, they simply do not have a proper view of reality.

Christians should accept this vision of the New Jerusalem as a two-edged sword and allow it to call them to a repentance which will enable them to see their Jewish neighbours as full brothers and sisters.

The two new church documents referred to above did not run into serious difficulty because they proclaimed the abiding validity of the Jewish covenant. The problems arose when this affirmation of Jewish faith was used to lend theological support for the existence of the Israeli state.

Pope after pope has refused to recognize the State of Israel — in large part because of fear that such recognition would be misconstrued to mean that the State of Israel is part of the divine plan.

It is important that we continue to disassociate the political reality of Israel from the religious validity of the Jewish faith. Not to do this is dangerous for world peace and stability — given Israel's militaristic policies.

Yet Catholics must admit they have an inherent credibility problem in their proclamation that they can be fully open to Jews without affirming the need for the Israeli state. It must be difficult for Jews to take our popes seriously when they see them treasuring the privileges that accrue to heads of state.

Surely there are great advantages to having the politically independent State of Vatican City, but, as the Archbishop Paul Marcinkus Vatican-Bank affair continues to embarrass Catholics everywhere, let us at least readily acknowledge the credibility problems inherent in it.

Ghetto mentality

September 18, 1989

The nearly 2,000 years of history of the Christian treatment of Jews have precious few moments we can be proud of. That the Jews have survived at all is one of the great miracles of history.

They have survived through their formation of closely knit ghettos. Everything about them was directed at strengthening their life together. Their language, their culture, and especially their religion (the multiple kosher laws) made integration with the larger community all but impossible.

Ghettos, however, are not an unmixed blessing. While they strengthen the community within, they also foster distrust and suspicion outside. The more people are excluded from a ghetto, the more they become suspicious. It is no secret that there were few Polish Catholics around to defend the Jews of the Warsaw ghetto when the Nazis entered the ghetto at the beginning of the Second World War.

The bridge between Poles and Jews remains very shaky even today, 50 years later. The recent exchange between Cardinal Jozef Glemp, the primate of Poland, and Polish-born Yitzhak Shamir, the prime minister of Israel, regarding Carmelite nuns and their convent on the site of the Auschwitz death camp, is an embarrassment to Catholics and Jews alike.

The reinforcing of that bridge is impossible without the breakdown of ghetto mentalities. Jews in the past needed some of the benefits of a ghetto in order to survive Christian persecution, but that is hardly the case today.

Jews have been given a homeland, and they have made the State of Israel one of the most powerful nations in the modern world. Today they do not bargain with anyone, the United States included, from a position of weakness.

The time has come for Jews to part with ghettos. The world can afford ghettos among the weak and helpless; among the powerful, they are a serious threat to world peace.

This parting with ghettos will entail for the Jewish people a radically different way of remembering the Holocaust. Many Jews today want the Holocaust to be a purely Jewish phenomenon. The presence of Carmelite nuns at Auschwitz becomes a desecration — no matter that hundreds of thousands of Catholic Poles died there alongside the millions of helpless Jews.

While we agree that great sensitivity must be shown our Jewish brothers and sisters as they try to internalize and enflesh the horrendous reality of Auschwitz into their lives — and likely this means that the Carmelites should move the quarter mile asked of them — we still maintain that the greatest good will be achieved from remembering Auschwitz (and the Holocaust in general) when Poles and Israelis, Christians and Jews together remember their glorious martyrs.

Christendom and Islam December 12, 2001

We worry about Islamic fundamentalism. And rightly so; we should all have learned that on September 11. But we can easily forget that moderate Algerians have feared it for a long time. Every time they go to the polls, Turks worry about Islamic fundamentalists. Saudi citizens have every right to be afraid. Jews are striking out at Yasser Arafat, kidding themselves that he can control those zealots who have been radicalized by decades of imprisonment in refugee camps. The United States has also been burned by its clandestine support of al-Qaeda in its simplistic Cold War policy.

It is important for us to realize that the whole Arab world has as much to lose as the West from Islamic fundamentalism. And, ironically, maybe we should be able to understand this right-wing fervour better than our moderate Muslim sisters and brothers. The high theology of Europe before the Renaissance differed little from that espoused by the terrorists today.

Christendom was the perfect world view. Everyone else was part of the *massa damnata* (condemned) crowd. Outside the church there was no salvation. Thus it made perfect sense to carry a Christian missionary or two on every colonizing ship.

And since the Chinese really were lost souls, it was perfectly acceptable to tell them just a century ago to accept the opium trade or face First World warships.

The first major incursion into the perfect world of Christendom was the Renaissance. It was a bitter pill to swallow, but church leaders had to concede, if not on the theoretical level at least on the practical, that the world had a life of its own. The church did not formally concede, however, until the Second Vatican Council. Until that time the world view of the *Syllabus of Errors* held official sway. Error had no rights and an infallible pope, the head of Christendom, had the final word on everything. He could pontificate not only on dogmatic and moral issues; he had the right (and duty) to render sentence on practically everything from democracy to inoculation (popes have decried both).

The Vatican Council formally left that world behind — but not without many a bishop or curial member still hankering for the old world of clearcut lines of authority and simple yes-and-no answers.

Had it had the chance, the church would have avoided the Renaissance like the plague. Nor did church leaders gracefully concede religious rights to Jews, Muslims, Hindus, and Buddhists. But over the past 50 years or so, the leaders of the mainline Christian churches have done so. Though Pat Robertson and Jerry Falwell could still see September 11 as God's answer to homosexuality and abortion, there is every indication that evangelical churches will come to see the evils of fundamentalism mirrored in the horror of that day.

The Muslim world needs to learn the lessons of the Renaissance; it needs to learn that religious people, other than Muslims, have rights. It is the challenge of the Christian world to assure moderate Muslims that all is not lost in giving up the notion of a perfect Islamic world, any more than Christians lost anything in giving up the notion of a perfect Christendom. Indeed, most Christians today would see the re-establishment of Christendom as a giant leap backward — a leap, ultimately, into the fascistic world of a Mussolini, if not of a Hitler.

We are not going to assure Muslims of this, however, by means of superior air power or smarter bombs — all used in a crusade against evil terrorists. The pope's call for Christians to fast in solidarity with their Muslim friends will take us a lot farther.

Chapter 8

The Ethic of Life

Immaculate Conception December 7, 1987

Catholic dogma deals with salvation in Jesus Christ, with the relationship of God to the human family.

The church, in proclaiming the Immaculate Conception of Mary, was not interested primarily in distinguishing her from the rest of humanity. Rather as an icon of the church she helps God's people understand and experience the meaning and power of Christ's saving grace.

In the middle of the last century many in the church thought any association with the intellectual thrust of the day to be a capitulation to evil. In their justification of this, they were tempted to latch on to the Reformation theology of original sin in all its rigour.

In the years following Martin Luther, the Protestant theologians almost vied with one another in giving the most absolute description of the depravity of human nature. Nothing could be expected from nature; we were saved because God would not judge us according to our nature but solely in terms of the grace given us in Christ.

Similar to the way evangelical theologians today have grabbed hold of this to produce their gospel of born-again fundamentalism which is bereft of much social consciousness, so the Catholic theologians of the 19th century saw this teaching as a way of freeing them from involvement in the issues of their day. With this theology of original sin, the way was open for the church to pile one *Syllabus of Errors* upon another.

The church, in proclaiming the Immaculate Conception of Mary, laid the foundation for a totally different theology of redemption, one rooted in our tradition. We are shown in the fully human maiden from Nazareth the full splendour of our nature. We are shown that grace does not replace nature, nor make it of no account. The grace given Mary enabled her to be true to herself, and gave her the self-confidence to say yes to the Advent messenger.

Grace in Christ is so personalized that it brings each person's nature to its own glory. Conversely, sin is what is not true about us; and it cannot fully rob us of the meaning given each of us in creation.

So in Advent we remember Mary as immaculately conceived. We admire her beauty, and thus find it easier to remember the working of God in our world, in our church, in our bodies — even though the sun is getting weaker and weaker, and the days colder and colder.

Need for "seamless garment" July 1, 1984

Few issues have ever created as much controversy in our society and in our church as abortion. It has become the polemical issue of the day, and, as with all polemics, positions have hardened.

There is a growing distrust of anything or anyone who does not advocate these hardened positions.

Many uncharitable remarks have been levelled at our brothers and sisters in the United Church of Canada. It has become inconceivable to many pro-life advocates that these Christians can be sincere in their beliefs, that they, too, are honestly struggling to proclaim the full vigour of Christ's Good News to this age.

The *Prairie Messenger* has also been questioned and for many found wanting. For some this has been a simple matter: not having a major anti-abortion article in the paper for three consecutive weeks was an ample sign that we are at least wishy-washy on the issue.

We, like many Catholics — including several national conferences of bishops — have refused to see abortion as a single issue. We believe the issue will be furthered if we, like Cardinal Joseph Bernardin of Chicago, insist on keeping all the life issues together in one "seamless garment."

Remembering the Immaculate Conception is a good starting point for a seamless-garment approach for developing an ethic of life. Beginning with the evil of sin or with a culture of death ultimately takes us nowhere. On the other hand, the Immaculate Conception calls us to build, not on some ethical abstraction, but on what is truest about ourselves.

Most Prairie pro-lifers have a broad notion of what the movement should entail. Many have given us exemplary Christian witness: they have supported unwed mothers, they have treasured the mentally handicapped, they have reverenced the elderly. It is perfectly understandable that they should feel hurt when other members of our church criticize their tireless zeal for the cause.

Cardinal Bernardin, however, names several other areas that must be included if the garment of life is to remain seamless: capital punishment, mindless militarization that robs the poor of their dignity, nuclear war and terrorism, by both guerrillas and governments.

These are not easy issues to include. Many advocates of these issues are every bit as narrow-minded as the most rigid anti-abortionists. Not too many anti-nuclear groups, for instance, are ready to study seriously the erosion of moral fibre caused by abortion-on-demand.

Several recent events indicate how crucial it is that these other issues be included. Leaders of the U.S. National Right to Life Convention made the re-election of Ronald Reagan their number 1 priority. Two weeks later the American president threatened to veto any bill that would allocate funds for any social welfare program in America if funds for this administration's covert activities in Central America were not tied to the bill.

Not without reason did the Laity Commission of the Catholic Bishops of England and Wales speak out strongly against single-issue voting in the last general election in Great Britain: "It would usually be imprudent, if not morally irresponsible, for Christians to vote on the basis of a single or narrowly restricted range of issues." Respect for life includes, they insisted, a whole range of questions which at least include "our defence policies, health care and welfare policies, our penal system, policies on race, handicapped people and others besides."

The pro-life struggle is too important to have it bogged down in partisan politics. The credibility of the champion of the unborn, Joseph Borowski, is too valuable to have it dissipated in his affirmation of America's dealings with Nicaragua.

Let us hope that the controversy that has raged in our letter column this past month makes us all realize that our disagreements do not help the pro-life struggle. We all lose credibility if we cannot work together.

There is, however, a painful corollary to the acceptance of the seamless garment of the Lord. If abortion is seen as a single issue it can be condemned in black-and-white terms from a position of innocence. If such issues as capital punishment, militarization, and social justice are included, the waters become much more muddied for all of us. We find ourselves part of the sin we know we must condemn. We find everything a little more blurry around the edges. The comfort of absolute certitude must be sacrificed for this struggle of life. And this sacrifice is the ultimate test for credibility.

With St. Paul, who early in his ministry was quite ready to condemn, we must learn why our Saviour did not come to us with a bright shining halo, but in the likeness of our sinful flesh (2 Cor 5:19-21).

Gospel of life
April 19, 1995

The pope, in the most strongly worded encyclical of his pontificate, cries out against the "culture of death" which he sees quickly taking hold of modern society. The powerful in the world, he notes in *Evangelium Vitae* (Gospel of life), have been able to control modern political processes, thereby in many countries encouraging the state to tyrannically arrogate "to itself the right to dispose of the life of the weakest and most defenceless members."

The pope, to emphasize this struggle, turns to military language; he notes that this culture of death is "in a certain sense a war of the powerful against the weak."

Three times in the course of the encyclical Pope John Paul II evokes the full power of his papal office to solemnly reaffirm "teachings that the church has always held." He declares "the direct and voluntary killing of an innocent human being is always gravely immoral"; "direct abortion, that is, abortion willed as an end or as a means, always constitutes a grave moral disorder"; and "euthanasia is a grave violation of the law of God."

Church leaders, in response to the encyclical, have taken up the pope's opening affirmation that these things have always been church teaching, that the pope is not saying anything radically new. Critics have tried to disarm the encyclical by noting that indeed there is nothing new here, that it is what is to be expected of the "conservative tradition that has been identified with the current pope."

The president of the Canadian bishops' conference, Archbishop Francis Spence of Kingston, bristled on hearing this criticism: "Is it conservative to be pro-life? Is it conservative to favour the weakest people in the world against those who are very strong? It's time to fight against the culture of death and have a culture of life."

On reading the encyclical one notes, however, that it is not as "traditional" as the pope and his critics, both friendly and hostile, maintain.

While the pope centres his argumentation on the two times when human life is most fragile — before birth and when approaching death — he nevertheless sees the struggle for life in much broader terms. Thus Cardinal Joseph Bernardin of Chicago rejoices to find the "consistent ethic of life," which he has always fought for, as the true framework of the encyclical.

Life is threatened, the pope notes, by the violence to "millions of human beings forced into poverty, malnutrition and hunger because of an unjust distribution of resources between peoples and social classes." The violence of war and the "scandalous arms trade" are also high on the pope's list of forces opposing life.

He speaks out so strongly against capital punishment that Cardinal Joseph Ratzinger has acknowledged that the corresponding chapter in the new catechism will have to be rewritten. While not denying absolutely the possibility of capital punishment being, in a particular circumstance, legitimate, the pope quickly adds that the conditions necessary for such legitimation are "very rare." He goes so far as to say that likely these conditions are "non-existent in the modern world."

The pope, echoing a basic theme of a previous encyclical, *Veritatis Splendor*, reminds his readers — not only Catholics but all "people of goodwill" — of the need for absolutes. Life can never be a relative value, and thus he teaches that human political laws which contravene God's law concerning the sacredness of life cannot be binding.

At first sight it would appear that the pope is calling on all who believe in the sanctity of human life to unite and become a major corps of conscientious objectors.

The pope, however, sees the faithful moving in quite another direction. Breaking important new ground in the pro-life struggle, the pope wrote: "In a case ... when it is not possible to overturn or completely abrogate a pro-abortion law, an elected official, whose absolute personal opposition to a procured abortion was well known, could licitly support proposals aimed at limiting the harm done by such a law and at lessening its negative consequences at the level of general opinion and public morality."

Pro-life zealots have at times been known for their all-or-nothing approach. Should a national conference of bishops, for instance, acknowledge that proposed new legislation, though far from perfect, is better than the previous law, they would often be labelled heretics, unfaithful to the Lord and the pope. This encyclical should go a long way in clarifying that.

Ultimately the pro-life battle will be won by changing hearts, not by forcing unwelcome legislation — no matter how perfect it might be — upon an electorate. And changing hearts — changing a culture, to use the pope's language — is never a once-and-for-all event. It is, rather, a gradual process, a moving forward step by step, and thus the pope explicitly acknowledges that often the best thing that can be done in the short haul is to work for a better law. And he asks the people of goodwill whom he addresses in this encyclical to be wary in issuing blanket condemnations.

The pope does not do this even with the women who have chosen to have an abortion. While never reneging on the absolute evil abortion is in our modern world, he calls for understanding of those who have procured an abortion. Citing what he calls mitigating circumstances of economic and psychological anxiety, the pope asks women to trust in God's forgiveness and gives the church the special task of "healing their wounded hearts."

John Paul speaks about a "network of complicity" that can lead a woman to abortion, including husbands, friends, family members, doctors, and legislators. Often, the pope notes, it is the father of the child who is to be blamed, either because he pressures the woman to have an abortion or because he lets her "face the problems of pregnancy alone." Abortion is often chosen, the pope notes, because of difficult or even tragic situations of suffering, loneliness, the struggle to make ends meet, depression, and anxiety about the future.

As the encyclical often points out, the church is called upon to war against the culture of death so evident in abortion. But all is lost if this struggle means that the church is not able, first of all, to convince the woman in pain over an abortion of the sheer mercy of our God.

The struggle against abortion and the whole culture of death may not harden the face of the church. The victory over this culture of death is a matter of conversion, a changing of hearts — something that can never be forced, something that always demands the ultimate in sensitivity and understanding.

Thus right before the church celebrates the passover of its Lord from death to life is perhaps the best time for the pope to issue his most challenging encyclical.

Easter calls us to the ultimate in faith. To believe that the corpse hanging between heaven and earth on the cross is really the wellspring of new life prepares us never to panic before the culture of death so pervasive in our society.

People who panic become cold and rigid and try to force their views on others. People who believe in the Gospel of Life are ready to gently touch the souls of their sisters and brothers and give them the courage to change their hearts.

The first call of *Evangelium Vitae* is to heal a culture, to affect once more the call of Easter: to transform death into life.

Birth control and the Gospel January 30, 1989

Redemptorist Father Bernard Häring made few friends in Rome in begging the pope to reopen church debate on birth control. The rhetoric coming out of the Vatican in recent years has been stronger on this issue than on any other. The pope himself has stated recently that expressing doubts on the church's ruling against artificial birth control "would render useless the voice of Christ."

To be sure, a reopening of the debate would cast some doubt on the church's teaching, but that is not the reason why many in the church want the issue looked at again.

It is not enough for the teaching church to be right about this or any other moral issue. It must also enable the church community to see the teaching as Gospel, as Good News.

Every confessor and spiritual director working with young couples in our country knows that the overwhelming majority of them do not experience it as such. For far too many it is experienced as bad news dangerously separating them from the institutional church.

Häring begs the church to re-examine how it should teach sexual ethics to prevent the current abandonment of the church "from assuming even more catastrophic dimensions." He has made this call for restudy out of love for the church. The last thing Häring wants is to weaken the teaching church in the eyes of young Catholics.

Weakness is a paradoxical word in the Gospel. Most often it is praised as a powerful vehicle for carrying the Gospel message. The weakness scorned by Jesus expresses itself in legal rigidity and self-fulfilment.

We pray that the church embrace that weakness which will enable it to speak humbly to its members about following a Lord made especially present to them in the glorious sacrament of married love.

Differing on birth control

March 22, 1993

Two events, more than anything else, have shaped the church these last 25 years.

First, the Second Vatican Council. Twenty-five years ago the church began the practical work of implementing the council. The first obvious changes were in liturgy, and most Catholics found great joy and hope in them.

It was an exciting time to be with a group of priests. They were optimistic about the future and thus were full of energy. Indeed this optimism reached well beyond the church. In the Constitution on the Church in the Modern World (entitled *Gaudium et Spes*, or Joy and hope), we were told to read the signs of the times, that is to find the beginnings of kingdom values in the secular movements of our age.

There were disagreements then too about what the church should be. But virtually everyone, from bishop to the layperson barely in the last pew in church, was convinced that the kingdom power unleashed by the council would carry us all over our problems and truly make our church new wine in new wineskins.

Then came — 25 years this coming July — *Humanae Vitae*, the papal encyclical on birth control. Pope Paul VI announced that he could not accept the advice of the theological commission he established to study the issue. He stated that artificial contraception was intrinsically evil.

The bishops of the world felt the immediate pastoral impact of this decision, and many national hierarchies wrote joint pastoral letters nuancing the papal teaching.

The Canadian bishops produced the most extensive pastoral letter and it was reprinted throughout the world. Pope Paul VI, speaking later to the president of the Canadian bishops, personally told him how pleased he was with the Canadian response.

But nuance has not characterized subsequent theologizing about this papal teaching. Rather it has become, as Jesuit Father Avery Dulles said recently to an international gathering of bishops, practically the "sole litmus test" for theological correctness.

And, almost in direct proportion to the highest church leaders' insistence on a rigid observance of the encyclical, the laity has rejected it. Ask any priest with even a smattering of pastoral experience and he will agree with Dulles's assessment that "the overwhelming majority of laypeople are at odds with the hierarchy on the question of birth control."

The laity simply has not received this papal teaching.

The resulting split between church teaching and the people as a whole has been catastrophic for the church. The excitement, the optimism that invigorates is gone. Not an insignificant part of the serious demoralization that now characterizes many communities of priests is the conflict in the church over *Humanae Vitae*. A major study of U.S. priests noted that they feel "betrayed" by their superiors.

To shore up its teaching on birth control, the highest levels of the church's magisterium have downplayed the role of the people in church teaching. The *sensus fidelium*, the guiding sense of the faithful, is for all practical purposes totally dismissed. The ancient notion — that church teaching, to have true certitude, is to be received by the people — is conveniently forgotten.

Without an active acceptance of the notion of the *sensus fidelium* we would have a lot of theological difficulties in our church. In AD 1203 Pope Boniface VIII, for instance, certainly tried to use all his papal authority to teach when he said, with fourfold vigour, "We declare, we state, we define and we proclaim that it is absolutely necessary for salvation that every human creature should be subject to the Roman pontiff."

A century and a half later the church was still not convinced, and so an ecumenical council, the church's highest teaching form, took up the issue and proclaimed (this time with only threefold intent) that "the Holy Roman Church firmly believes, firmly professes, firmly preaches that no one remaining outside the Catholic Church, not only the pagans, but also the Jews, heretics and schismatics — no one can become partakers of eternal life, but will go to the eternal fires prepared for the devil and his angels unless before the end of their life they are received into the church."

Not all church teachings are that sublime; Pope Gregory XVI, with full encyclical form, one day declared, defined, and proclaimed that vaccination was a grave evil, the work of the devil. God, he declared, used smallpox to punish the human race for its sins and people should not try to thwart God.

Such teachings are never officially retracted by the church. The day comes when those in authority simply acknowledge that the people, with their fundamental sense of the faith, know better.

The church, like all things human, must struggle to find its way. There is no easy way for the church to come up with all the right answers — and for it to pretend otherwise is to court disaster.

Pope Paul, let no one forget it, had some fundamental fears that were critically important. The pope saw — rightly, we believe — that our age had almost deified sex. Sex had become a plaything, and we all had a right to its pleasure. The pope feared what a contraceptive mentality could do if it had free rein; he saw what it had done in the world and he did not want to see the same thing happen within the church community.

Dulles rightly notes that a wholesale rejection of the papal teaching has left the church in a critically vulnerable position. The hierarchy, carefully chosen to uphold the encyclical, becomes more and more irrelevant; many people, not listening in one area, soon find it easy to uncritically reject uncomfortable teachings in other areas.

The church needs conflict, but it must be mature conflict. We cannot use a hierarchy that declares itself infallible independent of the *sensus fidelium*. We cannot have a people who pick and choose church teachings according to their own convenience.

Mature conflict, so essential to a growing church, is always difficult to achieve. But we must resist with all our strength the easy answer — and let us not forget that the dogmatism of a carefully selected hierarchy is as problematic as the relativism of a self-serving permissive laity.

Archbishop Rembert Weakland, in his pastoral letter on Catholic identity, states succinctly the need for dialogue if the church is to grow: "The conservative voices force the more liberal to examine deeply the roots of a practice before changing it. The more liberal voices keep the church from becoming stagnant and force it to be constantly re-examining its positions and the grounds for them."

As we mark the 25th anniversary of *Humanae Vitae*, everyone in the church is called upon to begin again. Let us not be afraid to struggle — we know it will always be a struggle to make our sexuality a true expression of the kingdom — but let us struggle maturely so that we can leave behind the destructive smallness of spirit that has marked so much of the last 25 years.

Humanae Vitae: 25th anniversary August 2, 1993

It has been a tragic 25 years for the church. For 25 years, people have been talking past one another; in this area of church life, on birth control, true listening to one another has been a scarce commodity.

The two principal articles on *Humanae Vitae* in the *Prairie Messenger*

The Ethic of Life

reflect this failure in communication. The lead story on page one, an account of the text which the U.S. bishops' Committee for Pro-Life Activities published to mark the anniversary, solidly backs Pope Paul VI's condemnation of artificial contraception as a great prophetic stand. Little — very little — is said in acknowledgment of the difficulties true Christian families encounter in trying to be obedient to this papal teaching.

The bishops spend much more time recounting the signs of sexuality gone awry: "non-marital cohabitation, out-of-wedlock pregnancy, abortion and divorce." The bishops note that there is "a state of confusion with regard to the meaning of human sexuality"; it is, they point out, "a clear rejection of moral principles and a trivialization of sex itself."

They don't directly say it, but the implications are clear: if a couple decides to practise artificial birth control, it is a sign that they suffer from this all-pervasive problem of sexuality gone awry.

Sidney Callahan, in our second article, writes from a totally different viewpoint. She speaks from her own experience. She had seven children in the first 10 years of her marriage. Her children ranged from 3 to 13 when Paul VI issued his encyclical. Natural family planning, it must be remembered, was 25 years ago far from the science it is today.

Callahan believes that one cannot analyze each marital sexual act in isolation, but rather must recognize sexuality within a Christian marriage "as ongoing within a whole complex relationship."

"Whatever celibates may imagine," she notes, "the challenge in modern marriage is not to control unbridled lust, but rather to cultivate joyful sexual celebrations of love on those occasions when it can be arranged. Under harassed family conditions arising from overwork and unpredictable child-rearing emergencies, it is not easy to find the time or energy to keep a loving sexual life alive and well."

Two worlds. Both will use the same words to describe the beauty of conjugal love, but still they are worlds apart. Ultimately they do not trust the other's experience. No one should be surprised that they are going to argue about who is right.

But two things are clear: 1) Callahan is not about to change the minds of the bishops on the Committee for Pro-Life Activities, nor are they going to make a dent in her thinking; and 2) Callahan and the bishops are both sincere in their Christian convictions.

This second point is critical. Without a deep appreciation of this point we will never remove the disastrous impasse that now imprisons the whole church.

On reading the bishops' text one senses they really do not believe that people can hold positions such as espoused by Callahan and maintain a modicum of Christian integrity. One senses, too, that the Callahans in the church are not about to look to celibate ecclesiastics for any direction in sexual morality.

This breakdown in trust has become more destructive to the life of the church than has been the fierce disagreement on the teaching of *Humanae Vitae* that spawned it. And there is no hope that the church will ever come to a healthy peace concerning its teaching on birth control until this latter problem is fully addressed.

There is a painful paradox in all this. To shore up the teaching contained in *Humanae Vitae*, the church has centralized authority as it has never been previously exercised in the church. Only clerics who are ready to publicly proclaim *Humanae Vitae* as a prophetic utterance are called forth to be bishops.

The role of the laity, as an integral part of the *sensus fidelium* (the sense of the faithful), is cavalierly disregarded. We hear more talk about the magisterium and the obligation of the faithful to be obedient to it than ever was the case when the Spanish Inquisition was in high gear. Precious little room is given for conscientious dissent. The presumption is that the church cannot be wrong.

Anyone with even the slightest knowledge of church history knows that this simply is not true. Again and again popes have uttered the darnedest things ever so solemnly through apostolic bulls and encyclicals.

Adults are not impressed with people who cannot ever admit they have made a mistake; nor are Catholics impressed with a church which feels it must proclaim its inability to err.

Leaders in our church are afraid that if they even admit to the possibility of having made a mistake that proverbial hole in the dike will quickly appear and usher in a total collapse.

They cannot face the paradox: the more the church shores up its impregnability, the weaker it is; the more it admits to the possibility of being wrong, the more capable it will be to initiate a sincere and honest dialogue that can lead to healing and strength.

Without this dialogue which actually takes seriously the experience of sincere Christian married people, the destructive mistrust that has followed in the wake of *Humanae Vitae* will never be removed from our church.

Condoms

February 26, 1996

The church has a difficult time communicating its message on the meaning of human sexuality. The complex nature of our sexuality is not well served in a world that loves short, 10-second TV bites of information. Let's face it: it's hard to nuance the use of a condom!

Thus it is understandable that the Vatican has seldom tried. Twelve years ago, it was roundly laughed at when it proposed a condom with a hole on both ends to gather a semen sample from a couple experiencing fertility problems. The laughter turned bitter, however, when Vatican theologians told East African men afflicted with HIV that they could not use condoms while having intercourse with their wives.

Recently the Vatican stepped in and ordered Archbishop Keith O'Brien of Edinburgh to dissociate himself from public anti-AIDS campaigns that included any use of the condom as a safety factor. The archbishop's argument for a limited use of the condom had followed the traditional moral argument of double effect — that is the permissibility of acting when one's otherwise legitimate act will also cause an effect one would normally be obliged to avoid.

Dr. Marc Gentilini, president of the French Catholic Doctors' Committee, takes up this argument and makes it succinctly: "The Roman Catholic Church can be against condoms as a means of contraception which prevents the transmission of life. It cannot be against the condom as a means of preventing the transmission of death."

Older Catholics remember the mothers who died because the fetus did not pass down into their womb but stayed in a Fallopian tube. These mothers died: they were told the child could not be removed because to do so was equivalent to having an abortion. Consequently neither mother nor child survived.

Now moralists use the argument of double effect. In performing the operation, the doctor wills the recovery of the mother but not the death of the fetus — even though that necessarily follows.

Women in marriages in which the husband has HIV are physically open to new life for only a few days in the menstrual cycle, but the husband's semen remains a poison each and every day. The church will only appear cold and cruel if it cannot distinguish between using a condom to prevent a deadly disease and using one to prevent conception.

Of course, public health officials must be forthright in indicating how poor a protection condoms are in the prevention of AIDS transmission.

The World Health Organization acknowledged recently that 30 million pregnancies result each year from contraceptive failure. The danger of failure is greatly increased with regard to AIDS, since the virus is much smaller than the pores in even the best of condoms.

The church has been right: it will always be nigh to impossible to have public campaigns which encourage the use of condoms by sexually promiscuous people without appearing to condone the promiscuity itself. But it is equally true: if the church cannot make a distinction between the various reasons for using a condom, it will appear as a cold, heartless parent who can stand idly by while many of its children contract the deadly virus.

We are convinced without a shadow of a doubt that the world is greatly in need of the church's message on sexuality. Thus the church simply may not needlessly destroy its own credibility. The French bishops have made an important decision when they decided to become directly involved in their country's struggle against the spread of AIDS.

When does life begin?

March 27, 2002

This is not only a philosophical and theological question. The world of the scientist also has something critically important to say.

Pope John Paul II has made it one of the goals of his pontificate to bring together the theologian and the scientist, telling both of them that truth is one and that they have much to learn from one another.

The scientist rightly has a problem with the religious world's too ready equating of the fertilization of a human egg with the conception of new life in the sense of ensoulment, the begetting of a new person with all the rights and dignities becoming human existence.

Scientists point out the difficulties intrinsic to that equation. A fertilized egg sometimes splits before the 14th day after fertilization, becoming identical twins. Less often two fertilized eggs can unite during this first fortnight and become one perfectly normal human person.

So the scientist has every right to ask the theologian: Does one soul split into two; do two souls unite to become one? Any religious body with even a smidgen of ontology in its theological wherewithal will have to acknowledge the difficulties inherent in these questions. Several years ago Cardinal Joseph Ratzinger of the Congregation for the Doctrine of the Faith did indeed acknowledge the scientific problems surrounding the moment of ensoulment.

Primate of the Anglican Church of Australia Archbishop Peter Carnley has used these problems to advocate the church's acceptance of serious study of stem cells obtained from artificially fertilized eggs. He makes an impassioned argument that this is not a situation of human beings usurping the place of God; rather, he sees it "as part of a process of co-operating with God in an exercise aimed at perfecting all things."

To be sure, it is one thing to use this 14-day period to justify, for instance, the use of a "morning after" pill, and quite another to permit the creation and study of embryonic stem cells in a concerted effort to find cures for human disease.

But the question remains: Should not our respect for human life strongly discourage us from entering this space and, like Moses of old, do no more than take off our sandals before the holy? Given our record as a modern society, it is imperative that we do so.

It is ludicrous to believe that a society, so blind that it cannot find the dignities and rights of a human person in a viable fetus ready to be born, should be given the luxury of discernment as to what is the proper treatment of a fertilized egg in the first fortnight of its existence.

Let's deal with the obvious first, and only then contemplate moving beyond the wisdom of Moses.

Accepting human sexuality
July 10, 1989

Most people will smile a little on reading about one of the latest dilemmas of the Vatican — on whether or not to fully restore Michelangelo's *The Last Judgment*. It is a question of restoring the saints to a nude state as painted by the artist, or of keeping them in their "respectable" clothing added later to assuage papal sensitivities.

Michelangelo, believing that nudity is part and parcel of the saints' glorious heavenly splendour, filled his painting with nudes. Not everyone thought this particular theological insight worth dwelling upon, let alone expressing it in living colour above the altar of Christian love and unity.

Even the stature of Michelangelo, the genius who figured out how to set a beautiful dome on the massive St. Peter's Basilica, was not great enough to halt a cover-up on his monumental work on *The Last Judgment*.

Pope Pius IV hired a nobody to paint clothing on his nude saints.

Ironically the bits of clothing Daniel of Volterra painted on Michelangelo's nudes reveal far more than they hide. They speak volumes about Pope Pius IV and his court. They speak of a church not at home with the human body, with the sexual nature of humanity.

Granted, God has planted the virtue of modesty deeply in our nature, a virtue that helps us maintain a privacy necessary for true human dignity. Modesty is to protect us from sexual exploitation. It takes, however, a great stretch of the imagination to see any of Michelangelo's nudes as exploiting human sexuality. If Pius IV found Michelangelo's work an assault on Christian purity, that was his problem, not the artist's. Pius IV's credibility, not Michelangelo's, was at stake.

Throughout the years the church has maintained the uncanny ability to shoot itself in the foot, to undermine its own credibility in matters sexual. It insists on "raising" sexuality to a spiritual level. Too often, however, this does not mean that sexual expression should be so profound as to touch the very spirit of a person; it means raising it above the body level. It means taking the passion, the uncontrollable ecstasy of abandonment, out of sexual intimacy.

In the last synod in Rome on the meaning of the lay Christianity, Mavis Pirola, an Australian member of the Pontifical Council for the Laity, made an impassioned plea before the bishops for the development of a spirituality appropriate to the married state. She said such a spirituality must begin with a stress on the sexual nature of the sacrament of marriage. "At the centre of a couple's relationship is their sexual responsiveness to each other, manifested especially in genital sex," she said. "Sexual intimacy is what distinguishes matrimony from all other Christian relationships."

She added that only a profound appreciation of sexual intimacy can underpin a teaching on the meaning of the transmission of life. There was little in the final communiqués from the synod that would indicate that the bishops heard what she was saying.

Our church, largely through the work of its celibate clergy, has provided teachings on the morality of every sexual act conceivable, even of the smallest details of life in the bedroom. To compare the extensiveness of the church's treatment of sexual matters with those of social sharing or justice or of war and peace reveals a church seriously hung up on sex.

As Pius IV lost credibility in trying to hide the glorious naked splendour of the saints at *The Last Judgment*, so the church has lost the ability to proclaim the human nobility of sexuality by insisting on finding sin everywhere. There is a tragic irony in this loss of credibility: not only has the church lost its power to teach the world about the beauty of sexual passion; it also has no one listening to its declarations of sin.

Strengthening marriage
May 26, 1999

Civilization is as healthy as its families. When the family as the primary social unit loses its moorings, the whole of human life is endangered.

Human values, even the central value of life itself, are handed on in a family setting. It is here that mysteriously most of us find the strength, the courage to ultimately believe enough in ourselves to find meaning in our very existence.

This cannot be taught; it can only be experienced — experienced in the unconditional love given by parents. And, ideally, parents find the grace to image — albeit imperfectly — the unconditional love of the God revealed in Jesus Christ in their own experience of marital love, in the marriage bed, and in their daily sharing in the myriad of little activities known as family life.

Pope John Paul II loves to see the Christian home as a domestic church. As we become in the Eucharist the one Body of Christ filled with the Holy Spirit, so in marriage the two become one flesh, one sacrament of Christ's presence. In the sacrament of marriage a home is formed, filled with the Holy Spirit, creating a new space in which children know not the power of sin as the world's strongest force, but rather come to trust in the victory of Jesus, the victory of love.

And, in the celebration of that victory, the children gradually experience the victory of their own personhood, as it emerges as their own supreme good, as the best gift which the God of all power and majesty could with wisdom divine create for them.

Much of this comes to fruition around the kitchen table where families so often gather to eat, to play, and to pray — and, at times, to fight and to cry, since these too are part and parcel of becoming an independent person.

Saying this in theological terms, the banquet table of the kingdom in heaven, the liturgical table in our churches, and the secular table in our homes take on one and the same meaning.

Only with such an identification can the Christian find the wherewithal to lead the world in a celebration of its secularity, of its core meaning. Catholics speak of the family as the primary social unit of civilization by calling it a sacrament, the mystery of the very presence of Jesus Christ with all pathos and splendour that was his death and resurrection.

Not without reason do the Easter Vigil readings always begin with the story of creation, with the proclamation of the absolute goodness God has planted in everything created.

We are not prone to find in the Eucharist the key to understanding and appreciating sexuality in the Christian home — and this appreciation should form the basis for our evaluation of the world.

No one will deny that human sexuality has often been misused. Pornography, for generation after generation, has been big business. But it doesn't take a church to tell people this is wrong. It does, however, take a church community to insist on human sexuality's unbelievable greatness and true glory.

For the church to have a credible voice in this critical dimension of human existence, it must move beyond a listing of sins. Once the church spontaneously views the marriage bed and its eucharistic expression as parallel sacramental expressions of the kingdom, no one will be tempted to question that it has something vital to say about life in this world.

Changing laws, changing hearts   February 8, 1988

The Supreme Court's recent decision to strike down Section 251 of the *Criminal Code* as unconstitutional took the country by surprise. Even Dr. Henry Morgentaler did not expect to win the case.

Section 251 never had many supporters. In possibly their only area of agreement, both pro-lifers and pro-choicers had declared it a bad law. The tragedy in the January 28 decision is certainly not Section 251 — we're glad to be rid of it — but the chaos that comes with its demise. As Archbishop Adam Exner notes, "Canadian law now gives no protection to unborn human beings."

To work for good legislation concerning abortion "is our common task now," said the president of the Canadian bishops, Archbishop James Hayes of Halifax, "and the future of our human society depends on how soon and how well it is done."

The Ethic of Life

But the archbishop does not end there. He gives us a second task: "In the process of working for new legislation, all Christians must also apply themselves to the continuing pastoral work of evangelizing modern culture regarding the God-given values and rights of every human life."

To get the perfect law through Parliament is not an end in itself. Laws, as Jesus constantly pointed out in his day, do not bring about the kingdom. For that, hearts have to be changed. And it is primarily to this that Christians are called.

In any case we are not going to get anything approaching a perfect new law unless, to use the archbishop's words, we "evangelize modern culture." Politicians, and even successful political parties claiming to have a solid pro-life plank, have shown us again and again that they are not ready for the prophetic work of bucking a selfish culture. And certainly not in times of close Gallup polls.

The first thing we must do is cut out inflammatory language. To call the Supreme Court decision "an uncivilized judgment" or to proclaim it "a licence to any doctor in the country to set up a corner butcher shop" is to hinder the cause.

It might do us all well to recall how St. Paul learned to be an effective reconciler, one who could change hearts.

In Second Corinthians, he relates how he argued with charismatic leaders who thought their weekday activities — even consorting with prostitutes — should not interfere with their Sunday ministry, so long as they could manifest the signs of the Spirit. Paul used all the righteous authority he could muster, even reminding them that Jesus personally had called him to be an apostle.

Still the people rejected him and suggested he go elsewhere to preach. He was forced to leave, and this failure nearly ruined Paul — or so he thought. His self-possession left him, or, to say it in Pauline terms, he was given a thorn in the flesh.

Again and again he prayed for strength, that this thorn in his side would leave him, but all he ever heard from God was: "My grace is enough for you. My power is at its best in weakness."

Finally Paul determined he had to go back to Corinth, weakness or not. And to his utter surprise the people listened to him and were reconciled. Paul ecstatically proclaimed that henceforth he would forever glory in his weakness, "for it is when I am weak that I am strong."

But Paul learned something else too. Now he understood why "God for our sake made the sinless one into sin, so that in him we might become the goodness of God." Paul learned that even God could not change us while maintaining a righteous position on high. He had to become like us, experiencing life as sinners experience it.

The struggle for hearts in the abortion debate will never be won by people who, from a position of innocence, call it a sin. Jesus knew it would not work for him and his mission — and deep down we know it won't work for us either.

The principal advantage of the seamless-garment approach to life issues is not that abortion is seen in a larger context — however valuable that may be. Nor do we advocate the seamless-garment approach because it forces us to nuance the human struggle and thus prevents us from condemning abortion in black-and-white terms.

The essential factor in including such issues as capital punishment, militarization, nuclear deterrence, and countless cases of social justice in one's struggle for life, in one's effort to evangelize today's culture, lies elsewhere. If we broaden our agenda beyond such things as abortion, homosexuality, and (for men at least) feminism and include issues such as those listed above, we suddenly find ourselves part of the sin we know we must condemn.

We lose our position of innocence, but in sacrificing that we gain what we were so sorely lacking: credibility.

Abortion as violence
March 14, 1988

The Supreme Court's January 28 decision to strike down Section 251 of the *Criminal Code* as unconstitutional has been hailed as a great victory for women. For instance, the Toronto *Globe and Mail*, in its most massive headline in years (a double, 65-point, five-column extravaganza), declared: "Abortion law scrapped; women get free choice."

The ruling of the Supreme Court justices is really not something new. Pro-life groups have for years continuously proclaimed the injustice inherent in Section 251. The law dealt exclusively with the pregnant woman.

The church must do more than flex its political muscle and force politicians into passing a more restrictive abortion law. It must change the hearts of Canadians and sway them to look upon abortion in an altogether new light.

Abortion is not primarily a matter of women's rights. It is about violence. And this violence so numbs our consciousness that we can all but forget that the victims are human beings in the early stages of their lives.

The American bishops stated this clearly in their pastoral on peace: "When we accept violence in any form as commonplace, our sensitivities become dulled. When we accept violence, war itself can be taken for granted.... Abortion in particular blunts a sense of the sacredness of human life. In a society where the innocent unborn are killed wantonly, how can we expect people to feel righteous revulsion at the act or threat of killing non-combatants in war?"

Violence always looks for immediate solutions. As with abortion, there is no long-range perspective. Needs must be gratified here and now. Free choice all too often means that one's current needs, seen in the narrowest of terms, have been given absolute value.

This violence not only leads to the death of countless unborn babes; it also spells the death of our civilization.

The legitimation of violence in our society which flows directly from our acceptance of abortion is indeed a women's issue. Women have never gained anything by society's acceptance of violence; instead they become — as history teaches over and over again — its targets.

To quote the American bishops again: "Violence has many faces: oppression of the poor, deprivation of the basic human rights, economic exploitation, sexual exploitation and pornography, neglect and abuse of the aged and the helpless and innumerable other acts of inhumanity."

To fight abortion we must see it for what it is — part of a whole degenerating culture which is so at home with violence. We live in a world where nuclear weapons are called instruments of peace, where economic control of banana republics is proclaimed a love of democracy, where the death penalty is heralded as the guarantor of life, where wanton cutbacks in social services are termed freedom of opportunity, where high sticks and brawls on the hockey rink become authentic signs of manliness.

Pro-life groups are afraid the call for a consistent ethic in society will weaken their struggle against abortion. But if the struggle against abortion is seen first of all as a struggle to change hearts — and this is the course Jesus always chose — presenting abortion as a legitimation of violence, in a world that is all too full of it, can only strengthen the fight for human life.

Addressing sexual abuse

June 12, 2002

This issue of the *Prairie Messenger* contains two painful stories of sexual abuse by members of the clergy. In both stories the church hierarchy was inclined to believe the abuser rather than the abused.

In both instances, even after the abuse was acknowledged, members of both clergy and laity continued to question why the abused insisted on speaking out. It seemed that the abused were out to get even, they concluded, even to the point of harming the church.

Both stories deal with victims who continue to worship regularly in the church community and who have in considerable part adjusted to their new circumstances. Yet both insist that their stories be told — not for their own good but for the good of the church. One of them is a strong supporter of "one strike and you're out"; the other can visualize priests truly repenting and being healed and in fully public and specific ways continuing to serve the church in priestly fashion.

Both stories indicate that the abused felt used by both the abuser and the church hierarchy. And in both instances they had more trouble coming to terms with an abusing church than with the priest who abused them.

This latter point must not be forgotten. Sexual abuse is horrific and emotionally devastating, but the damage can be contained and positively addressed. It is the abuse of power by the hierarchy in "dealing" (or not dealing) with the problem that has given the abuse such destructive force that those affected lose all hope of personal healing.

Much more destructive of church life than the sexual abuse is the abuse of power that accompanies it. Until this is acknowledged there is little hope for healing in the Catholic Church. The American bishops have gone to Rome to address the problem. They have come back with a ready scapegoat — homosexuality — and with a get-serious, get-tough policy — one strike and you're out. Nothing, however, is being said — publicly — about bishops who have secretly moved abusing priests from ministry to ministry. Until that changes, the problem will not lose its destructive force in the church community.

While the church must look at why homosexuals choose the priesthood in numbers far beyond what sociological percentages would predict, there can be no question of the power for good these men have been in the presbyterate. To equate homosexuality and pedophilia is pseudo-psychology at its worst.

We must also look at the "one strike and you're out" solution. At first

The Ethic of Life

sight, it looks as if the church is finally getting serious and is acknowledging that every child and young person has an inalienable right to feel safe in the church community. And that this right precedes any right of the abuser or of the clerical order itself.

But this "solution" is really not addressing the key problem of hierarchical abuse of power. As long as that is not addressed, the bishops indeed need a "one strike and you're out" procedure. Otherwise, when things become public — and they usually do — it is the bishop who will be caught holding the bag. And that will never do!

But in all this mess one question must be asked: What would Jesus do? It is inconceivable that the constant companion of prostitutes, tax collectors, and sinners would ever choose a principle that places the individual — no matter how sinful — after the well-being of the community, be it the apostolic college of the Twelve Apostles or the sacred church that developed from it.

"One strike and you're out" is too simplistic, too easy — especially for a hierarchical world that still believes that all wisdom and power has been given to it.

To be sure, if we must continue to live in a church mindset that centres all wisdom and power in the episcopate, and thus perpetuates a secretive "Father knows best" world, we will never be able to gainfully employ a priest abuser again; we simply could not take the chance.

But what happens if the bishop sees himself as the gatherer of the church's many gifts and the harnesser of its collective wisdom, if the issue is brought into the open and judgment is made not by a clerical group of men with obvious vested interests but by a true representative sampling of the whole community? In this way, all the gifts of the church would be available to deal with this terrible problem.

This would mean that all is public — including the sins and crimes of the priest abuser. There is, by the way, a third story in this week's PM. In this story a parish community wants its priest back as their leader in prayer, even though he has been found guilty of past sexual abuse. The parish community believes he has God's calling to lead them toward the kingdom.

As with the sentencing circles of the Native peoples, the welfare of both the perpetrator and the victim must be foremost in people's minds, and not the safeguarding of a hierarchical world which Jesus explicitly questioned: "You know that among the pagans their so-called rulers lord it over them, and their great men make their authority felt. This is not to happen among you" (Mk 10:42-43).

Once the church identifies the problem as one of power abuse rather than specifically one of sexual abuse, we will be a long way along the road to healing.

Dignity in dying
February 28, 2001

Jesus summed up the paradoxical nature of human existence succinctly in his famous statement: Those who try to save their life will lose it; those who lose their life will save it.

That paradox, running straight through the centre of the human heart, is ancient teaching. The familiar story of Adam and Eve eating the "apple" highlights this.

As our first parents aged in paradise they started to fret about not being as full of life as they used to be; and, quite understandably, the darkness (mystery) surrounding their limited self-knowledge also started to annoy them.

Whereas in the past it was no problem for them to ignore eating from the tree of life and from the tree of knowledge in the centre of paradise, now suddenly they wanted mastery of their lives, now they wanted knowledge and control over their future.

It was not difficult for the devil to entice them to part with God's wisdom that they should accept their paradoxical nature (not eating of the tree of knowledge and life) and go rather for straightforward, simple answers to life. Indeed, what could be simpler? What could be more attractive than taking complete hold of one's own life?

Paradox, the devil told them, is God's way of controlling human existence. Taking ownership of one's future through full knowledge, the devil assured them, would put them on a par with God.

Of course, the promise of "having one's eyes opened and being like gods" proved to be an empty dream, but still we are continually tempted to eat that fruit which we are told will destroy us.

Euthanasia is really not about the prevention of pain-filled dying. All of us want that, and we rejoice that modern medicine continues to find more humane ways of controlling pain.

At its core, euthanasia is about control — about the belief that to die without control is unworthy of human existence. As the devil told Adam and Eve that it was "inhuman" on God's part for them to have to submit to weakness and old age, so the promoters of euthanasia find the "loss of control" that is part of dying an unnecessary attack on human dignity.

To die with dignity is the battle cry of the Hemlock Society. In this regard it is important to study closely what is happening in Oregon where the terminally ill have been given the legal right to ask and receive from their doctor life-ending drugs.

Almost all who have asked for these drugs have stated that they did not want to be a burden on their family or on society. The "right" of patients to choose death is very quickly turning into a "duty," that they should not allow themselves to become a burden to others.

As the devil did not transform our first parents "to be like unto gods," so the promoters of euthanasia are not providing new dignity to the dying in causing them to worry about becoming a burden to others.

This worrying about being a burden to others can much more easily be transformed into a classical expression of deep depression than it can be transfigured into a joyous experience of previously unknown human dignity.

As Dr. Peter Quelch, director of palliative care at the Richmond Hospital in British Columbia, notes, most calls for euthanasia come not from the experience of pain but from the loss of meaning in their lives, from that terrible feeling of being no more than a burden.

Jesus did not deem equality with God something to strive for. As he emptied himself to die like one of us, so must we resist eating the fruit that will destroy us; so must we prepare, through the daily paradoxes of life, to die one day with true dignity, the dignity that comes from trusting in the Lord.

We are, we must remember, not disciples of a calm, hemlock-drinking Socrates, but of a crucified Lord who cried out to his disciples, pleading with them to spend but one hour with him in his travail.

Most of us will be tempted at death to see ourselves as no more than a burden. As Christians we pledge to stand by one another and show the dying through our love incarnate that they are anything but a burden, that indeed we will miss them dearly.

Sue Rodriguez

February 21, 1994

She caught the attention of the nation. People everywhere empathized with her plight.

And a great many Canadians, finding her call to be able to die with dignity a noble aspiration, fully respect her decision to ask a doctor's aid in taking her own life.

It is easy for those who support Sue Rodriguez in her choice to see it as a strong endorsement of her as a person. MP Svend Robinson, who was with her when she died, has spoken out passionately on how nobly she died, on how she was in control of her own destiny.

Death is never something we easily come to terms with. The desire for life is planted deeply within us — even Jesus in the Garden of Gethsemane cried out for the cup he knew he had to drink to pass him by. When death faces us we desperately hope it will be easy. The Greek term euthanasia means "an easy death."

But God with inscrutable wisdom did not promise any of us individually that it would be easy — and God certainly did not promise that to us as a society. We as a society will never find death easy, and any structures we might create in a vain hope to make it such not only are doomed to failure but also carry within them great dangers to our fragile hold on human meaning and purpose.

It is so easy to see Sue Rodriguez's last days as empty days, days when human meaning and purpose had passed her by. Lou Gehrig's disease slowly but inevitably shuts down the body's muscular functions. She could no longer speak clearly; she could not control her daily bodily functions; she needed help to do the simplest things.

None of us wants this to happen to us. Just as none of us wants to parent a severely handicapped child; just as none of us wants to walk into the scary darkness of Alzheimer's. It's so tempting to grasp the easy answer: with the best of intentions we welcome death as the solution to meaningless existence.

Yet paradoxically these afflicted ones carry with them our pledge of meaning. In our struggle individually and as a society to treasure their human meaning and purpose, we safeguard our own.

As the Canadian bishops' response to Rodriguez's death notes, acceptance of her solution as a valid one puts a great deal of pressure on the most vulnerable in our society. The old and the sick must ask themselves

— and this becomes all the more true if they suspect that Alzheimer's is setting in — if it is right and proper for them to become a burden to family and friends, if indeed they too should be asking themselves whether they should ask for euthanasia, for the easy death.

There are so many pressures in modern society which cheapen the value of human life. The pope said much the same thing in his first encyclical; he questioned many of the socio-economic biases we call progress, and noted that our future lies "in the priority of ethics over technology, in the primacy of persons over things, in the superiority of spirit over matter."

We live in a world that virtually as a policy cheapens human life for the sake of profit. It is not easy for us to maintain the value of human life independently of its productive capacity. There are moments in all our lives — and not just when we are ill and thus unproductive — when we question our own worth.

It is not by chance that Jesus spent so much time with the poor and marginalized in his own society. He did not pick up little children just because he thought they needed a blessing.

He knew we all need that blessing, that we all need affirmation as we brush up against our weakness and mortality.

Human dignity is not advanced by praising the noble death of those who choose euthanasia. It is rather in our finding as a society the meaning of each person suffering from Lou Gehrig's disease. It is in treasuring the severely handicapped child and in honouring the Alzheimer's sufferer in our midst that the blessing of human meaning and purpose is secured.

Jean Vanier, who has dedicated his life to honouring the mentally handicapped, has something to say about a society toying with accepting active euthanasia as a good: "A society which discards those who are non-productive and weak risks an exaggerated development of reason, organization, aggression and the desire to dominate. It becomes a society without a heart, without kindness — a rational and sad society, lacking celebration, divided within itself and given to competition, rivalry and, finally, violence."

Honouring the dead

March 6, 1995

There has been in the Catholic Church of late a great shift in practice as to how the body of a deceased relative or friend is reverenced. We have moved swiftly from a church in which cremation was virtually prohibited to a community of believers in which many are now opting for cremation for themselves and their loved ones.

In 1963 the church officially changed its policy, a policy which presupposed that anyone who asked for cremation was effectively denying a key tenet of our faith, the resurrection of the body. This was indeed seldom the case, yet a major shift in the way Catholics reverence the dead has occurred without sufficient regard for the consequences of such actions.

The German bishops, uncomfortable with some of the practices that are developing without due thought, have recently issued a pastoral on the customs of Christian burial. The bishops stress the importance both of funeral rites dealing explicitly with the body and of the existence of named gravesites.

A critically important element in the daily practice of a theology of resurrection unto eternal life is maintaining an explicit relationship with the deceased who have played a key role in our formation. Absolutely central to our Catholic faith is an everyday belief in the solidarity of the living with the dead, that, whether we live or whether we die, we remain one in Christ Jesus.

The German bishops argue strongly against unmarked graves. People need focal points, a place where they can pray, somewhere where they can place a bouquet of flowers.

Most of us have experienced how differently people treat remains and the body. Not to spend ample time with the body of a deceased loved one usually takes its toll. A healthy grieving process is often impeded or seriously delayed by a too hasty cremation.

We must be deeply sensitive toward the people who ask for a speedy cremation soon after their death and who say they do not want a designated gravesite. It may be, as the German bishops note, a cry of depression, an admission that they are fundamentally lonely people who regard themselves as little more than a burden to others.

Funeral rites ultimately are for the living, not for the dead. Our funeral plans must respect the needs of those who come after us. The church's funeral rites, developed over long centuries, should not be easily dismissed.

At first sight it may appear that individuals who ask, for example, to have their ashes scattered over their favourite golf course have come to healthy terms with their death.

But we must be most discerning here. Death is never to be taken lightly. To try to do so, either for ourselves or for those we must grieve, is to court disaster.

To be sure, the church was right in concluding that a desire for cremation is seldom a sign of lack of faith in the Lord's resurrection. But much more is at stake in cremation than finding a simple way to save money. Funeral rites and marked gravesites have centuries of human wisdom behind them, wisdom we disregard at our own peril.

Capital punishment revisited
February 23, 1987

First-degree murders have declined marginally since the death penalty was abolished in Canada. Police slayings have decreased quite substantially since 1962. During that year, the last year the death penalty was carried out in Canada, 11 police officers were murdered on duty.

Most years since then have seen less than half that number gunned down; 1982 and 1983 had one each year; 1984 was the worst with nine.

Yet today, if polls are to be believed, Canadians have dramatically changed their opinion as to the rightness of capital punishment. When Parliament abolished it, Canadians readily went along with their Members of Parliament. Nor did they in the following decade clamour for its restoration. But now, even though crimes for which the death penalty would be applied have decreased, it has become politically expedient to favour capital punishment. We must, as a nation, seriously ask ourselves why.

Deterrence can hardly be the answer. No matter how bull-headed one might be, it is difficult to ignore major studies in Canada, the United States, and Great Britain, all of which have clearly demonstrated that the persons committing first-degree murders will not be deterred by the consequences of their crime — even if the death penalty is one of them.

Is it that we have become more vengeful? Is the call for the restoration of the death penalty no longer fundamentally a question of deterrence but rather a cry for vengeance, a sign that violence has taken hold in our hearts? Let us hope not. As Christians we know that Jesus would have nothing to do with such vengeance.

We believe the present hankering for capital punishment is more a sign of panic than an indication of hardened hearts. We see around us a social unrest global in character. We know in our bones it is going to mean changes — major changes — to our way of life.

The changes are going to be most dramatic in the United States, and so it is not surprising that this country knows more violence than any other nation in the First World — and that the re-introduction of capital punishment there has not stemmed this violence in the least.

The Canadian bishops, already in 1973, told us that in looking at capital punishment "the focus should be on us. Should Canadians as a community," they asked, "try to break the escalating spiral of violence by refraining from violence even as a deterrent?"

The Quaker John Bright said much the same thing quite eloquently over 100 years ago: "The real security for human life is to be found in a reverence for it. If the law regarded it as inviolable, then the people would begin also so to regard it.

"A deep reverence for human life is worth more than a thousand executions in the prevention of murder, and is, in fact, the great security for human life. The law of capital punishment, while pretending to support this reverence, does in fact tend to destroy it."

We must not allow our current panic to lay aside wisdom such as this. The Soviet dissident, Andrei Sakharov, had a lot of time to meditate in prison on the true nature of capital punishment. "I regard the death penalty," he said, "as a savage and immoral institution. A state, in the person of its functionaries, takes upon itself the right to the most terrible and irreversible act — the deprivation of life. Such a state cannot expect an improvement in its moral atmosphere."

Applying capital punishment April 21, 1987

In February Amnesty International released its study of the application of the death penalty in the United States. The report, *United States of America: The Death Penalty*, stated that there were certain injustices inherent in the application of the death penalty.

Racism, the report affirmed, was rampant. The socio-economic status of the condemned also played a major role in the application of the death penalty, it stated.

Now Canada has a study of its own. Professor Kenneth Avio of the University of Victoria has studied all 440 cases of capital punishment in Canada between 1926 and 1957. He has also studied the cases in which the federal cabinet commuted the death penalty during those same years.

The results should make parliamentarians think twice before re-introducing the death penalty in Canada. Native Indians, Ukrainians, and

French Canadians, Avio has demonstrated, "were executed in disproportionate numbers to English Canadians."

Disproportionate is hardly the right word. In one of his examples — the slaying of an English Canadian — he noted that a Native perpetrator had a 96 percent chance of facing the death penalty. An English Canadian killer faced only a 21 percent risk of being executed.

But should one expect a different result? Avio uncovered frequent memos from the Ministry of Indian Affairs, advising the courts and the cabinet that Native people "need special deterrence."

Canadians of eastern European descent and French Canadians did not fare much better. The following case is not atypical. In 1942 a sentencing judge "informed" the federal cabinet that the defendant was typical of Canada's Slavic immigrants "with low moral standards — a bullying, cruel type greatly given to drink. There is a danger to the public of extending leniency on the commission of major crimes by these people."

Avio has shown in his study that those who have died in Canada at the public executioner's hand have come disproportionately from the ranks of the poor, the minorities, the powerless. Even if our MPs are not convinced by the traditional arguments against capital punishment, the spectre of its uneven application in our land should haunt them, and drive them to find a better way for establishing justice and order.

Chapter 9

Call to Justice

A spirituality for justice
September 12, 1994

Catholics often view spirituality in the narrowest of terms. Rather than perceiving it as a call from the Spirit for the life of the world, we tend to see it as soul work, as the fulfilment of the personal task of saving one's soul.

Seen within such a narrow framework, a Jesus-and-me attitude toward our faith appears perfectly normal. And once this rugged individualism has been legitimized, we can begin making clear distinctions between a mission of justice and a call to charity.

In such a world Christians are not called to critique and change the structures of the world, structures that are robbing increasing numbers of peoples of a human level of existence, but are simply called to charity, that is, to sacrifice a small part of their good fortune as a donation toward the less fortunate.

When justice and love become separated, everything loses its rightful place in the kingdom.

The call to justice comes to be seen in economic and political terms, not only by those who are less than eager to see social justice as an essential element in the call to Christian perfection, but also by those struggling to make justice a central focus of church life. It is not an accident of history that so many justice workers in our church cannot rise above the daily frustrations and in a rather short time burn out.

Frustrations there surely are. Parish workers (and editors of Catholic newspapers!) can so easily capitulate in the face of the relentless criticism that their struggle for justice is based not on the Gospel but on a political preference.

But not only justice becomes a dirty word when justice and love are separated.

Love too can become a hollow excuse for maintaining structures from which we have personally received multiple rewards. And thus, for instance, we can give generously to food banks while screaming about reducing welfare because we know two or three people who have abused the system. We might even be able to couple our donations to charity with a blanket condemnation of Native peoples. We don't notice that a propensity to stereotype people really vitiates our acts of charity.

Only a passion for justice can purify our love; only that love which can understand and appreciate the cross of Christ can make our struggle for justice the mark of the kingdom.

The definition that Jean Vanier's Faith and Sharing group has given for charity is a good starting point. L'Arche sees the Gospel as "a call to live and share the truth of the Good News of the poor." It is believing "that each person has a unique and undeniable value and reveals something of the infinite mystery of God." Jesuit Father Walter Burghardt, a tireless crusader for social justice, gives flesh to such thinking in his tract on a social justice spirituality.

He tells the story of a rabbi meeting two drunken peasants. Had he stereotyped them, as we are so wont to do, he would have learned nothing. But rather he listened and thus was able to learn the meaning of love. The peasants were in a drunken embrace proclaiming their love for one another. But when one declared he did not know what hurts his friend, he (and the rabbi) heard a nugget of wisdom: "If you don't know what hurts me, how can you say you love me?"

Justice is never cold philosophical or political theory. Nor is love ever abstract charitable donating. It is knowing what is hurting our brother and sister. It is admitting with Burghardt that "the plight of the poor is not primarily a part of reality that calls for charity, but part of disordered systems calling for justice."

A true Christian spirituality is never limited to God-experiences in our interior lives. The Spirit always calls us beyond ourselves and beyond our churches to work for the life of the world. Did not Jesus, in giving us his flesh to eat, in calling us to celebrate the Eucharist as the centre of our faith, remind us that his flesh is always given "for the life of the world" (Jn 6:51)?

Ten Days for Development

February 3, 1986

The Ethic of Life Dom Helder Camara, former archbishop of Recife, Brazil, once said: "When I give food to the poor they call me a saint; when I ask why the poor have no food they call me a communist."

The archbishop answers his critics by allying himself with Pope John: "Those who use anti-communism to defend their own self-interests are not willing to listen to the words of John XXIII in *Pacem in Terris* (Peace on earth) which state that the most serious social problem of our time is the gap, increasing daily, between the developed and underdeveloped world."

A generation ago the British economist Barbara Ward dedicated almost all her energies to teach the church about development. And with utter conviction and zeal she urged the developed countries in the West to dedicate 1 percent of their gross national product (GNP) toward international development.

The times were good and many countries took up her challenge. Even though few reached the goal of 1 percent, the level of aid then far outstripped today's contributions.

Development officials in every corner of the world today are having trouble getting aid. They must exercise extreme caution lest the establishment label them communist and cut off what little aid they were getting. Western governments are anxious to justify their cuts in this manner.

There is an amazing amount of money, thank God, available for emergency charity, but long-term development funds which would do much to prevent tragedies are getting ever more scarce. Camara had a word for this phenomenon too: "We need justice, not charity."

The anti-communist propaganda and the diminishing funds are not the only obstacles faced by those concerned about the widening gap between the rich and the poor. In the years since Ward's death countries have become much more adept at tying their aid to their own development rather than that of the recipient.

The Canadian bishops (in Witness to Justice, 1979) have condemned this: "It is estimated that approximately two-thirds of Canadian bilateral aid to the Third World is spent right here in Canada on goods, commodities and services. Most of Canada's 'aid,' therefore, never really leaves this country but is funnelled directly into Canadian business.

"In effect, Canada's aid and loan programs affecting Third World countries help to further facilitate the accumulation of wealth for Canadian businesses and perpetuate patterns of economic dependency for Third World countries."

And what makes this emasculation of Barbara Ward's dream all the more reprehensible: developed nations have learned to make huge profits from these underdeveloped nations.

Camara has a word for this too! "When you compare what Latin America receives in foreign aid with what it loses as a result of its lost raw materials, you understand the absurd fact that it is Latin America which is giving aid to North America."

The raping of underdeveloped countries has stretched their social and political structures beyond endurance. But this radicalization of their societies is not without its benefits for the developed world — it produces a world ready to buy the First and Second Worlds' armaments. Thus the poorer nations not only give aid to the developed countries, but also help pay their military budgets.

With this the vicious circle is complete. The militarization and ensuing violence tell the First World that the critics of Dom Helder were right. You cannot be too careful about communism taking over such countries as Brazil, Nicaragua, or the Philippines.

As we observe these Ten Days for World Development, a Canadian ecumenical project, we would do well to meditate on the words Pope John Paul shouted out during his homily in Edmonton: "In the light of Christ's words ('I was hungry ... I was thirsty ... I was a stranger ... naked ... sick ... in prison' — Mt 25:35-36), this poor South will judge the rich North. And the poor people and poor nations — poor in different ways, not only lacking food, but also deprived of freedom and other human rights — will judge those people who take these goods away from them, amassing to themselves the imperialistic monopoly of economic and political supremacy at the expense of others."

The Berlin Wall comes down November 20, 1988

The principal sign of the Cold War struggle between East and West has come tumbling down. Between November 10 and 12 of this year an estimated 3 million East Germans crossed through new openings in the Berlin Wall for one gigantic, spontaneous weekend.

All this seemed impossible just a month earlier. Erick Honecker continued to maintain one of the most rigid regimes in eastern Europe. But it did not take Honecker long to realize it was all over when he heard tens of thousands of East Germans marching through the streets of Leipzig taunting him with shouts of "Gorby! Gorby!"

Ultimately the success of the winds of change in Poland, Hungary, and East Germany — and Cardinal Frantisek Tomasek of Prague says that Czechoslovakia will not be far behind — are due to Mikhail Gorbachev. This Russian politician has steadfastly pushed for a new order despite unsettling movements for freedom within the USSR, despite the extreme weakening of the Warsaw Pact. He has declared unilateral nuclear test bans, unilateral weapons reductions.

We in the NATO alliance can take no credit for the thaw in the Cold War. It is the work of Mikhail Gorbachev.

Of course, the Cold War is not now suddenly passé. We know Gorbachev is for real, but we must ask: Can he hold on to power, or will the old guard topple him as so many previous general secretaries have been unceremoniously replaced in the past?

Without doubt Gorbachev, if he is to further his mission of ending the Cold War, needs help from the West. He needs to show the Soviet people that we are responding to his challenge of peace.

A simple first step for Canada would be a public declaration that we are terminating the permission we gave the Americans to test their prize first-strike weapon, the cruise missile, on Canadian soil.

And if we really believe the Cold War should be ended, if we indeed want to take the leadership role in the work of peace, we should as an early second step call home from Germany our troops that are "guarding" our side of the wall.

The most troubling part of ending the Cold War is the resultant chaos to our economic well-being. We have to acknowledge how much of the western economic growth is dependent upon the creation of instruments of death, upon support for the military establishment.

Saskatchewan leaders, should they be interested in a new order of peace, ought to inform Ottawa that Canada must stop shipping uranium to the United States. More than four years ago, CTV's W5 gave the whole country clear evidence that Canada's uranium was being used in the production of nuclear weapons.

Of course, this will be costly for Saskatchewan, but then peace has not come cheaply for Gorbachev either.

In 1983, Saskatchewan's bishops along with most of the other church leaders in the province called for a moratorium on uranium mining. If the recent spill at Wollaston Lake cannot convince us of the foolhardiness of uranium mining, let us hope the current call to be prophets of the new age of peace will prod us toward greatness.

Cold War camouflages neo-colonialism
November 20, 1988

The American bishops, in their pastoral letter on war and peace, declared that one of the worst aspects of the Cold War was its camouflaging of the rape of the Third World by the First and Second Worlds. The Cold War, they proclaimed, was being used by their country to justify an unjust foreign policy, especially in Latin America.

The pope has been even blunter. In his last social encyclical, *Sollicitudo Rei Socialis* (On social concern), he condemns "the neo-colonialism" of both NATO and the Warsaw Pact. For the pope the Cold War is primarily about economics. He, too, speaks of it as a camouflage, "legitimating this neo-colonialism that has impoverished so many millions of people."

In his January 1986 World Day of Peace message, the pope declared that injustice to the South is the major threat to lasting peace.

Little will be achieved in the warming of the Cold War if we do not allow it to take the blinkers off our eyes and help us acknowledge the tremendous evils that have been wrought on the poor by the "ideologies of the superpowers" — to use, once more, the words of the pope.

The ending of the Cold War, if we are truly honest, will be costly indeed. But then, if we compare it with the real costs of the Cold War, it is likely the best bargain this millennium.

Progressive taxation
May 27, 1985

Progressive taxation has not had a smooth history in the western industrial world. The famous 1909 budget of British Prime Minister Lloyd George, which brought with it the philosophy that taxation was not only a vehicle to provide governments with working capital but also a means whereby the poor might share more equitably in the wealth of a nation, created a constitutional crisis.

The budget weathered the crisis, and later became a model for Canadian income tax legislation.

Until recent times, few politicians have questioned the principle of progressive taxation. When Alberta businessman Peter Pocklington proposed a flat 20 percent income tax during a Progressive Conservative leadership race, Canadians overwhelmingly saw the proposal as patently unjust.

While at least in theory the progressive-taxation principle has been adhered to, there has been a constant chipping away at it. Tax loophole after tax loophole has been created. While the reasons for these are always couched in national economic terms, the result is always the same. With each tax shelter the poor pay a higher proportion of the total tax burden.

Many governments have come to rely on sales tax for an increasing proportion of their tax revenue. This flat tax, too, has undermined the principle of progressive taxation.

The process has gone so far that few of the very rich in this land pay any income tax at all. The progressive taxation system has been so abused that even a flat tax begins to sound fair. We almost forget that it was the injustice of flat taxation that led to taxation reforms in the first place.

In their study of the U.S. economy, the American bishops call, in the chapter on the present crisis in agriculture, for a greater application of progressive taxation. They want to see it applied not only for income tax purposes; they also support a graduated land tax.

In order to maintain the family farm they call for a taxation system that will discourage the accumulation of large landholdings.

If the tax were higher for the 5th quarter section of land than for the 1st, and substantially so for the 10th, there is a chance that farming would remain a way of life, and not be totally converted into agribusiness.

The same justice that demands progressive income taxation also demands a new approach to land taxation.

Since farming is principally concerned with the production of food for the whole human family, it is all the more urgent that a land-ownership reform be undertaken in Canada.

What Pope John Paul II said to the Newfoundland fishing community, when he spoke at Flatrock in September 1984, applies equally to Prairie farmers: "Large industrial fishing companies are exposed to the temptation of responding only to the forces of the marketplace, thus lacking at times sufficient financial incentive to maintain production.

"Such a development," the pope said, "would put the security and distribution of the world's food supply into even greater jeopardy, if food production becomes controlled by the profit motive of a few rather than by the needs of the many."

Most tax reforms over the last 25 years have been based on the principle that the rich know what is best for the country and should be free to use their wealth to develop the nation's economic base. Likely the present federal government will continue to undermine the principle of progressive taxation since it has never wearied of reminding us to rely on the financial acumen of the private sector.

How different this is from the pope's vision among the poor fishers of the sea; how contrary it is to the call of the American bishops to strengthen the small family farmer. Contrary to current political thinking, these church leaders still believe that the surest way to a healthy, just society is to give power and dignity to the individuals at the lower end of our economic substructure.

U.S. farm subsidies

May 15, 2002

With a logic that only the initiated in all things American can fathom, the country that puts import duties on steel and softwood lumber because it believes in free trade now has increased its farm subsidies more than 75 percent, enriching the pork barrel by $190 billion (US) over the next six years.

Canadian farmers who have been screaming at Ottawa for years for greater subsidies will be surprised that the U.S. bishops' National Catholic Rural Life Conference takes a dim view of the moneys being promised farmers.

They have two main objections: first, that in Congress's haste to shore up low grain, livestock, and other commodity prices, the American government is actually contributing to overproduction — and thus lower prices and the need for ever greater subsidies.

Their second objection deals directly with "the pork barrel." Very little of the money will be going to small family farmers. The new bill has virtually no limits, no caps on payouts, and the lion's share of the new money will go to agribusinesses, not family farmers.

Even before this 75 percent increase in "farm" subsidies, six-figure payments were going to the likes of John Hancock Life Insurance Co., Chevron, banker David Rockefeller, and basketball star Scottie Pippen.

Talk about corporate welfare! Not surprisingly, the American government notes that it will have to cut social security in order to afford its new expenses. But its farm subsidy program fades in real significance when compared to the new military budget. That is being increased this coming year by $48 billion — to a grand tune of $396.8 billion. This is more than the rest of the world's military budgets combined.

And if Canadians are disturbed by the money our federal government spent in Quebec advertising, know that there is no direct governmental supervision of the Pentagon budget — even though fully one-quarter of that budget was not accounted for this past year. This alone is more than the U.S. government spent in total on education last year.

It will certainly not be of much comfort to Canadian farmers to know that most of the money from the U.S. government will not reach the pockets of needy family farmers south of the border. Last year nearly three-quarters of the farm-subsidy money went to the richest 10 percent of American "farmers." Commentators believe this discrepancy will only increase with the new program.

There is much that Canadian farmers have to fear from this $190 billion increase in subsidies. Now, more than ever, it will be possible for the United States to export its food so cheaply that no farmers anywhere else in the world will possibly be able to compete.

But it will also put great strain on other Canadian structures, most notably the Canadian Wheat Board. Government programs that do not have a cap per farmer have always had a detrimental effect on rural communities and family farms. Land prices inflate, farms grow ever larger, and rural communities collapse for lack of bodies. And the larger the farm, the less care can be lovingly given to the land. Monoculture and ever heavier doses of fertilizers, pesticides, and herbicides will be needed to camouflage the not-so-gradual destruction of the land's ability to feed the world.

And, all the while, agribusiness entrepreneurs (and not true in-your-boots farmers) drink freely at the government well, while conscientiously reminding their neighbours that there is no such thing as a free meal.

It is questionable whether the Canadian government, even if it had the desire (which is highly doubtful), could come close to matching its southern neighbour's largesse. But painful as it might be, Canadian farmers should take to heart the criticism levelled by the U.S. bishops' National

Catholic Rural Life Conference. Programs without rigid limits or caps per farmer will in the end do more harm to our rural economy and lifestyle.

We need more help from our government. But it will take men and women who truly see tilling the land as a heavenly calling to structure our country's limited resources in such a way that the moneys spent by governments will truly revitalize rural economies and ensure future generations that their land is not being raped of its fertility.

Feeding the hungry   June 19, 2002

In 1996 the nations of the world, under the aegis of the United Nations Food and Agriculture Organization, pledged to cut in half the number of hungry people by 2015. UN General Secretary Kofi Annan, seeing that this goal was not being met, called a special "hunger summit" in Rome, the headquarters of the FAO.

If nothing is done, Annan said, we will have almost as many hungry people in 2015 as we had in 1996. Annan's wake-up call challenged world leaders, noting that a reduction of 400 million hungry from the current 815 million would not greatly impinge on life in the First World.

The pope clearly became Annan's greatest fan. In a strongly worded message to the conference, the pope first of all apologized for not being able to attend in person, citing his poor state of health. To make up for this absence, it seems, he fine-tuned his words, reminding the world leaders that it is not for lack of production that so many are hungry.

In the bluntest of terms, the pope told the conference attendees that the secret to success is to reject self-serving policies and choose instead solidarity with the starving.

Then in language that surely would make liberation bishop-theologian Archbishop Helder Camara smile in his grave, the pope reminded his audience that "solidarity is not charity but justice, a justice based on the acknowledgment that the resources which God the creator has entrusted to us are destined for all."

The pope did not hide which side he was on in the socio-philosophical debate that raged at the conference. He explicitly endorsed the concept that the poor and the starving have an inalienable right to food. Indeed, he developed this concept even further: unless the governments of the

Call to Justice

world guarantee this right to food, he said, there can be no true hope for peace.

The United States, however, used its muscle to force a watered-down definition of this human right; the hungry, according to this way of thinking, do not have a "right to food," but rather the "right to have access to safe and nutritious food."

At first glance, this appears to be a minor change, but the NGOs and several leading economists were not fooled by the rhetoric. Two items important to the American delegation underpinned this change: first, the freedom to develop genetically modified foods and, second, the right of America to subsidize its agricultural community so that its own production would indeed dominate the world's food trade.

The American delegation presented the struggle as one between capitalist and socialist principles. Likely it was because of this that the pope and the Vatican delegation uncharacteristically went to the liberation theology manuals for their language.

But it was not only the pope and the NGOs that fought against the American "compromise." Jeffrey Sachs, no stranger to capitalist principles — it was he whom Washington sent to Russia and other ex-communist states to help them in their transition to free-market economies — gave at the FAO meeting his own interpretation of September 11.

That horrific day, he said, should have been "a wake-up call to the United States" on the need to address the consequences "that arise from poverty, despair and failure in the developing world."

Canadian farmers know only too well how the U.S. farm subsidy bill is hurting them. The NGOs at the Rome meeting tried their best to show how profoundly this U.S. subsidy program is negatively affecting small farmers in the Third World. They simply cannot compete.

While Canadian farmers acknowledge that, when push comes to shove, Canada (and the European Union, Australia, and Argentina) cannot compete with Washington, Third World nations cannot even begin to struggle.

Genetically modified (GM) foods are also a problem. While they were presented at the Rome meeting as a great blessing — because of greater yields — they are in fact just another way in which First World corporations gain control and ownership of the food trade.

Sachs, while not able to fight this self-serving two-pronged approach to food distribution, begged for a little altruism. If the First World nations increased their contribution from 5 cents to 10 per $100 of their annual earnings, 8 million people would be saved yearly from succumbing to AIDS, malaria, and the other deadly diseases endemic to the developing world.

It's not the whole, but it is something.

The pope and the NGOs did not win the battle in Rome. Nor, most likely, is the cause of the poor to win out in the forthcoming meeting of the G-8 in the Rockies near Calgary. But progress is being made, albeit slowly. The protestors in Halifax recently and those who will march in and around Calgary can see already a new future. Let us encourage these young people — and those among them who are not so young!

We can be certain that the pope will give a clear call to the church's youth as they gather with him in Toronto to celebrate the Good News of that strange Messiah who totally identified himself with the powerless.

Same dignity given to all

April 15, 1998

Gays and lesbians can bring the best and the worst out of people. Phone-in radio programs in Alberta recently revealed how polarizing an issue the banning of any discrimination of homosexuals can be.

Formed by God's grace to counter polarization and to build community, the church as institution must be deeply concerned since its members differ so strongly on how they are to treat homosexuals — especially since such a high percentage of them see their religious faith as a central element in shaping their mindset.

It cannot go unnoticed that many of the people who work so hard to transform society in ways that will promote healthy family life are at the same time deadly afraid that full recognition of the human dignity of gays and lesbians will foster a moral collapse of that society. It is not by accident that abortion, homosexuality, and "radical feminism" are so often lumped together in the pro-life struggle.

The Supreme Court's decision that Alberta must include full legal protection for its gays and lesbians should be good news for the church. That homosexuality is so easily blackened with the same brush that condemns abortion should make all of us re-examine our strategies, our tactics, for it is incontestable that homosexuals and heterosexuals share exactly the same dignity — which we in the Judaeo-Christian world see as that grace which makes us images of God.

The Edmonton social justice commission calls the court decision a blessing, a victory for all Christians who want equal rights for all. We must be especially vigilant in not allowing opponents to this decision to equate equality with special rights. No one is calling upon civil society to grant gays and lesbians special privileges.

Gays and lesbians foster the best and the worst in us. It is so easy to see "the worst." Few gays and lesbians have escaped being bloodied, physically and/or emotionally, by the insensitivities of their "straight" neighbours. But there is also "the best." Getting to know a gay or lesbian personally invariably challenges our mindset. Any priest or spiritual counsellor who has ever listened to a gay or lesbian's story about the pain, the loneliness, the despair they have faced precisely because of their sexual orientation will be less inclined to hasty judgments in the future.

Beneath our fears of moral collapse should the full human dignity of gays and lesbians be respected are those suspicions that these people are more inclined to sexual promiscuity in general and pedophilia in particular. These fears are not likely to be eased by learned arguments in a book — or in a good homily, for that matter! Only hearing and sharing the pain their orientation has caused them will open our hearts.

It was not by chance that Jesus was so often found with the two groups that made his contemporaries worry about moral collapse. They dreaded tax collectors not only because they cleaned their pockets but also because they strengthened the Roman system and undermined the people's dream for a holy nation of their own. No explanation is needed as to why they dreaded prostitutes!

Jesus came with a downright scandalous message about the graciousness of his God. To enflesh this message, to challenge people so that they would know if they really accepted it in their heart of hearts, Jesus often associated himself with prostitutes and tax collectors. The Lord left no room for those who said they liked the message — if only he would stop associating with those people who were undermining society.

After listening to the hate-filled rejection of gays and lesbians that filled our airways following the Supreme Court decision, one cannot but think that if Jesus were to come back again he would often be found in the company of gays and lesbians.

Of course, Jesus is not going to come again in the flesh; he sent his Spirit to create a church that would follow in his footsteps.

Racism in the church June 18, 1983

Bishop Blaise Morand of Prince Albert has made understanding the Native community in the Prince Albert Diocese one of his first priorities. He acknowledges he does not know how best to catechize them. But he is convinced that our present tools are not up to the task.

Why he sees them as inadequate is significant. The bishop feels they carry too much of our cultural baggage. They speak to the Native community, he notes, of "the white God."

Northern dioceses have been working hard of late to correct this. Much less, however, is heard of efforts in our southern cities with their large Native populations.

The church cannot wash its hands Pilate-style of the blatant racism that is raising its ugly head in almost every corner of our land.

If the church deeply felt the need to unite all peoples in the one Body of Christ it would have a catechism with a Native face. It would also have given all of us of European origin a God with some distinctively Native or Métis features. Only an appreciation of what is best in each civilization will give us a true image of the God we should be worshipping.

Racism is the opposite of this. Rather than project the goodness of others into our God image, we project what we cannot face within ourselves.

Carl Jung, the psychoanalyst, repeatedly observed in his clients that whatever sin, whatever evil, they could not face in their hearts, they tried to free themselves of by projecting it onto the handiest scapegoat.

In this the Métis and Natives have served us well for many years. We have taken advantage of their great gifts — tolerance, disdain for social climbing, and deep desire for peacefulness — and made them our scapegoats, the bearers of our sins.

No wonder our jails are full of them.

Futility of violence at Oka September 10, 1990

The whole country took a deep sigh of relief when on September 1, the Mohawk women stepped between the Canadian army and the warriors. Had they not taken charge, a senseless, tragic bloodbath would have soured relations between the principal nations in this country for many years to come.

The needless calling in of the army had already poisoned relations. It has been painful to see the Quebec government, which has rightly treasured its people's national identity, so ready to manipulate the negotiations that they were doomed to fail.

One would have hoped that the province, which has preached its doctrine of national identity so powerfully and persistently to the rest of the country, would have been more ready than the rest of Canada to appreciate the national aspirations of its first citizens.

Rather, it appears the Bourassa government wanted the last-minute negotiations to fail. The Quebec premier, practically in his own name, called in the Canadian army — after the Mohawks had already started to dismantle the barricades leading to the Mercier Bridge and after they had put an honest, comprehensive proposal on the table re the barricades in Oka.

There was no justification in Prime Minister Brian Mulroney's acceding to Quebec Premier Robert Bourassa's pressure to engage the army. The potential of this move to greatly increase the level of violence was simply too high.

The relative ease with which our government leaders resorted to violence should make us hesitant to criticize the warriors' taking up of arms. Natives have suffered devastating hardships at our hands over many, many years. And who would dare compare the hardships endured by Canada's Native peoples with the 50 days of inconvenience experienced by the residents of Chateauguay in commuting to Montreal. Yet this led to pelting old men, women, and children with rocks — while the Quebec police stood back doing nothing to stop the violence.

We decry the warriors' resorting to violence, but, all the same, we non-Native Canadians must honestly ask ourselves: Would anything less have got our attention? Have we not proven again and again that we were not ready to listen to their right to be treated as nations?

We simply must acknowledge the nature of the treaties we signed with our Native peoples. They were nation to nation. Canada's aboriginal peoples never negotiated away their right to self-determination as nations. That we were so sure they would assimilate, disintegrate, or disappear and thus forfeit everything to us is irrelevant.

They are nations — and that is not something we can negotiate about. Yes, we decry the warriors' resorting to violence, but we do acknowledge that in applying traditional just war principles the Mohawks surely had a better case for taking up arms than the Canadian government had in sending its battleships to the Persian Gulf.

The first peoples in Canada are nations, nations to whom we are deeply indebted. Let us hope the age of paternalism came to a crashing end in Oka. May the federal government's purchase, at inflated prices and with Indian money, of the land which Oka entrepreneurs tried converting into a golf course be the last paternalistic act of the "Great White Father."

The self-determination of our Native peoples on a realistic land base must be taken as a given. Just settlements are required now in every corner of our land. The federal government, in trying to justify its practical non-involvement in the Oka crisis, has stated that it has nearly completed two land claim negotiations. According to the government's timetable it would take another half millennium to deal with the more than 500 outstanding Native claims. That is hardly justice, hardly something to brag about.

The surest way to end futile violence in our land is to convince our Native peoples that we do indeed want them to be once more nations confident in themselves — with a self-assurance that only personal dignity can provide.

If we believe this, we will anticipate the new beginnings of honest negotiations with an immediate restoration of federal funds to Native publications and education. That would be a good sign that the Canadian people want future citizens, in studying our history, to come to see the chapter on Oka as one of the bright turning points in our common story with the First Nations of this land.

Ovide Mercredi's tears
December 18, 1995

It was an electric moment at the Sacred Assembly earlier this month in Hull, Quebec. Amid many tears, Ovide Mercredi, chief of the Assembly of First Nations, spoke of his upbringing as a Catholic.

He had much to weep about. He said that as a youth he had many questions about his Native culture and spirituality. No answers to his questioning were forthcoming, he said, "and I am less of a human being for it."

Instead of answers he was given "indoctrination." The church told him: "The drum was evil, the sweet grass was evil, and the songs [his] people sang were evil."

We know, in this regard, that Mercredi is right. Our church did those things. All of us, too, though to a far less significant degree, experienced that church. Not only Native peoples were taught that almost everything was a sin. At times it seemed that the goal of church preaching was to extend the lines outside the confessional box. It became a mark of good pastoring to have long lines every Saturday night for confession.

Not only Native people learned that they were "no good." All of us learned that, and in the process we were given a God to be feared, a God who — despite what Jesus in the Gospels said to the contrary about his Father — was much more adept at punishing our sin than in forgiving it.

We were all victimized. But it must be said over and over again: no one paid a price like that exacted of Canada's Native peoples. Especially for the zealots of single-minded thinking (Mercredi uses the term "indoctrination"), Native spirituality was, in the general condemnation of "earthly" things, singled out for special denunciation.

Yes, our church was far from perfect. It did indeed play a role in victimizing Native peoples. And it is scant consolation to realize that few of the victimizers realized what they were doing. The very fact that it was done in such a doctrinaire manner indicates all too clearly that the practitioners were sincere — all too sincere. True believers are usually known for their zeal.

Where do we go from here? First of all, we must stop the process of victimization in the depth of our soul. It matters little whether one had been victimized to a lesser degree and was given, for instance, a God who could not be trusted, or to a much greater degree and had one's cultural roots ripped out and thus was demeaned as a human person.

Victimization is never an excuse for self-pity and ongoing anger or bitterness. Understandable as these emotions are, they only perpetuate the process of victimization.

All of us have had imperfect parents, imperfect teachers, an imperfect church. But no one, no elder, no church, no government — no one but we ourselves must now step forward and take responsibility for our lives. For all of us, Native peoples included, that will entail noting what was good about the church and about our experience of education and upbringing.

Of course, that does not mean governments and churches need not seek to right the wrongs that have been perpetrated.

Governments must come to respect the treaties they signed — or, in many cases, did not sign. Nothing will bring about reconciliation and healing faster among Canada's Native peoples than their sensing that governments wish to deal with them justly.

What about the church? Much more than an apology is needed.

First of all, it must admit its tendency to "indoctrination." This is by no means a dead issue. The *Prairie Messenger*, in warning about a narrowness of vision that can accompany religious enthusiasm, has been roundly accused of doing the work of the devil.

Secondly, the church must curb its habit of more often pointing out sin than the kingdom. As long as the church is perceived as being a greater authority on what is sinful in the world than on being skilled in revealing the kingdom at work in the fleshly lives of people, the danger of repeating the terrible blunders done our Native peoples remains a distinct possibility.

Thirdly, the church must not only respect Native culture, it must be seen to respect it. In church language, to respect a culture means to inculturate the Gospel within it. Pope John Paul II said in 1982 that "a faith which does not become a culture is a faith which has not been fully received, not thoroughly thought through, not faithfully lived out."

There can be no inculturation of the Gospel among Canada's Native peoples without the church recognizing Native Elders. The Vatican's answer in 1993 about safeguarding priestly celibacy throughout the Roman Rite was simply beside the point when the bishops of western Canada and of the North unanimously asked for a married clergy among our northern Native peoples.

Finally, the church must free itself from being perceived as a church of the well-heeled. When the private schools were stripping the Native peoples of their culture and dignity, church and state were seen to be working closely together.

That link no longer exists, yet the church must constantly ask itself: What proportion of its energy and funds goes toward maintaining its established First World parishes, and how does this compare with its expenditure on missionary and aboriginal work? If a diocesan church spends little on its social justice office, should it be listened to when it apologizes to Native peoples?

Bishop Remi De Roo of Victoria was eloquent in his response to Mercredi's tearful litany of Catholic shortcomings. We have, he noted, wonderful heroes of faith. De Roo mentions two in our day: Archbishop Oscar Romero and Bishop Samuel Ruiz.

To be sure, with true Advent eyes we should be able to see that a new church is being born in the slums of Latin America.

But we Catholics in Canada are not called, first of all, to have prophetic eyes to discern a new church born in far-off lands. We are to see in Mercredi's tears the work of the Spirit calling for a truly indigenous church in our midst.

We have a new patron in heaven, St. Eugene de Mazenod, founder of the Oblates. His followers have done much to lay the foundations of the church among the Native peoples of Canada. Let us never cease to pray for the courage to welcome in our midst a church — our church — which can truly celebrate, in the words of Pope John Paul II, "that Jesus Christ is himself an aboriginal."

Tracy Latimer
November 28, 1994

The tragedy of the Latimer family has touched the whole nation. It has filled our newspapers and television programs. It is the burning issue of radio talk shows and of small-town coffee shops and sophisticated city restaurants.

Much of the debate has centred on the father, Robert Latimer, and on the fairness of his second-degree murder conviction for killing his daughter Tracy, which carries a minimum 10-year jail term. Far less discussion, especially in the national media, has centred on Tracy and the meaning of her life (and death).

As Heidi Jantz, who also is severely handicapped with cerebral palsy, notes: situations like that found in the Latimer home can be rectified "only if the media and society as a whole start ascribing genuine value to the lives of people with severe disabilities."

Jantz certainly has a point. We were not given authentic news reports on the Latimer trial. We were given commentaries. And, if one were to take them at face value, one would have to conclude that Tracy's life was not worth living.

We are on very slippery ground indeed when we as a society start making value judgments about the comparative worth of any human life.

One can talk to countless families who have a severely handicapped person in their midst — and the overwhelming majority of them will declare unhesitatingly that, despite the many difficulties, this person has become a great and unexpected blessing who has played an important role in the close bonding of their family. Priests in small-town Saskatchewan who have been graced with presiding at a funeral liturgy for one of these little ones soon realize that their whole parish has been positively touched by that person — in ways far beyond the capacity of the so-called "normal" people of the parish.

Rather than demean the value of the severely handicapped, the whole community, and not just one family, is called upon to concretely respect their human dignity. Treasuring handicapped people must surely include making certain that their pain is controlled with medication and physical therapy paid for by the state. The immediate family must also be given public support. We may never take advantage of a family's love and allow those closest to the disabled one to break under the strain.

The local community and our government's Social Services department must bear a significant share of the guilt in the tragedy that struck the Latimer family. This dark day in our history should make all of us reconsider the ease with which governments are dismantling our social safety net.

But while we must recognize the obligations we all had toward Tracy, this will never significantly mitigate the seriousness of her father's crime. As journalist Dale Eisler notes: we are in deep trouble if we believe that, "because of her condition, Tracy did not warrant the full protection of the law like any one of us," and thus "the gravity of the act itself" was diminished.

Those in our society who are now fighting legalized euthanasia have argued that it will not end there. Soon, they argue, we will pass beyond those explicitly asking to end their lives to those not capable of expressing themselves but who, according to some arbitrary standards, do not enjoy a sufficient quality of life.

The tragedy of Tracy Latimer reveals how true this can be. We may never say that she had less of a right not to be murdered than any other citizen in the land. It is a terrible and frightening world indeed that can proclaim that being disabled makes one less a person.

Penal reform

April 19, 1996

Only the United States has a higher incarceration rate than Canada. All other nations lag far, far behind these two North American neighbours who pride themselves in being among the most advanced countries in the world.

We are similar to the Americans in another way: the jails in both countries are filled with people belonging to minority groups. Though aboriginal people are a minority in Saskatchewan, the overwhelming majority of those in its jails come from that social stratum.

Long ago we gave up calling our prisons reformatories, since it is nigh on a miracle if more than one or two here or there come out of prison better persons than they were when first incarcerated. We know our prisons are in fact a rich breeding ground for future crime. We even know what an occupational hazard they are for the guards. Ask any prison chaplain whether it is not an even greater miracle if several years of prison work transform guards into more sensitive people.

If one were to believe the media, one would have to conclude that Canada has a spiralling crime rate and that the country is filled with people crying out for vengeance. Both prejudicial viewpoints are not, thank God, sociological facts — and therefore one must ask why these myths are being promoted as gospel. Just who do our media owners believe is to profit from this blatant distortion of the facts?

We know, too, how expensive it is to keep people in prison. It's not surprising that there is another way in which we love to ape our southern neighbour. We want to be like them in making use of the death penalty, even though we know only a half-dozen other countries (like Iraq and Iran) still engage in this practice of ultimate violence. Indeed, the cries for its reinstatement are increasing in direct proportion to the advancement of that social instability which inevitably emerges from the ever-widening gap between the haves and have-nots in this country.

With our prison system being such an abysmal failure — and an extremely expensive one at that — we must ponder why we do not, as a society, ask ourselves some fundamental questions about prison reform. Could it be that our marketplace mentality has so accustomed us to see the human person as nothing more than an economic commodity that we find it impossible to view in any other fashion the poor and underprivileged who fill our jails?

Indeed, to many of our well heeled, that miracle cure of all our social ills, namely privatization, quite naturally springs to mind. For who would question this truth: only a fool would think that the state could incarcerate people more cheaply than can the private sector.

But that's not the only certitude in this regard. We can be equally assured that these new private-sector wardens will not strive to work themselves out of a job by rehabilitating too many of their "clients" (read: economic commodities). That we can even entertain the idea of a prison system in which private financial success depends on having more prisons and more prisoners should jolt us about the seriousness of the problem.

Though it means addressing some issues that touch the very substrata of society in Canada and the United States, we simply must look afresh at our penal system which is based on retribution and nourished by one of our baser urges — the cry for revenge. We must ask ourselves why it has been such a colossal failure.

Rittenhouse, a Toronto agency dedicated to questioning our punitive model of criminal justice, outlines four alternative models that have worked — and worked well — in other parts of the world. Rather than centre on punishment, all these models concentrate on "healing justice," on healing both the victim and the offender.

All four models will have difficulties in acceptance that have nothing to do with their effectiveness.

One flows out of the Japanese culture. The Japanese were not among our favourite people in the last world war — and their current success in outdoing us in the marketplace has not exactly endeared them to us either.

Another model stems from the Mennonite tradition and its espousal of pacifism, a concept directly at odds with what we hold dearest. As citizens of today's world, we are certainly more at home with blood-curdling cries for vengeance in the hockey arena than we are with a Christ who asks his followers to turn the other cheek.

Though they have high success rates in cultures similar to our own (such as New Zealand), the last two models have one mammoth strike against them: they stem from aboriginal cultures.

There is much evidence that sentencing circles in Canada and Maori conferencing in New Zealand do indeed work. But what will it take before our "superior" culture, which has filled its prisons with aboriginal people, has the moral integrity to study seriously the wisdom of the very people it is so prone to see as a central problem?

Penal reform is not just about moving from punitive justice to healing justice. It is a call for healing at the very core of our not-quite-so-superior culture.

Turning play to violence

April 11, 2001

It is said that 19th-century America developed baseball, while 20th-century America developed football.

Catholics were never a dominant force in 19th-century America and

Call to Justice 219

no Catholic college has ever been known for its baseball. Football — now that's another matter. The very bricks from that secular shrine of American Catholicism, the old football stadium at Notre Dame, are still revered in countless Catholic homes. Enlarging that stadium into a first-class temple was easily financed. Bricks from the outer wall of the original model were sold at exorbitant prices.

Recently, however, football has come on harder times, deemed increasingly inadequate to express mythically the soul of America. It was not sufficiently macho; it did not glorify violence well enough.

The owners of the XFL have promised to correct all that.

Now cameras and mics are everywhere so no hit be missed. So what if a cameraman gets run over on the field, or a sound girl at the very edge of the field becomes a bloodied part of the very sound she is collecting — the game then takes on some true blood and guts, some reality!

Of course, the cheerleaders now must stress not the beautiful but the erotic, since we are celebrating that machismo which makes the male of the species the great manifestation, the very epitome of humanity.

It's only logical that if the cameras are allowed on the field of battle and in the male-bonding locker room, they should find their way into the cheerleaders' locker room too. Fair is fair.

It is this world, which finds baseball about as exciting as watching paint dry, which finds it necessary to spice up football (make it more violent) so it may more adequately express the American dream. Yes, it's into this world that eager American entrepreneurs are now selling Canadians' sporting passion — hockey.

And, in the process, we are losing part of our soul. It is, we are told, inevitable. We are no longer talking about play — something so essential to our human development. No, we are talking about violence — something, whether we admit it or not, which is destructive to human growth and maturity.

Rev. Tom Ehrich talks about taking his son to a Carolina hockey game. Rather than cheer on great plays, he hears the announcer give the official interpretation of what is happening on the ice. "This is war!" screams the announcer. "Revenge!" flashes on the mega-screen.

His nine-year-old son has been captured, as was the Roman Forum before him, as were the participants in Hitler's liturgies in mid-century. "I love the fights," he tells his dad.

Canadians love to recall the great days of the 1972 Canada-Russia series, especially since we won the last game. Indeed, there are great moments to remember, such as the New Year's match in the old Montreal Forum, when the Canadians and the Russians duelled to a 3-3 tie in perhaps the greatest hockey game ever played.

But we forget other events, such as the day the leaders of the National Hockey League decided there was only one way to win. They had to slash and break the ankle of the best Russian player — and forthwith accomplished the deed all the while proclaiming that by winning we were illustrating the superiority of our capitalist system over that evil empire of the East.

To be sure, the Carolina announcer is closer to the truth than we would like to admit. Much of what is called hockey today is more about war and revenge than it is about play.

Play is not reserved solely for the young. All of us need to play. The child in each of us must never be allowed to die.

Play is based on three rather simple elements: entering the world of make-believe through one's imagination, experiencing one's limitations, and bonding more closely with one's community.

The "adult" in us, however, is quite capable of warping all three. We can so easily forget that it really isn't essential to move a piece of pigskin 110 yards, or to put a hunk of rubber into a net. We tend to make these so real, so important, that "players" are paid 10 and 40 times higher salaries than are paid to our national leaders. We so esteem putting that soccer ball into the net that we riot and kill people "to establish" our true superiority. Who today wants to play Great Britain in soccer? Great Britain, one of the founding cultures of our nation!

Children at play tend to even the sides to add excitement to the event. Adults, not eager to brush up against their mortality, look for the goon to ensure their victory.

Play is meant to bond the younger with the older, the skilled with the not-so-skilled, the extroverts with the introverts. And in all this, human growth takes place. But many adults find this useless. We need to develop the best, they tell us, so we can be assured of winning (and thus express our superiority).

We as a society pay a heavy price in making our great sports less and less a game and more and more a business. Play is supposed to humanize us.

But instead, as Ehrich puts it, we enshrine "road rage" as normative; we declare revenge a value; we indulge blood lust. We fight back, or better yet, shoot first. Hating is always easier than loving. Revenge is easier than compassion. Bluster is easier than listening. "Death to the infidel" is easier than "love your neighbour."

A sober reading of this week's *Prairie Messenger* on Americans struggling with the death penalty should give us some hint of the society we are creating for our children when we take the play out of their games and insist on symbolizing what we know in our heart-of-hearts is the worst about us.

No wonder we have become so barbaric as a society that we can truly regress to that level of human consciousness that actually believes a "justice" system can be built on revenge.

Events of September 11 September 19, 2001

Nothing can, in any way, justify the violence inflicted on Americans September 11. With the Latin Patriarch of Jerusalem, "we were deeply saddened when we watched the extent of the catastrophe inflicted upon innocent people, which was caused by horrible acts of terrorism.

"It is unimaginable," he added, "to see how catastrophic the extent of terrorism could reach."

Perhaps the president of the Canadian Conference of Catholic Bishops, Gerald Weisner of Prince George, said it best of all: "When faced with events such as this atrocity, words cannot be found."

Yet, no matter how evil these acts of terrorism were, they can in no way legitimize U.S. President George W. Bush's declaration that the war to follow will be "a monumental struggle of good versus evil." As long as we in the First World insist on calling ourselves "the good," we have nothing to learn from this tragedy.

It is perfectly understandable that our first reaction was anger. Nor is it any surprise that we lie so easily to ourselves, telling our inner hearts that we will be at peace once we mete out a fitting vengeance.

Cardinal Theodore E. McCarrick of Washington has served well not only his troubled city but the whole religious community in forcefully reminding us that "we resist the temptation to strike out in vengeance or revenge."

Bishop Amedee Grab of Church, Switzerland, president of the Council of European Episcopal Conferences, goes further. Rather than simply resist the temptation to strike out in vengeance, he challenges the First World to actively seek for peace. "On an occasion such as this," he says, "humankind needs to pause and ask how to break this cycle of inhumanity and destructive violence and discover new ways of embodying Christ's peace and justice on earth."

It is easy, but not of much significant value, to ask what would lead these men to such acts of desperation. It is not evil persons per se who are likely to sacrifice their lives for a cause larger than their own person. It takes some nobleness of character, however skewed, to come to such a state.

And let us not blame it on the Muslim faith. In this regard it is good for Catholics to remember the IRA. It was not the Gospel of Jesus Christ that led them to kill in the name of God, but a long history of injustice at the hands of the English. The teachings of Mohammed should no more be blamed for this violence than should the teachings of Jesus be used by the U.S. military establishment in its quest of a holy war. It is important for all to remember that Catholic and Muslim leaders in America have jointly condemned the terrorist attacks as "evil and diametrically opposed to true religion."

No, religion is not what has made these terrorists so desperate that "they felt they had nothing to lose." Archbishop Renato Martino, the Vatican's representative at the United Nations, challenged us to "identify the problems at the roots of terrorism and find solutions."

The First World will not be able to do this so long as it sees itself as "the good." But not only the nations are called to conversion. The church, too, must change — and change radically. The churches will not have the saving power to lead the nations of this world to face their hands-on involvement in the terrorism that is rampant throughout the world unless they come to follow the Prince of non-violence.

Christianity has for a long time transformed Jesus into a teacher of the just war (and virtually every war was somehow deemed justifiable). The starkness of September 11 has ushered in a new era. For the churches that will mean paying the exceedingly high price of recognizing Jesus for what he surely was: a pacifist who went the extra mile with those who had enslaved him.

Waging a "just war" September 25, 2002

From the time of Christ until the overwhelming influence of St. Augustine at the end of the fourth century, virtually all Christians were pacifists. It was an uncontested tenet of their faith life: while the terms were not clearly defined, they believed that Jesus was fundamentally a pacifist and that they should live accordingly.

Indeed, it is difficult to imagine that the itinerant Preacher who called upon his disciples to offer the "other cheek" would find some way to justify the carpet bombing of hapless people. Even as he faced an imminent violent demise, the Lord chastised Peter for drawing his sword, reminding the leader of the apostles that "those who live by the sword die by the sword" (Mt 26:52).

St. Augustine, however, found the early church's imitation of Jesus's personal conduct too simplistic. He believed in the sacramental principle that the city of God had become an integral part of the earthly city, that Christians were called to be active, responsible citizens in the world.

To achieve this, Augustine believed, Christians should be ready to serve in the emperor's army, even if it meant going to war.

This was no minor paradigm shift for the Christian community who had all their lives — and not without social cost — thought that war was wrong. Augustine countered this thinking by proposing the concept of a "just war." Few Christians would have followed him had he not made war very difficult to justify.

Augustine would no doubt be horrified to see what has happened to his just war theory. He was convinced that if Christians assumed a responsible place in the political arena, the world as he knew it — safeguarded by his just war theory — would become a place where true peace reigned.

Anything but that happened. Among the classical religions of the world, Christianity became the most bellicose of all. The history of the Christian world is one long story of war. There simply are no extended periods of peace in Christian history. Today we tend to equate the Muslim faith with a holy *jihad*, the urge to make the world an Islamic state through warfare. Even a cursory look at history shows any honest student that Christianity has spawned many more wars than Islam ever has.

Perhaps most frightening of all in a study of Christian history: there are practically no examples of church leaders intervening, telling their governments that the current war does not meet Augustine's criteria.

Human life is never clear-cut. There is always some ambiguity — just enough, it seems, that church leaders cannot outright condemn any military action. But also, alas, just enough to justify a prayer or two and a generous outpouring of holy water. Perhaps, for Catholics anyway, the saddest moment for the just war theory came in 1936 when the pope went to Rome's port to bless Mussolini's flame-throwers, weapons to be used to subdue the primitively armed people of Ethiopia.

Augustine had outlined seven principles, all of which were to be present if a war were to be justified: just cause, comparative justice, legitimate authority, right intention, probability of success, proportionality, and last resort. Very few wars meet all these principles.

It is interesting that Augustine made just cause and right intention two separate principles. It seems that armies have always had difficulty in making the two mean the same thing. Governments can mouth just causes, but all too often these are not their true intentions or the reasons they actually go to war. One cannot imagine, for instance, that any of the world's powers would be concerned about Saddam Hussein were there no oil in Iraq.

Most pacifists today centre their concerns around comparative justice and proportionality. They believe modern weapons are so destructive of civilian life that nothing can justify war.

Rev. Andrew Greeley, in a *Prairie Messenger* column, questions this: "The weakness of pacifism is that, if all wars are evil, then one cannot make a particular case against a specific war." He gives the war against Hitler as an example of a just war.

The Second World War was a war of great powers fighting great powers, and all sides paid a heavy price. Ask that generation of Russian women; with the Russian army losing more than 10 million men, Mother Russia became a land of widows and spinsters.

Even those who had no problem justifying the Second World War have had to acknowledge some evil side effects. In the classical struggle between Churchill and Hitler, it was not Hitler who became more like Churchill but it was Churchill who became like his adversary. Churchill ordered the horrendous firebombing of the historic German city of Dresden, a non-military target, simply because it was the same size as Coventry, which Hitler had bombed earlier in the war.

It is interesting to note that in justifying the Gulf War a decade ago, the American government painted Saddam as a reincarnation of Hitler and spent $10 million selling its case to its own people. Central to its propaganda was the lie about Iraqis pulling Kuwaiti babies out of incubators. One must ask: if Saddam was so evil, why did the American government have to lie to its people?

To be sure, few people question Saddam's unsavouriness, but can that alone justify the Allied actions in the Gulf War?

The Allied forces, Canada included, rained 88,500 tons worth of bombs on Iraq, pulverizing it into a state of pre-industrial chaos. Back home we saw nightly on our TVs images of smart bombs hitting their targets. But in reality only 7 percent of the bombs dropped on Iraq were smart ones. These smart bombs hit their targets 90 percent of the time, the Pentagon claims.

Dropped from far greater heights than were the bombs in the Second World War, the dumb bombs — a mere 81,980 tons worth (laced as they were with depleted uranium) — had according to official estimates a 25 percent accuracy rate.

When one remembers that most of the bombing was directed at Iraqi city targets, one begins to get a hint of the destruction wrought on the Iraqi people. During the Gulf War the Allied forces lost fewer than 40 men, the majority of them by "friendly fire," while the Iraqis suffered an estimated 100,000 non-combatant casualties.

Augustine along with many others would have a hard time even calling that a war — just or unjust. It should more aptly be called a massacre.

Yet, when we went to "war" a decade ago, we could at least talk about Saddam having a huge modern army. It took no spies to determine what he had — 95 percent of Iraq's arsenal had been provided by the five permanent members of the UN Security Council. (Apparently Saddam only became a Hitler late in his career — after he refused, perhaps, to privatize the oil patch?)

Today Iraq lies in ruins; American and British bombers continue to bomb reconstruction projects, under the pretext that they are preventing Saddam's rearming of the country.

It is to this land, already vanquished in war, that President George W. Bush wishes to extend his "war against terrorism." If the Gulf War, the war in Serbia, and the recent war in Afghanistan are any indication of what the president means by "war," pilots will once more unleash carpet-bombing on a defenceless people.

The objection of the institutional church was long in coming — the pope was a lonely voice throughout the Gulf War — but this time the American bishops have spoken out: "It is difficult," they said, "to justify extending the war on terrorism to Iraq, absent clear and adequate evidence of Iraqi involvement in the attacks of September 11."

The just war theory has been a disaster throughout the centuries since Augustine; it has not enabled Christians to deal morally with war. But if the example of Christ is too much for us to accept, let us at least rejoice that church leaders throughout the Christian community are doing today what precious few ever did in the past: declaring a particular war in the planning patently unjust.

Nuclear weapons
June 5, 2002

We panic at the thought of India and Pakistan, both nuclear powers, going to war, even though both have said they will not be the first to use nuclear weapons.

But still we panic. And rightly so. Ask Belgium what international safeguards mean. In both the First and Second World Wars the "law of war" superseded all civilized international law.

It is not because we do not trust the Indians and Pakistanis as civilized peoples that we fear their using nuclear weapons. Rather we know that in war people do things they would never contemplate in peacetime.

That is not to say that there is not at least a trace of racism at work here. Why did the world not panic when President Bush announced that the United States is contemplating a defence policy that includes both the nuclearization of outer space and the possibility of using nuclear weapons on a first-strike basis?

Is the United States more trustworthy than India or Pakistan? Its history of aggression would indicate otherwise. This does not imply that the American people are warmongers. As a people they are anything but. Yet if you had asked the American people in 1940 if they would drop the equivalent of nuclear bombs on the hapless citizens of Hiroshima or Nagasaki, they would have shuddered at the thought.

No people should trust themselves with nuclear weapons. While the peoples of the world rejoice that the United States and Russia are talking about a two-thirds reduction of their nuclear arsenals, it is important for this to be put into its proper context.

Most of the weapons slated for elimination are outdated and would never be used in a nuclear war. Both nations have enough modern weapons to totally obliterate the other — and the rest of us on this planet as well — without having to resort to the weapons now on the negotiating table.

And how much safer will the world be if the United States, while eliminating older nuclear weapons, is developing newer ones to constantly orbit the earth in outer space?

Nothing can justify the creation or the contemplated use of nuclear weapons. May the conflict between India and Pakistan solidify, in the minds and hearts of all the peoples of the world, the humble conviction that no people should ever trust themselves — let alone anyone else — with nuclear weapons.

Depleted uranium weapons   January 17, 2001

Officially, as far as NATO is concerned, the problem does not exist. Handling depleted uranium weapons does not jeopardize the lives of soldiers.

Yet the BBC stands by its recent news report that seven Italians, five Belgians, two Dutch nationals, two Spaniards, one Portuguese, and one Czech national have already died from cancer after serving in the Balkans. Five French soldiers have advanced cases of leukemia.

None of this is officially acknowledged. But denying it has become ever more difficult because of reports coming out of Bosnia and, more recently, out of Kosovo. In Hadzici, Bosnia, which suffered heavy bombardment by DU shells, more than 400 civilians have died. The town has begun to panic; more than 10 percent of the people have fled Hadzici.

The armies of the world still have not faced the Gulf War Syndrome. They have not had to face the role DU weapons played in it, since the world community does not seem very interested in hearing of the tens of thousands of Iraqis who are dying in the regions that experienced heavy DU bombardment.

Ten years have passed since the Gulf War, and we are still not ready to face the wanton destruction we inflicted on that nation, an ongoing destruction because of DU weaponry. Let us hope that the serious health problems of NATO soldiers can do what the deaths of countless Iraqis could not do — lead the world community to ban all DU weapons.

Protesting in the streets   April 18, 2001

An ugly concrete and steel fence surrounded much of beautiful old historic Quebec City during the free trade Summit of the Americas. These days that gives a mixed message. On the one hand, the city remains the cultural birth centre of the nation with a wonderful mix of the old Europe and the new America. Clearly, something precious was here that both the French and the English wanted.

Yes, there was something honest about the guns on the Plains of Abraham. That classic battle was definitely about big business and government. Both the English and the French governments saw profit signs before they worried about les habitants and Native peoples.

Today, however, all subtlety is lost. The concrete and steel fence tells it all. The ordinary citizen's voice is not wanted as big business and government work out a new marriage relationship.

We are reminded again and again that the protesters represent no one but themselves. Money, it seems, has given legitimacy to big business; governments claim to represent the people through national elections.

And so, the powers that be tell us that controlling (stifling) the protesters is a matter of basic principle. Indeed, it is a matter of democracy.

Pope John Paul II has spoken out repeatedly about democracy. But he has a very different definition of what it entails than the one we are given today in the media. The concrete and steel fence denies everything the pope says about democracy. According to the pope, democracy is about having a say in the matters that affect one's life. To have the right periodically to choose between different political parties, all of them closer to big business than to the concerns of little people, is no guarantee of democracy.

Of course it is nigh on impossible to so structure society that true democracy is guaranteed — even if the powers that be were interested enough to at least half-heartedly try to achieve it! And so we need safeguards; yes, we absolutely need safeguards.

One of history's clearest safeguards is people protesting on the streets. In recent times, we have seen the importance of street demonstrations. East Germany tumbled the day the youth paraded through the streets shouting, "Gorby! Gorby!" The old guard with all the power and legitimacy of government could not withstand the "student punks" it utterly detested.

Slobodan Milosevic was head of a powerful army, but he could not resist the unarmed people in the street. According to our western news sources, these people are to be praised. They are presented as heroes of democracy.

But let us remember the days of the Vietnam War. This was no ordinary war; it was part of the great Cold War.

Throughout most of human history armies were mustered only in time of war. War is an expensive proposition, and taxpayers are never eager to pay for large standing armies. That's what made the Cold War so brilliant. It enabled the military to maintain huge armies with unparalleled, ongoing massive budgets. America still claimed to be a democracy but at the same time had a military establishment solidly in place.

Ask any American general from the '60s and he will admit that the military leaders felt fully in control. If they didn't like a government in Brazil, they overthrew it. If Chile wasn't to their liking, they shot the democratically elected president and replaced him with a thug, General Augusto Pinochet.

Who would have thought that students in the streets would challenge this military establishment? We know the results — even if we still do not accord these protesters the same respect we have given to East German and Yugoslav demonstrators.

It is interesting to note that the demonstrators on the streets of Quebec City today insist that they are concerned about democracy. They see the concrete and steel fence as anything but a safeguard for democracy.

They see the summit — quite accurately, we believe — as a sellout to international business conglomerates. Free trade, according to their understanding, is freedom for the world of commerce without any national government control.

We see the great dilemma we find ourselves in as soon as "market forces" are freed from any moral shackles. Percy Schmeiser, a Saskatchewan farmer, has experienced the consequences of governments giving away ongoing rights over seed to companies such as Monsanto.

We see what happens when huge companies control the life-and-death medicines needed by poor African AIDS victims. Soon they will also control vaccines which, we believe, must not be owned by anyone.

We see the results in Ecuador, a country decimated by the adoption of the American currency. No poor Ecuadoran would ever see the adoption of the American dollar as a free democratic act.

It might be a lot messier, but Canada's democracy absolutely needs the people out on the streets of Quebec City. We need to take these demonstrators every bit as seriously as we took the people in East Germany and Yugoslavia.

We must ask ourselves why we "need" that concrete and steel fence. That fence speaks eloquently about government's failure to listen to anyone other than those with huge vested interests.

Yes, our democracy is at stake.

Morality of the marketplace

August 28, 2002

In 1991, to mark the 100th anniversary of Pope Leo XIII's epoch-creating social encyclical *Rerum novarum* (Of new things), Pope John Paul II issued his third social encyclical *Centesimus annus* (The hundredth year).

Excitement filled the air in the days preceding its release. The Berlin Wall had recently fallen, and the pope was expected to use the occasion to celebrate the victory of the capitalist system over the immoral principles of atheistic communism.

The pope, however, had been closely watching the events unfolding in his own homeland. The capitalism coming to birth there had few, if any, of the humanizing niceties of capitalism as the West had known it in the glory years of the mid-20th century. It was obvious to the pope that western capitalists were eager to turn eastern Europe into another Third World colony.

Rather than praise the capitalist system for its superiority, the pope warned western nations not to see the collapse of communism "as a one-sided victory of their own economic system, and thereby fail to make the necessary corrections in that system."

Instead of glorifying the amoral forces of the marketplace, he placed the human person at the centre of all economic activity. The pope spoke of a "human ecology" that must mark all economic dealings.

In this regard, it is interesting to note what the pope thought of his own teaching. He said it was wrong to see the social teaching of the church as a mere extension of church doctrine. It is to have a central place, he noted, "it is genuine doctrine ... an essential part of the Christian message."

The pope could not have been more incisive than when he called for a "human ecology" at the heart of all economic activity. It is a myth to speak about amoral forces objectively running the marketplace. We know from the Enrons, the WorldComs, and the Arthur Andersens that something else is at work and it is anything but a superior amoral force above and beyond the foibles of human hearts. It is greed with an all-too-human face.

One generation ago, CEOs made "only" 40 times as much as the average worker in the company. Now they make 500 times as much and that should alert us to the fact that something is fundamentally wrong.

But before we make too many righteous judgments concerning the morality of the current system's CEOs, let us look again at how we play the stock market. We, too, act as if the central actions of the marketplace were amoral. We buy and sell without regard for the workers of the companies concerned. We believe we can operate freely with our money, buying and selling company stocks as if there were no moral ramifications.

An alternative to capitalism   June 21, 2000

At least in theory, if not in practice, socialism provided a counterbalance to unrestrained capitalism before the fall of the Iron Curtain. Since that event, seen as a victory for the western way of doing business, capitalism has reigned more and more supreme.

At an ecumenical meeting in Hofgeismar, Germany, which studied the worldwide effects of global capitalism, Rev. Philip Potter, a former general secretary of the World Council of Churches, told the churches they must find a way to challenge the "unjust structures" which are literally impoverishing more than a billion people.

"Since economic life has been taken away from the state, whose leaders are answerable to public opinion," Potter noted, "it is harder to challenge today's injustices."

The Hofgeismar meeting stated unequivocally where laissez-faire capitalism is going. "Globalization," it declared in its final communiqué, "is ruthlessly pushing the world into a unipolar, barrierless global society in which financial capital and international debt are devastating nations and becoming destructive of the material basis for human life.

"We resist the assumption," the statement continued, "that the world economic system should be primarily orientated toward the accumulation of wealth for the benefit of a small minority, rather than toward the satisfaction of basic needs of all human beings and the nurturing of God's creation.

"We resist the idolatry of capital and the new religion of consumerism, which defines the purpose of life in terms of material possessions."

Just as the pope has done consistently since he noticed with alarm what the world economic community was doing to his Polish homeland after the fall of the Berlin Wall, the Hofgeismar meeting called for a new modus vivendi: "We resist the assumption that fair competition is possible in a world dominated by Mammon, where transnational realities transcend national regulatory mechanisms and the powerful impose the rules of the economic game, with the unavoidable result that the rich become richer and the poor become poorer."

Of course, an alternative to the current system built unabashedly on greed will not happen overnight. We must begin somewhere, and where better than by challenging the worst aspects of the system.

As could be seen from the recent "Asian crisis" that eventually harmed even the world's second strongest national economy — that of Japan — something must be done immediately to put some controls on the $1.65 trillion (US) which freely flutters daily from stock market to stock market looking to make a profit, often by undermining national economies.

Already back in 1978 Nobel Prize-winning economist James Tobin suggested a tax of one-quarter of 1 percent on all stock market transactions. To date, only two countries, Finland and Belgium, have endorsed the Tobin Tax on financial transactions.

The tax — one-quarter of 1 percent! — is surely very low, but given the $1.65 trillion in liquid cash flowing each day from computer to computer, it would produce over $400 billion a year.

That alone would pay off all the debts of the 50 poorest nations while leaving significant sums to ensure all peoples clean water and the basics in education.

More than a year ago the Canadian Parliament passed a private member's bill calling for the implementation of the Tobin Tax. So far our government has done nothing to give substance to this far-seeing measure.

The Tobin Tax is a good first step. It not only provides a substantial amount of capital to help the victims of the current system; it also pricks the conscience of those who play the stock market. It concretely reminds them that some responsibility should always accompany the accumulation of wealth.

Without this acknowledgment of responsibility, according to Julio de Santa Ana, a leading ecumenical theologian, we are heading for "a major crisis." We must not, he says, allow the current process of the capitalist economy, which aims at subordinating all other interests, to dominate, since "it aims at freedom, but imposes oppression; it aims at happiness, but creates pain and suffering; it says it affirms life, but it brings death."

Chapter 10

Heroes of Faith

Pope John XXIII (1881-1963)   June 6, 2001

The Romans never take their religion too seriously. But they are proud to belong to Rome, the primatial See of the Catholic Church and are ready to take family visitors to see St. Peter's Basilica.

To North American eyes these visits resemble a family picnic more than a pilgrimage to a holy place. They talk, they laugh, they visit. When they fill St. Peter's Square it is a festival. How else, they ask, should one celebrate one's faith?

Things were different this Pentecost Sunday. Thirty-eight years after his death, Pope John XXIII was solemnly carried through the square to his new resting place on the main floor of the basilica. A few people started to clap, but they soon noticed that this was not considered the appropriate response.

The people of Rome stood silent as their favourite pope, perhaps of all time, passed by. The stillness, the reverential awe of the occasion was broken only by the Romans silently crossing themselves.

It seemed right to them to stand in respectful silence, privately making a personal act of faith. In a way they were welcoming John home, to a place of prominence in the largest church in Christendom.

For years they had carried flowers down to the crypt under St. Peter's, only to have them immediately removed by one especially hired for that purpose. But the curial move to prevent a "cult around John XXIII" from developing was doomed to failure.

The Romans also saw through the smokescreen of beatifying their hero together with the pope (Pius IX) they had come to hate with a common passion. It was as if Pius IX was not part of the ceremony; it was John, and only John, they wanted to see honoured in a special place in St. Peter's.

John had imaged a church they could identify with and love.

Good Pope John followed one of the most respected popes in the long history of that office. Pius XII stood perfectly erect, with not an ounce of fat on his ascetic body. Pius ate all his meals alone, in silence. According to the books on classical ascetic theology, Pius XII was the saint — and the Curia was anxious to raise him to its altars. But not the people of Rome.

While many throughout the church were shocked to hear that John lasted but four days in eating alone in silence, the Romans understood why John needed a bottle of wine and friends at his table.

While North Americans had bought into the image of holiness Pius so painstakingly manifested, and thus were a wee bit scandalized at the fat and jolly pope who succeeded him, the Romans celebrated their new pope. They now had a bishop whose very humanity celebrated life — and faith.

The Romans understood perfectly well that strange passage in Luke's Gospel: "They are like children in the marketplace chanting, 'We played pipes for you and you wouldn't dance; we sang dirges and you wouldn't cry.' For John the Baptist comes, not eating, not drinking wine and you say, 'He is possessed.' The Son of Man comes, eating and drinking and you say, 'Look, a glutton and a drunkard, a friend of tax collectors and sinners'" (Lk 7:32-34).

Ironically, much of the church community had over two millennia come to see John the Baptist as the higher image of holiness. And in the process had so recreated the image of Jesus that any accusation of gluttony or drunkenness made no sense at all.

While we do not know much about the personal life of Jesus, this passage from Luke makes it clear that Jesus liked a fine meal — with a goodly supply of wine. It is not an accident of history that Jesus was often invited to parties. He certainly was not a spoilsport or a wet blanket; people enjoyed his company.

While Pius XII reminded the Romans of John the Baptist — who could be admired from afar — John became the embodiment of a Christ who came to call people to the banquet of the kingdom. And they knew the Lord could not do that as a killjoy. Their Jesus, they were certain, knew how to party.

The people of Rome could not believe their good fortune in getting a pope who knew how to make his faith a down-to-earth celebration. While they too would have been scandalized if their pope had returned to the ways of the Renaissance popes, whose courts intentionally sought to outclass those of any mere earthly king, the Romans were tired of the super seriousness of a century-long parade of men who seemed afraid even of smiling too freely.

It's interesting to hear John speak about why he called the Second Vatican Council. He did not give any high philosophical or theological reason. He had no special agenda that he wanted to introduce in the church.

His reasoning was much more basic, much more human in the way the Romans had come to understand and appreciate it in their pope.

John told them he had called the council because he felt he was "in a sack." He was suffocating in the Vatican. In a thousand little ways, the Curia was asking him to eat alone, in silence, while they would, with years of professional expertise behind them, take care of the church.

His gut reaction told him that this was wrong. The pope should never be in a sack. His famous images of throwing open the windows to allow fresh air in and of giving the Spirit the freedom to blow where she will were not abstract concepts. For John, they were experiences of daily life — experiences that soon rang true to people everywhere. Not only to Catholics.

Before Pope John it was unheard of for a religious leader of any other branch of Christianity to grace the steps of the Vatican. The Archbishop of Canterbury, Arthur Michael Ramsey, was the first to come calling on Pope John.

His visit was ignored by the official Vatican newspaper, *L'Osservatore Romano*. When John complained about that, a one column-inch story on the back page noted that a certain Mr. Ramsey had come to visit the pope.

With the calling of the council, John made it clear that leaders of Christian communions were not only welcome at the council but were to be given prime seats. Many a Catholic bishop, seated almost out of sight of the proceedings of the council, was envious of their special placement. How did John steal the hearts of so many? Not through his theology — when he died people did not really know if he was a liberal or a conservative theologian.

He did it by living and breathing the optimism of a humanity at home with itself. Most of all, he did it by imaging a Christ happy to be born in the likeness of our flesh.

Yes, the Christ he knew was not the Christ of Christian polemics who had come to justify, indeed, to necessitate the divisions in the church community. The Christ Pope John knew transcended all our petty theological arguments; his Christ could, by celebrating the gifts of others, lead all of us to believe and hope in a kingdom made unmistakably visible in the changing of our waters of worry into the very best wine of the wedding feast.

John opened the windows to allow the freshness, the optimism of the Spirit to permeate the church. May no one ever be allowed to close them again. We do not have to fear that that will happen, as long as the Romans continue to come to St. Peter's to party with their "good Pope John."

Dorothy Day (1897-1980) September 4, 1983

Dorothy Day, the American Catholic activist and intellectual, was always a symbol that spoke loudly to friend and foe alike. Few ever questioned the authenticity of her symbolic life. Many did not like what they saw and heard, but they respected her integrity; but calling her a saint — well, that's another matter.

Dorothy Day herself made little of references to her sanctity; as she put it, "When they say you are a saint, what they mean is that you are not to be taken seriously."

That so few have thought Dorothy Day a fit candidate for canonization paradoxically makes her canonization all the more important. We need a new image of sainthood for this post-Vatican II era.

Historically canonization had precious little to do with affirmations of being in heaven. Canonization was concerned with mentioning individuals publicly in the Canon (eucharistic prayer), of placing them in the celebrations of our story, the saving passover of the Lord.

Readiness to celebrate the communion of saints is one of the great glories of Catholicism. Each age needs its icons of holiness, its courageous forerunners who challenge us to newness.

Dorothy Day all her life faced the issues that today confront the church — with unbelievable steadfastness, with good humour, and without bitterness or cynicism, the mortal sin of today.

The church today has lost much of the power it had in previous eras. Dorothy Day knew the strength of powerlessness.

The church today is struggling to find a new marriage of religion and politics. We need a union of the two that will work both in Poland and Nicaragua. Dorothy Day was political to the marrow of her bones, feeding daily at the table of the Lord.

The church today is struggling to lose a clericalism that aped the hierarchical notions of the world, and be first of all the "body of the faithful" as the new code of Canon law loves to view God's people. Dorothy Day was lay — as no one had been for hundreds of years — and she brought the church into the centre of today's world.

The church today is struggling to have a word of peace for a world living under the constant threat of nuclear self-destruction. Dorothy Day lived peace. Her message was always the same throughout her years; she had the same message for the Second World War as she had for Vietnam.

Can we choose less today and live? We need her strength, her vision, her life-image in our Canon of the Mass.

Karl Rahner April 15, 1984

The day was November 20, 1962 — the pivotal day of the Second Vatican Council.

The council fathers had been discussing for a week On the Sources of Revelation, a schema written by the Theological Commission under the presidency of Cardinal Alfredo Ottaviani, who at the time held the powerful post of prefect of the Holy Office of the Inquisition. It was obvious to everyone that a crisis was at hand.

Theologians like Jesuit Father Karl Rahner had spent most of their energy the first months of the council preparing bishops for this critical moment. Rahner urged bishops to reject totally the commission's draft text.

The vote came on November 20. Of the 2,209 fathers voting, 1,368 called for a rejection of the text. That was close to 62 percent of the assembly, but technically 67 percent was needed to reject it. It was announced that the next day discussion of the schema would continue.

But that night Pope John XXIII did what 62 percent could not do; he personally intervened and withdrew the text.

It would take another year of inside manoeuvring before Rahner would be asked to lead the work in drawing up a new schema. In April 1964, the text, which was almost totally Rahner's work, was given to the council fathers. The final Constitution on Divine Revelation differs little from Rahner's text.

Gone was the idea that revelation was essentially doctrine which Jesus proclaimed to his apostles and which in turn was handed down to the church by bishops, the successors of the apostles.

In place of this, revelation became the self-disclosure of God in a believing community. Building on the work of Dominican Father Yves Congar, Rahner saw tradition as embracing the full life of the worshipping community. Apostolic tradition is preserved — nay, is kept alive — in a community that "devoutly listens," that "celebrates all that she is, all that she believes."

This theological change underpins all the major reforms of Vatican II. The church today is still struggling with its ramifications. The church is in deep debt to Rahner; not only did he have the personal brilliance to work through the issues, he also had the ability to convince a great many quite ill-prepared bishops of the absolutely critical nature of that November vote.

These past weeks in the *Prairie Messenger*'s parish-based Lenten study, we have been working on the World Council of Churches document Baptism, Eucharist and Ministry (BEM). Leaders of various Christian communities in Canada have been presenting material for discussion. Much has centred on ministry in the churches. In this we have been experiencing some of the fruits of Rahner's labour. Now Catholics have a new way for evaluating the ministries of sister churches not in communion with them. Following the lead of the council document, On Divine Revelation, we are able to distinguish between the succession of churches in the apostolic tradition and the succession of a particular apostolic ministry, such as the office of bishops.

To a large extent Rahner's work has helped us go back to the patristic viewpoint which saw the church itself, God's people, rather than the hierarchy, as the primary bearer of God's saving Word. There is no longer a need for the mechanistic theory of apostolic succession as being bishop to bishop, as in a pipeline.

This was not all theory to Rahner. He believed in the little people in the church. He was as much at home writing simple works of spirituality as he was when challenging the world's leading theologians to re-examine their preconceptions.

Canonizing Romero (1917-80) March 26, 1990

It is not just the poor in El Salvador, who make up the vast majority of people in that country, who believe Archbishop Oscar Romero is a saint. Throughout Latin America he is venerated as the martyr who stood by those unjustly exploited by the rich and powerful of this world.

To a large extent it is irrelevant to them whether or not the official church canonizes him. He is already the patron saint of the millions and millions trapped in the slums which are largely the exploitative work of First World financial dealings.

Through most of our church history the declaration of sainthood was a rather informal local process. The people picked their heroes. Canonization was an acknowledgment by the church leaders that their example would be a useful one for all Christians to emulate.

There were problems with this discernment process taking place on the local level — especially with religious orders. When they smelled that a dollar could be made with the canonization of one of their own, little could stand in their way.

But there are problems, too, when the process is effectively removed from the local church and moved thousands of miles away to Rome. Schools of thought and the availability of money become the key issues in canonizations — not local needs, not even the virtues of the one being considered.

And so, founders of religious orders (which are willing to pay out large sums of money) are now the most likely candidates for canonization. Celibates have a 1,000 percent — and then some — better chance of canonization than a married person.

Romero is the giant figure in the Latin American Christian community. Nothing the official church does is going to change that. Not to canonize him says virtually nothing about the archbishop but volumes about the church. It speaks about a church not at home with Romero's love and concern for God's poor, about a church which in the crunch still believes it is best (safest) to nestle with the rich and never offend them — as the canonization of Oscar Romero surely would.

Who is a martyr? March 22, 2000

Our current pope, who suffered greatly at the hands of the communists who took over his country after the Second World War, had plenty of reasons to completely distrust the government leaders in Poland. While the communist government in Poland was never as virulently anti-religion as were the administrations in Ukraine and in the former Czechoslovakia, it was surely intolerant enough to radically colour the pope's thinking.

We should not be surprised; nor should we stand too smugly in judgment over John Paul's administration for being totally wary of all things communist but not nearly so concerned about right-wing administrations.

Yet it is painful to read Archbishop Oscar Romero's account of his visit to John Paul. He tells the pope how the Salvadoran government forces killed one of his priests, claiming he was a guerrilla. Romero says the pope was ready to believe the government, and instructed him to develop a better relationship with that government. Of course, the pope would never have given this advice to any bishop living in a communist country, but saw no difficulty in doing precisely this in Latin America.

So Romero stood alone, and the Salvadoran government knew it. He was there for the picking.

But was he a martyr? Can one be a martyr at the hands of Catholics?

It is interesting to note that this past week the Vatican gave notice to the communist government in China that it would be proclaiming 120 of that country's citizens as martyrs. Among that number are many who died in the Boxer Rebellion in 1900. The Chinese did not kill these missionaries for their religious convictions. Rather it was because of their close identification with the colonial forces which were forcing an open door policy on their country.

It seems one can die a martyr for political reasons if the political stance is correct (though it is hard to imagine how one can see anything positive in the open door policy forced upon China).

How is one to judge whether Romero is simply a political martyr or truly a martyr of the faith? Maybe there is a better way to ask the question: Who can with practical certitude judge the authenticity of Romero's faith?

Traditionally, the Curia alone makes the final decision. This, we believe, would not be wise in this case. One only has to look at the latest appointment to Romero's old See, the Archdiocese of San Salvador, to see why.

The Curia did not even appoint a Salvadoran to the post. It chose a Spanish nationalist, a member of Opus Dei, a man close to the very army responsible for murdering Romero. The little people in the country have plenty of reasons to believe that Archbishop Fernando Saenz Lacalle is trying to restore the church Romero eventually rejected.

Is Romero a martyr of the faith — even though it was Catholics who plotted his assassination? We must seek the answer from the poor, the crippled, the lame, and the blind. They will tell us if they experienced in Romero either the Lord and his reign of graciousness or simply a strong-willed political despot.

Of course, to listen to the answer of the peasants of El Salvador will have tremendous ramifications for the whole church of God. Martyrs have a way of doing that to the church.

Henri de Lubac (1896-1991) September 16, 1991

One of the giant figures of the Second Vatican Council, Jesuit theologian Henri de Lubac, died recently. Since the council he has been praised by Catholics of virtually every theological stripe. So much so that it is difficult to remember that it was not always so. For the 15 years preceding the council he was forbidden to teach or publish anything dealing directly with Christian thought.

De Lubac ran into trouble with his views on the close inner relationship between the natural and the supernatural. His thinking was far closer to that of St. Thomas Aquinas than to that of the Roman curial theologians. Historians of theology justly wonder if it really was de Lubac's work, *The Supernatural*, that led to his temporary disciplining. A good case can be made that de Lubac's real mistake was coming to the support of his Jesuit colleague Teilhard de Chardin.

In any case, it was decreed that de Lubac's theology was incompatible with the church's teaching on original sin, and he was given no alternative than to study non-Christian religions if he was to stay in his field, theology.

But as the event that was the Second Vatican Council got out of the control of the Roman Curia, what was heresy suddenly became basic to the fast-emerging vision of the church. The fundamental optimism, the solid appreciation of nature, that de Lubac struggled so hard for came to underpin the critical theological documents of the council. One of the key persons the bishops of the world turned to was de Lubac, after Pope John XXIII called on them not to listen to the prophets of doom.

De Lubac's treatment by the highest-placed leaders in our church should have sensitized us to the pitfalls of blanket condemnations of theologians. Today, however, we are not just condemning individual theologians; it has become fashionable to make sweeping broadsides against theologians in general.

It has even become accepted theology to declare that theologians are not part of the magisterium or teaching authority, that that belongs exclusively to the bishops. Even Cardinal Alfredo Ottaviani, whose staunch defence of pre-council orthodoxy got de Lubac into so much trouble, never went that far.

When de Lubac was later offered a cardinal's red hat, he told the pope he would accept it only if he did not have to be ordained a bishop. He would have nothing to do with the current emasculation of the episcopal office whereby curial bureaucrats are called to this level of ministry and are given fictitious sees that have long ago gone out of existence — and then these "peopleless" bishops are declared part of the magisterium.

Faithfulness to Christ cannot be achieved by decrees from above. Faithfulness is a struggle engaged in by the whole church. There will be mistakes, but a careful discernment of the people's sense of the faith by the bishops of the various dioceses will keep the church from making fundamental errors.

That cannot be guaranteed by clamping down on theologians, as was so clearly shown in the Curia's treatment of de Lubac, among many others.

Let us be faithful to the powerful witness de Lubac gave the church by not repeating the same errors of method today.

Christiane Brusselmans (1930-91)   Nov. 18, 1991

The first schema (discussion papers) of the Second Vatican Council spoke almost exclusively of revelation as doctrine, as a body of truths held by the church. During the council the emphasis shifted sharply and the final documents spoke in much more personal terms.

They spoke of a God revealing himself in a trusting, believing, and prayerful community.

It was one thing for the bishops in council to proclaim a new direction for the church; it was quite another to embody this new emphasis in the life and liturgy of the church.

The laywoman Christiane Brusselmans, at home with both the ancient church and the modern church, played a key role in creatively bridging the theories of the council with the ordinary Christian in the pew.

Largely through her vision the church revived the catechumenate for adults seeking baptism and spoke once more of an "order" for bringing them into the church, the Rite of the Christian Initiation of Adults. In pre-council days the term "orders" was used exclusively of the priestly ministry.

Brusselmans also worked hard to apply these new processes to children. Her creativity once again shone forth, and her influence on the initiation of children to the various sacraments will likely endure for many years to come.

Life was never easy for Brusselmans; she often struggled with long periods of deep depression. Her driving creativity was often a desperate effort to rise above her own personal problems.

She did not win her last struggle; last month at the age of 60 she took her own life.

This tragedy fills many in the church with dismay — and rudely reminds all of us that life is always a mystery. We celebrate her greatness, and marvel how much she was able to do in spite of — or, maybe, because of — her personal handicap.

She has powerfully taught the church to celebrate its risen Lord; we have no doubt that this same Lord, in his own mysterious manner, will find marvellous ways of thanking this great servant of the People of God.

Dom Bede Griffiths (1906-93) May 24, 1993

Few people this century match the stature of the late Bede Griffiths. Though he progressively moved further and further away from the centres of power and influence, he actually moved ever nearer the heart of a new beginning for the human family. Only in the years to come will we realize just how indebted we all are to this prophet.

Griffiths was brilliant as a student at Oxford. His education was classical in the finest tradition, yet the more he learned, the more he was left unsatisfied.

St. Bede's *History of the English People* continued to intrigue him and played an important role in drawing him to the Catholic Church and, shortly after his entrance into the church, to the Benedictines at Prinknash.

Griffiths thought he had found his home with them. He tried desperately to settle down. So long a traveller, he wanted to be at home.

Years later in India he writes of that time at Prinknash. "I had begun to compromise with western science and industrialism and to imagine that they could be used 'in the service of God.' But I now think this is an illusion. The present state of the world is not due to some defect in the use of science and technology which can be corrected. Western science and technology are based on a false philosophy which has undermined the whole of western civilization.

"The only hope lies in a deliberate break with the whole system. This will come only when the western world has undergone a radical change of consciousness — a change which will probably be accompanied by a breakdown of the present system — and has recovered the wisdom of the ancient world, the world not only of Christian Europe but of India and China and Islam."

Long before the Second Vatican Council declared that Catholics had much to learn from other religions, Griffiths had begun to look to the East for some critical correctives of western Christianity. In 1955 he went to India and in time set up a Christian ashram.

Griffiths was always the Christian and, though he donned the clothing of the Hindu ascetic and ran *Saccidananda Ashram* more in the manner of a Hindu contemplative centre than as a Benedictine monastery, the daily Eucharist remained central to his spirituality.

But he was not hesitant to criticize his church. He was convinced that as long as the church in the West was dominated by the ways of the West it would never fulfill its destiny to be the sacrament of harmony and love for the whole of humanity — as stated in the opening paragraph of the council's Constitution on the Church.

Western society, Griffiths believed, was at an impasse, a dead end brought about by rationalism, legalism, ritualism, and faith in power structures.

It was these worldly features and not a faithfulness to its Christian origins, Griffiths held, that led the church to absolutize its dogma and structures.

Griffiths was not popular in many circles when he insisted again and again that, "though the Absolute can be found making itself known and communicating itself in a religion, the religion itself can never be absolute in the sense of being free from historical and cultural conditions."

The western world (and Griffiths included in that the former Soviet Union) and the church, too, had become too aggressive, male dominated, exploitive, and feverishly active. Griffiths called for a marriage of East and West.

Not many at the Vatican were happy to hear this monk sitting beside a sacred Hindu river declare that the Roman church, if it is to be true to its calling to catholicity, would have to discover once again how to be attuned to the intuitive, the mystical, and, yes, the feminine in its soul.

Griffiths could see no ready vehicle to help the church go beyond its static and rigid notions of structures, formulas, doctrines, and ideologies other than the religious literature of the East.

Griffiths was no pessimist. Though western civilization, through its marriage to industrialism, "has set itself on a course which is leading to disaster ... a new hope has dawned," he said in a 1980 introduction to his autobiography.

This new movement, he believed, "extends throughout the world among people of all religions and of no religion. It is a movement toward a science and technology which will cease to exploit nature and will learn to live in harmony with nature.

"It is a movement toward a unified vision of life, in which the whole human family and nature are seen to be part of a cosmic order — what in India was called *rita* and in ancient China *tao*."

Griffiths believed in a golden string holding him and all of creation in order. We would do well to treasure the words Griffiths used to end his autobiography (*The Golden String*). In typical fashion he quotes from another. He closes his story with the advice of a monk in Dostoevsky's *The Brothers Karamazov:* "Have no fear of another's sin. Love the person even in his sin, for that is the semblance of divine love, and is the highest love on earth. Love all God's creation, the whole and every grain of sand in it.

"Love every leaf and every ray of God's light. Love the animals, love the plants, love everything.

"If you love everything you will perceive the divine mystery in things. Once you perceive it, you will begin to comprehend it better every day. And you will come at last to love the whole world with an all-embracing love."

It is not easy to hear a great mystic criticize our world and our church so fundamentally. He did it, not out of bitterness or anger, but out of that love proclaimed by the Russian monk.

In his last book, *The River of Compassion*, Griffiths wrote: "The more we are integrated with our inner centre, the more we are open to others and to the whole of creation ... one with creation, with humanity and with God. To become aware of this essential oneness in the whole creation and in every being, that is the goal.

"The real world isn't illusory, but thinking it is final is illusory; the true *sannyasii* in attaining pure love through pure abandonment, is then available for everyone and everything."

Throughout his life Griffiths hung onto that golden string. His life attests to the truth he proclaimed. And so, we can live without fear. Though a particular view of society and of church may be dying about us, we should not be afraid to go to the centre of our being and feast on the absolute.

In Proverbs we read: "Where there is no prophetic vision, the people are abandoned" (29:18). Though our civilization may be crumbling, we do not feel abandoned. We have been given a prophet.

Griffiths, alone beside an Indian river, has given us the strength to believe in a new world in which people count more than anything else, a new church aglow with catholicity, a new heart open to East and West, North and South, a new spirit capable of transcending to God.

Cardinal Yves Congar (1904-95) July 13, 1995

With the passing of Yves Congar an era comes to an end in the Roman Catholic Church. He was a giant at the Second Vatican Council, one of the pivotal theologians who both laid the foundation for the council and took a leading role in formulating the final documents promulgated by the bishops.

Congar often claimed that he did not say anything new; with just a touch of irony he prided himself on being "a prophet of tradition." How can I be called "progressive" he would ask, since "I am completely in favour of tradition"?

Though he grounded all his theology in the great pastoral bishops of the patristic era, and went to great pains to show that his thinking was consistent with the medieval theologians favoured by the Roman Curia, he still managed to raise the ire of the Vatican. One member of the Holy Office of the Inquisition even bragged that he could find three heresies on every page Congar wrote.

During his personal prayer on the eve of his ordination in 1930, Congar felt a call to work for the reunification of Christians. In his first major work, *The Disunity of Christians: Principles for Catholic Ecumenism*, published in 1937, Congar single-handedly opened the church to a new era. But he paid a heavy price for this watershed work. He drew the attention of the Roman authorities and they were not ready for what they saw.

Only one thing saved him from sharing in the fate of his confrère, the

French Dominican theologian Marie Dominique Chenu. He had been conscripted into the French army at the beginning of the Second World War, was almost immediately captured by the Germans, and was held as a prisoner of war for more than five years. The Vatican did not want to add to his already abysmal state.

Neither embittered nor daunted by the treatment his writings were given in Rome, Congar further developed his work on ecumenism. Though much of what he wrote in *True and False Reform in the Church* (1950) would in time become central to the council's teaching, he soon felt the full impact of an encyclical of Pope Pius XII, *Humani generis* (Of the human race). In a very thinly veiled condemnation, Pius called the Dominican's work an example of "false irenicism," advocating peace and conciliation over fidelity to the truth.

This criticism forced Congar to deal with what he considered the central issue concerning the church's task in the world. It was not the hierarchy which would ultimately bring the church into the secular life of the world, he argued. It is the laity who, in Christ, will save the world.

In the seminal work preceding the council, *Lay People in the Church* (1953), Congar argued that through baptism each Christian shares effectively in the threefold Office of Christ. For those wont to see this threefold function as the work of the hierarchy, Congar coined a new word; he called their view of the church "hierarchology."

That kind of reversing the tables was certainly not appreciated and in 1954 Congar was put under strict church censure. There he remained until a new pope, John XXIII, personally contacted him and asked him to help him prepare for the council he had called.

And as the cliché goes, the rest is history.

Maybe it was because Congar was so closely involved with the council that he never viewed it as the great watershed most people see it to be. He believed that the church must continue to grow and develop. To his mind, for the church to stand still and wallow in the rich theology of the council spelled death just as assuredly as getting stuck, for instance, in the theology of Pope Pius IX's *Syllabus of Errors*, which condemned the modern world in virtually everything it did.

So till old age completely incapacitated him, Congar kept working. And, as always, he touched on what he thought were the key issues of the day: episcopal collegiality, authority as service, liberation theology, the charismatic movement, the role of the Holy Spirit as the guide of the church community, to name just a few.

He also worked to set up a forum in which theologians could take risks. With other leading theologians from the council, such as Jesuit Father Karl Rahner and Cardinal Joseph Ratzinger, he founded the scholarly journal *Concilium*.

Congar accepted a red hat from the pope a little more than a year ago — on one condition: that the honour would not be tied to his being ordained a bishop. Congar told the pope his calling was to be a theologian, not a hierarch, in the church.

Congar lived many painful years of mistrust between the hierarchy and the church's leading theologians. Congar never looked for the red hat; the honour he wanted was for theologians to be given their rightful role in the church. He died fearful that once again this key function in a healthy church was in jeopardy.

Joseph L. Bernardin (1928-96) January 8, 1995

Cardinal Joseph L. Bernardin has been a leader in the American church for many years. He oversees Chicago, one of its key dioceses, has led the U.S. bishops' conference as its president, and has chaired the writing of one of the most important pastorals issued by the American bishops, their 1983 letter on war and nuclear defence: The Challenge of Peace.

But here, in giving the reasons why we chose him for *Prairie Messenger* churchperson for 1995, we limit ourselves to events of this past year.

The year began with a dramatic reconciliation. Steven J. Cook, a young man dying of AIDS, had levelled a $10-million lawsuit against the cardinal accusing him of sexual abuse in the mid-1970s when Bernardin was Archbishop of Cincinnati.

Cook had been receiving counselling from an unlicensed psychologist who had used hypnosis to help him remember his past.

Bernardin denied all charges. He was, to use his own words, "publicly humiliated before the world." But he did more than fight the charges through the normal legal channels; he wrote the young man, telling him that he "harboured no ill feelings toward him" and that he would like to see him. For reasons still unknown, Cook never got that letter.

The cardinal did not know Cook's address or telephone number, so he tried other means to make contact. He found a priest in Cincinnati who knew Cook's mother, and on December 30, 1994, the cardinal and

Cook met, each bringing along a friend to the meeting.

Cook told the cardinal he was far from certain that he should trust "the memory" he had been given under hypnosis. He said that "a big burden had been lifted," that he felt healed now and was at peace. He also asked the cardinal to tell the story of his reconciliation with the church and with him.

Bernardin could have left it there; his name was cleared. But he stayed with Cook, promising "to walk with him in the weeks and months ahead."

And he kept his promise. Cook died during this past year — knowing he had a close friend in the cardinal.

Bernardin looks back on his first meeting with Cook as a high point in his life. "I have never, in 43 years as a priest, witnessed a more profound reconciliation," he said. "The words I am using cannot begin to describe the power of God's grace which was at work that afternoon. It was a manifestation of God's love, forgiveness and healing which I will never forget."

Bernardin sees the event as a blessing in his life, but close friends wonder whether the stress did not play a role in his being stricken with cancer later in the year. The case had hung over his head for more than two years before being so wonderfully resolved.

In June Bernardin was in hospital with cancer at the head of his pancreas, in his bile duct, and on his right kidney. He underwent radical surgery and began both radiation and chemotherapy treatments. His type of cancer was one of the most serious — the survival rate only 25 percent after five years.

In typical Bernardin fashion, the cardinal declared: "It is a wonderful thing in my life. I consider it a great blessing."

It has given him, he claims, a whole new mission. He doesn't work 16-hour days in the office anymore. He tries to limit it to three or four. But the time gained is put to other things. Each day he writes notes and calls and visits other people with cancer. He jokingly tells his friends that he has become "the unofficial chaplain for all cancer patients in Cook and Lake counties," the two counties of the Chicago Archdiocese.

Doctors have told him he could come in through a private entrance to receive his own cancer treatments, but he insists on coming in the same door every other patient must — even though it now takes him between 20 and 40 minutes to walk past the people in the waiting room. "I am a priest first and a patient second," he says, "so I am happy to see these people.

"I have found that since the cancer experience," he adds, "I'm much better able to counsel and help other people. I guess I have a certain credibility."

One of the great affirmations of the cardinal and his work in the church came March 30 with the pope's publication of his encyclical, The Gospel of Life.

Bernardin acknowledged that he had "a uniquely personal interest in this encyclical. For more than 11 years I have developed what I have called a 'consistent ethic of life,' a theological basis for linking all life issues, however diverse they may be, from conception to natural death."

Indeed the framework of the encyclical follows closely Bernardin's thought. The cardinal rejoiced to see that the pope clearly noted that to protect life the struggle must have a context, a broad context, one in which the church can "consider the violence against life done to millions of human beings, especially children, by poverty, hunger, unjust distribution of resources, discrimination, war, the arms trade, environmental harm, drugs — and a vast array of other evils."

Bernardin has long realized that the struggle against abortion will always have a political dimension. And he has continued to insist — often contrary to other highly placed church leaders — that the social teachings of the church, and not right-wing, economically conservative thought, should provide this political framework. The pope in his latest encyclical clearly favoured Bernardin's viewpoint.

Not long before he entered hospital, the cardinal spoke to the U.S. National Federation of Priests' Councils on the meaning of priesthood. He told them there were two essential dimensions to their lives as priests: "to be bearers of the mystery of God and to be doctors of souls."

"The priest," he said, "is not primarily someone who works, preaches, ministers, counsels. Rather, he is someone who, at the core of his being, has been set on fire by God and who invites others to catch the flame."

This, Bernardin has been for us. And at a time when many despair of the church as institution, the cardinal has shown us how beautiful its human face can be.

We are proud to proclaim Cardinal Joseph L. Bernardin our churchperson for 1995. We beg all our readers to pray that the cardinal succeed in his uphill struggle with cancer so that for many more years he can be for us what he strives to be as a priest: "a symbol of hope in a world where frequently there is so little hope."

Rev. Bernard Häring (1913-98)   July 15, 1998

Like many of the great theologians working in the church before the Second Vatican Council, Redemptorist Father Bernard Häring laboured under a great cloud. Many in the Vatican found his work suspect. But he had a great ally in high places. No less a church leader than the Vatican exile Cardinal Giovanni Battista Montini of Milan — soon to become Pope Paul VI — wrote the introduction to the Italian edition of Häring's epoch-making work *The Law of Christ*.

Häring played a key role at the council. Many bishops, arriving in Rome, were dumbfounded at what was soon to take place. The schema sent out to them before the council made sense to them. But all these schema were thrown out, and their neo-scholastic training had ill-prepared them for the new thinking contained in the revised texts.

The liturgy, the patristic writings, and indeed the scriptures themselves were now being used very differently than they had been in the old Latin textbooks familiar to all clerics ordained before the council. These sources had become the very foundation of the council thinking, not simply proof texts to bolster up propositions arrived at through neo-scholastic philosophical thought processes.

In the first euphoria of the council, many bishops saw the need for a radically new approach to scriptural, liturgical, and dogmatic studies. They were more hesitant, however, to see an equally thorough reworking of moral theology. The conviction that natural law, that is, rules of conduct inherent in human nature itself, was the underpinning of all moral equations was too deeply embedded in their Catholic ethos.

Nor were they ready to have someone tell them that the very notion of "nature" which permeated their textbooks had little in common with the thought of St. Thomas Aquinas. For Aquinas, nature and supernature were not two realities, one above the other. Nature, for the greatest of the scholastic thinkers, was perfectly predisposed to be enriched by grace.

In the manuals the bishops brought to the council, nature had lost much of the lustre Aquinas had insisted was there — even after the original sin of Adam and Eve.

With the Nominalism of the Renaissance and the theory of the total depravity of humanity brought on by sin, nature had to be corrected by grace to have any significant value.

The results of this disastrous shift of meaning, Häring noted, could most clearly be seen in marriage, a truly natural phenomenon. Intercourse now had no self-sustaining value of its own; it could be justified only with an openness to conception of new life.

But Häring went far beyond the correction of a notion of nature in his moral theology. He gave an altogether new basis to moral theology — the very person of Jesus Christ. He said the Gospels should be taken seriously when they proclaimed that Jesus was the new law, that his call to discipleship should underpin all our thinking.

Häring faced squarely the inherent difficulties in making the person of Jesus central to Catholic moral thought. He acknowledged very openly that it was impossible to build neat moral systems on a human person. The ambiguities inherent in human existence — ambiguities not foreign to our Saviour who assumed fully our life — were accepted as positive factors leading us to trust more deeply in God.

For Häring, moral theology took on a whole new atmosphere. It no longer focused on defining and pointing out sin as its first and foremost function; rather, moral theology now came to be centred on values. So positively did Häring view our human existence that he made human freedom the basis of morality.

Häring's mindset can most clearly be seen in the council document The Church in the Modern World. (This should not surprise us since he served as secretary to the commission that drafted this text!) When the council document asks us to read the signs of the times, it is telling us to find what is good in the various (worldly) movements of our time. Today so many in the church are back to the old pessimism that concentrates on what is bad, on seeing the church's role as primarily pointing out what is sinful in our midst.

The *Prairie Messenger* is carrying a major excerpt from Häring's 1990 "confession of faith." Over the last years Häring has once more come under a Vatican cloud of suspicion. Much more is at stake in this than his views on birth control. Häring believed the whole basis of his moral theology — a basis he resolutely believed was fully endorsed by the council — was under attack. He believed that his accusers in the Vatican were undoing the council and were returning to a fundamentally pessimistic view of nature and, more specifically, of human existence.

Many might be disturbed by the pessimistic neurosis he claims to find so pervasive in the church. But a closer reading of Häring's text should reassure all Christians.

This moral theologian is ever true to his principles; he cannot but live in hope for a glorious new age for the church — an age based on freedom and trust.

Cardinal Basil Hume (1923-99)

June 23, 1999

To be sure, the Second Vatican Council emphasized papal primacy. But it equally stressed episcopal collegiality. And it did not try to work out a balance between them. Following a Lord who delighted in parables and paradoxes, the council gave us both poles and let the Spirit in each age find the necessary balance.

It is interesting to note that Cardinal Basil Hume, in his final major address, centred his message to the U.S. bishops on subsidiarity and collegiality. (Hume had agreed to give several talks to the American episcopacy before he knew he was dying of cancer. On learning he had a very short time to live, he videotaped his final message to this group of colleagues.)

When one is dying, one sticks to essentials. Hume made it abundantly clear what he thought was the critical challenge facing the church's bishops. He started his talk with an affirmation of subsidiarity as a basic social principle: that tasks should be carried out at the lowest possible level. And quoting Pius XII, one of the strongest popes ever to sit on the Chair of Peter, Hume noted that this principle applies "not only to society, but also to the life of the church within its hierarchical structure."

For this to happen in the church, Hume calls for a strengthening of national conferences of bishops, suggesting that their leaders meet every two years or so to jointly take responsibility for boldly guiding the church through the challenges facing it. The council, he reminded the U.S. bishops, did not "cast the pope and bishops in the roles of chief executive and branch managers."

In a column marking the feast of Sts. Peter and Paul, Rev. Richard McBrien reminds us that "the governing structure of the church must function not only to preserve the unity of the church, but also to promote and enhance its diversity. To achieve unity-in-diversity, there cannot be only one centre of authority, imposing a single form of practice upon the whole church."

We have lost a great prophet in the passing of Cardinal Basil Hume; we must honour his final address to the churches — actually given on videotape one day after his death — in which he reminded us that the council stressed papal primacy and collegiality. "The challenge for today," he said, "is for these two to live side-by-side."

Dom Helder Camara (1909-99)

September 1, 1999

What is the point of your presence, Lord,
if our lives do not alter?
Take away the quietness of a clear conscience.
Press us uncomfortably,
for only thus that other peace is made
— your peace.

- Prayer of Dom Helder Camara

It is debatable whether any living person, with the possible exception of the pope himself, has shaped the church as profoundly as has the little apostle of the poor of Recife, Brazil: Archbishop Helder Camara.

During his 90 years with us he made the above prayer his own. Continually he asked the Lord for an uncomfortable conscience, and in the process began a process of conscientization (consciousness raising) that has powerfully disquieted the church in every corner of our world.

In the slums of Rio de Janeiro he suffered a conversion that left a glorious mark on the whole church. In his youth, like many of the bishops, he had been a fascist, a member of the Green Shirts. But his association with the poor changed all that. With the trust and devotion of the poor in Rio's slums, Helder found new meaning for his priesthood.

Long before the Second Vatican Council, long before theologians were speaking of collegiality, Helder was shaping a national conference of bishops in Brazil. He knew that no one diocese alone could change the socio-economic system imprisoning millions in dehumanizing poverty.

Brazil had never seen a bishop quite like him. And abroad, he also caught the attention and unflinching support of Msgr. Giovanni Battista Montini. Both before and after his election to the papal office as Paul VI, Montini would do much to strengthen the Brazilian prelate's work of remoulding the church. Not long after becoming pope, Montini named Helder to the important See of Recife, a city central to Brazil's impoverished northeast.

Helder became archbishop shortly before the CIA-inspired military coup in Brazil. His outspoken defence of the poor soon turned the military — and not an insignificant majority of the bishops — against him. But one important bishop, occupying the Chair of Peter, stuck with him.

With no official church censures available to them, the military — with the co-operation of many bishops — declared him a non-person. No one in the media was allowed to mention him or print his name. As far as the Brazilian media were concerned, Helder did not exist.

Slowly, and with the help of the strongest men in the land that Paul VI could find and name as episcopal co-helpers with Helder, the little archbishop of Recife rebuilt once again a church sensitive to the poor as God's special sacrament of salvation.

Helder knew from his own personal experience the power of God's poor; now he proceeded to employ it for the good of the whole Brazilian church.

As Helder's influence rose once more in the Brazilian church, so his work among all the bishops of Latin America prospered. The charter texts of pastoral theology passed at Medellín and Puebla by CELAM, the Latin American bishops' joint organization, clearly bear Helder's gracious mark.

A poet in his own right, Helder could take the theology of the scholars and turn it into songs and prayers which his beloved poor could cherish.

Pope John Paul II accepted Helder's resignation, at 76, as Archbishop of Recife. It has not been an easy retirement. Canadian missionaries from Muenster and Saskatoon witnessed many tears as they continued to visit one of the great heroes of their lives.

A new brand of bishops was being appointed. Even CELAM came to be dominated by bishops with a deep distrust of a church brought to life in the slum meetings of the poor.

In his own archdiocese most of his structural work has been dismantled. Rome has closed the two seminaries Helder had built — even after a local study declared them sound theological institutions.

The new archbishop does not look to the poor for guidance; he believes in ruling from above. In this new turn of events Helder was ordered to do something no powerful military ruler ever accomplished. The new archbishop sent an auxiliary bishop to Helder and told the prophet of the poor that he must keep silent.

In deference to the institutional church, and through prayer able to believe that his new superiors were acting in good conscience, Helder was obedient to his successor.

But for one who prayed repeatedly never to be ruled by a quiet conscience, silence was not really a possibility. Long before this visit from the auxiliary bishop, mere human words were no longer Helder's chief means of communication. Anyone who had met him and allowed him to enter their hearts knows that his whole being sang loudly and mightily the song of God's love for the poor.

And this final vocation of Helder's, the suffering prophet in a body crippled by old age, has not been sterile. He has gained the respect of people in the highest positions in Rome and in Brasilia. The Brazilian government has taken the extraordinary step of declaring three days of public mourning for this prophet of God.

Yes, Helder has made the song of God's love for the poor a powerful tool of church renewal. We believe no one in the church or in society today will be able to prevent that song from shaping the church of the new millennium.

Jean-Marie Tillard (1927-2000) November 22, 2000

Canada has lost its leading theologian; the church, according to Archbishop of Canterbury George Carey, must now go forth without "one of the most distinguished ecumenists of the 20th century."

Dominican Father Jean-Marie Roger Tillard began his teaching career in Ottawa, lecturing on patristic sources, principally those dealing with liturgical matters. A strong believer in the ancient Latin axiom *lex orandi, lex credendi*, that in liturgical prayer and celebration (word and sacrament) the church ritualizes what it believes in the depth of its heart and consciousness, Tillard's early publications centred on the eucharistic prayer, seeing it in relationship to the Jewish *berakah* (blessing or benediction).

Not only did he provide a base for a very different eucharistic theology — he noted that the whole prayer was consecratory, calling upon us, as church, to stand in awe in God's presence — Tillard, very early in his theological career, also saw the ecumenical possibilities in visiting these ancient texts together with one's separated brothers and sisters.

Tillard never lost his moorings in the writings of the first centuries of the church. As his confrère Dominican Father Gabriel de Chadarevian noted at his funeral: "In the courses he gave us, they were full, full of tradition." He gave people a deep love of their theological tradition.

His command of the liturgical patristic sources stood him in good stead as the Second Vatican Council began its deliberations on liturgical matters. It did not take the Canadian bishops long to realize what a treasure they had in the *peritus* (theological expert) they had brought with them to Rome. As Archbishop Marcel Gervais of Ottawa noted at Tillard's funeral, this young theologian meticulously took them step-by-step through the issues being debated. The bishops, he said, were "eager to fully participate in the reflections that would lead to the development of the various work plans."

After the council the bishops continued to listen to him and at various times sought him as a ghostwriter. Tillard, Gervais noted, "continued to put his talents as a thinker and as a writer in the service of the bishops of Canada."

Not long after the council Tillard began his work with the Faith and Order Commission of the World Council of Churches. While the Catholic Church has not, on the worldwide level, joined the WCC, it has worked closely with the Faith and Order Commission. From 1977 until his death Tillard served as vice-moderator of the commission.

Perhaps his greatest work in this regard was the major ecumenical document Baptism, Eucharist and Ministry (BEM). In penning this document, Tillard earned an international reputation as an incisive thinker who could find ways to express the mystery at hand so that all sides could understand and, most often, also accept.

The current director of Faith and Order eulogized Tillard: "Father Jean will be remembered by his Faith and Order friends with thanksgiving for his passionate commitment to the search for the visible unity of the church, for his penetrating insights, his flair and imagination, his humour and his ability to find appropriate ways to move beyond theological expressions crafted in isolation to common theological affirmation and agreement."

His work with BEM, especially the section on ministry and authority, led him to tackle one of the key issues dividing the churches, the role of the papacy.

In 1982, Tillard published the truly monumental ecumenical book *The Bishop of Rome*. It is not an exaggeration to say that the Catholic Church was never the same after the publication of that book. It gave great encouragement to ecumenists — maybe most of all to our Anglican friends.

Tillard was soon conscripted to do much of the writing for the Anglican-Roman Catholic International Commission. Perhaps his greatest contribution here was his work on The Gift of Authority.

While Tillard's work on the papacy often received warmer applause outside the Catholic Church than inside it, this did not deter Pope John Paul II.

From time to time the current pope has clearly shown that he is personally troubled by the way the papal office is exercised. While in Canada, he told an ecumenical gathering in Toronto: "I am an optimist about our unity, and I hope the pope is not the biggest obstacle." So it should surprise no one that when the current pope wished to write an encyclical on ecumenism he would seek Tillard to ghostwrite it for him. Nor should we be shocked that in *Ut Unum Sint* (That they may be one) the pope would ask Christians, one and all, to engage with him "in a patient and familial dialogue" to find new and better ways in the exercising of papal primacy for the good of the whole church.

The pope considered Tillard a friend, and long before the official Vatican condolences were sent to Canada marking his passage to glory, the pope had already sent his personal fax to the Dominican community.

The day before Tillard died, the pope's chief ecumenist, Cardinal Edward Cassidy, addressed the American bishops, chiding many of them. In words that would have cheered Jean-Marie to his core, the cardinal told the bishops: "The church cannot be true to itself unless it is ecumenical."

Thank you, faithful servant.

Mother Teresa (1910-97)

October 22, 2003

It is common knowledge that Pope John Paul II did not want any celebrations marking his 25 years on the Chair of Peter. When he saw that he was not going to win that round with the cardinals, he made the beatification of his close friend Mother Teresa the key event in a week of celebrations.

While, on the one hand, this was a gracious act on the part of the pope, it was, on the other hand, only right and proper. For, in a strange way, the pope needed a Mother Teresa out there among the Catholic troops, doing exactly what she did in such a saintly and heroic fashion.

The pope's philosophy of life has been solidly focused on the value of every human life. He has struggled to incarnate this teaching throughout his papal visits; he has insisted, everywhere he has gone, that he spend quality time with the marginalized.

It is one thing for the pope to spend quality time with the marginalized; skeptics, however, could always pass this off as theatre, as show. That criticism could never, with any plausibility, be levelled at Mother Teresa, who incarnated John Paul's basic philosophy of life to a "T."

John Paul needed a Mother Teresa. For that matter, all of us needed a Mother Teresa — and our age sorely needed her.

Her single-minded concern for the poorest of the poor and the lowest of the low did much, much more than help these destitute people find meaning in an unjust world. It went a long way toward assuring each of us of our personal dignity.

Personal dignity is a gift of God; it is not bestowed by wealth, education, or status in birth. So many people today appear bereft of dignity because they seek it by placing themselves above their neighbour. We compete with one another in a thousand ways and wonder why at the end of the day we feel empty and unfulfilled.

Mother Teresa refused to be dazzled by the great in this world. She afforded them the same dignity that she witnessed in the dying in Calcutta's worst slums.

Often people were quick to criticize her for associating with the Ronald Reagans and the Jean-Claude "Baby Doc" Duvaliers of this world. And no one can deny that people such as these were eager to use her for their own political ends.

But the first question we must ask is: Did she try to use them to build up her own person? The resounding "no" we hear around the world to that query surely speaks highly of her greatness.

This is not to say that Blessed Teresa's mission of charity was the full and total expression of the Gospel. No less a person than her close friend Pope John Paul himself has often reminded us that the Gospel calls us beyond a simple charity model to one of justice and empowerment. As Christians faithful to the Gospel of Jesus Christ we must repeatedly ask: Why are more and more people being trapped each day in the inhumanity of today's slums?

We must, with equal insistence, ask: How can these people be empowered to take hold of their lives and escape the injustice of the gutter?

Mother Teresa did not ask these questions. She did not see this as her mission. But that is not to say that she saw them as secondary or unimportant. She marked out her turf and gave herself totally to that task.

She would no more talk politics with Reagan or Duvalier than take sides in the theological debates that divide so many in the church. Many highly placed clerics would have loved to hear a word from the most prominent woman in the church about her views on women's ordination, for instance, but she remained silent.

Blessed Mother Teresa, however, forcefully attacked abortion. She saw this as her turf. Her goal was to touch humanity at its weakest. She saw the unborn in exactly the same light as she saw the dying destitute — as full expressions of personal dignity. In a similar vein, she fought euthanasia and capital punishment, finding one as dehumanizing as the other.

We live in a world that regularly devalues the human person. In business, amoral market forces take precedence over the personal dignity of the worker. In the "reforms" of our welfare systems, the dignity of the poor is routinely trampled.

We surely need people in the church who cry out for justice. We need prophets who analyze our social, political, and economic policies, who show us the deficiencies of these policies and how they create countless new slum dwellers each day.

But it is well for us to remember the numerous examples in history of what can happen to these champions of justice if their work is not complemented with the compassionate touch of a Mother Teresa.

Prophets of justice need Mother Teresa — and the Mother Teresas of this world need the Archbishop Helder Camaras who cry out for justice. No one can fulfill all the calls of the Gospel; each of us has our charism, our gift to give to the world.

Charisms flourish where they are taken as part of the whole. Any attempt to canonize one's charism to the exclusion of others is to demonize it. Yet it is true to say that none of the charisms have meaning in the absence of Mother Teresa's. All need the compassionate touch of the lover.

Blessed Teresa found the overwhelming beauty and dignity of humanity in the unborn, in the poorest of the poor, in the abandoned dying. And — we must never forget — in Baby Doc Duvalier and Ronald Reagan. And in you and in me.

What a great gift this has been to our world! Compassion is our vocation whether we are rich or poor.

And how did she achieve her goal? By transforming her self-proclaimed stubbornness and rigidity into a single-minded service to the human spirit she found in each of us. Through this transformation of her weaknesses she was able to give the Other in us her undivided attention.

In our Judaeo-Christian tradition, such worship of the Other is called holiness. John Paul was right again in seeing the beatification of his friend as a fitting climax to his 25 years on the Chair of Peter.

Mother Teresa's demons September 12, 2001

Both the Archbishop of Calcutta and the administration of the Missionaries of Charity appeared embarrassed. They went to great lengths to tell the world that Mother Teresa was not "possessed" with demons, that a true exorcism was not administered to her several months before she died.

Mother Teresa herself had no such scruples. As the early accounts of the prayer service noted, the saintly founder of the missionary sisters "happily agreed" to being "exorcised." She was deeply troubled in spirit, so much so that she could not rest, let alone sleep. Should such news disturb us? Only if we have a false view of holiness. A view that places the holy above struggle, seeing all need for struggle as a sign of imperfection.

The long history of hagiography soundly contradicts that point of view. Rather than view the last days of the saints as peaceful, as if the victory had long ago been won, the stories of the lives of the saints repeatedly speak of struggle, often of struggle to believe the very basics of the faith.

The mark of Mother Teresa's holiness was not that she was above the struggle, but that she hid nothing of her weakness from her sisters. Her call for exorcism should not embarrass us. Rather, we should see it as an open cry to her loved ones to stand by her in prayer as she fought off her demons.

Of course, no one around her thought she was possessed, needing a "real exorcism." But that does not mean we are not to take Mother Teresa's ordeal at face value.

This story of Mother Teresa's last days should provide everyone with "a reality check." Death, we must never forget, has its moments of darkness. Such is the price all humanity must pay for sin.

This sobering truth should mark our lives. And as we stand by our loved ones as they approach death, we must walk with them both with tender compassion and with a gentle honesty of spirit.

Cardinal Franz König (1905-2004) March 24, 2004

Cardinal Franz König of Vienna, the last cardinal to be given the red hat by Pope John XXIII, died peacefully in his sleep on March 13. A cardinal for 45 years, König continued to use the status given to him to fight for the church he had long envisioned. Trained not only in theology but also in the social sciences, he brought these two disciplines together to put flesh on his ecclesial dreams.

From the earliest days of the Second Vatican Council until days before he died, König remained a force to be reckoned with. At the council he argued for decentralization of power and joined forces with Archbishop Maxim Hermaniuk of Winnipeg in fighting for collegiality among bishops. For these concepts to take hold in the church, he saw the need for greater involvement of priests and laity in the nomination of bishops.

After the council he became deeply involved in social justice concerns, East-West relations, and peace issues. This led him to champion Karol Wojtyla as pope, and today it is generally accepted that he was the "king" (könig)-maker in the election of John Paul II to the Chair of Peter.

The council left an indelible mark on the cardinal, determining the way König would lead the rest of his life. Not convinced that the church had made its case well with regard to birth control, in 1992 he publicly challenged no less a person than the head of the Congregation for the Doctrine of the Faith (CDF), Cardinal Joseph Ratzinger, to an open debate on the church's distinction between "artificial" and "natural" birth control.

Ratzinger accepted. Though nothing substantive came out of the debate, Ratzinger was the great winner. His willingness to debate the issue did not weaken his power in the CDF but, rather, greatly enhanced it. König thought little about it; he took the notion of debate as a natural process in the post-Vatican II church.

His last great public service to the church of ideas came in the recent discussion on the role of inter-religious dialogue. Jesuit Father Jacques Dupuis was under investigation by the CDF. The congregation felt that the Jesuit theologian had given too prominent a place to non-Christian religions at the expense of the uniqueness of Christ. König, already well into his 90s, did not agree and used the most respected (lay-led) Catholic journal in the world, London's *The Tablet*, to support Dupuis's cause.

Dupuis was caught off guard. He had never met the cardinal and certainly had not looked to him for support. But he was soon to learn that this was no faint cry from a distant past, but an articulate, modern, passionate voice calling the church to newness, to wholeness.

A great spirit has moved upon this earthly church — a presence revered by more traditional Catholics, a prophet respected by those who saw the council as the great opening of windows to fresh air.

For no one was this a day of sadness. There surely were smiles throughout the heavens at the sound of Blessed John XXIII popping open a bottle of the best wine of the kingdom to welcome his friend home.

Sparring cardinals honoured

January 2, 2002

Jesus usually refused to enter into polemical arguments. He was more at home in the world of parables and paradoxes; he used miracles to call the people to conversion.

Jesus never let himself be pinned down. He feared simple answers; any truth that failed to include the paradox central to all human life he viewed as potentially diabolical.

If one day he preached "Blessed are the peacemakers, for they shall inherit the land," and noticed that the apostles relaxed, thinking, "Here is a truth we can finally understand," Jesus would be quick to add: "I have come not to bring peace but the sword."

Parables, paradoxes, and miracle stories served Jesus's intentions well but, let's admit it, they do not provide the foundation on which one can easily build a church institution. Institutions, we tell ourselves, need clear lines of authority — and the simpler this line of authority, the better.

But things were never simple in the ancient church. Church governance was by necessity extremely decentralized. It was no use dreaming of a powerful papacy, since it was practically impossible for a pope to intervene in the day-to-day affairs of sister churches, given the contemporary state of communications.

In the ancient church, Rome was viewed primarily as one patriarchy — albeit a most important one — among five patriarchies which complemented one another and together reflected the catholicity of the church.

Antioch, a hard-nosed business community, gave the church a love of rhetoric and pageantry. Constantinople wonderfully transformed these art forms into liturgy through song and rich symbolic activity.

Alexandria, home of the philosophers, gave the church a mystical bent and taught that all theology should end in prayer. (Not surprisingly, it was this church that first blessed the monks who sought God in the desert.)

Jerusalem, in the heart of the land where Jesus preached, quite naturally stressed the cross of Christ as the path to resurrection, and called upon the whole church never to settle down but to remain continuously on pilgrimage to the New Jerusalem.

Rome, the empire's centre of law and authority, blessed the church with stability and a concern for unity and peace. Rather than being exuberant in its rhetoric like Antioch, or flamboyant in its liturgy as Constantinople sometimes became, or daring to dream new visions for the church as Alexandria was wont to do, or lost in otherworldliness as Jerusalem often was, Rome held back, striving to maintain an even keel.

Yes, Rome was always conservative, and this served the church well. Its love of order and diplomacy made the western patriarchal see an effective arbiter among the local churches.

But early in the second millennium, for a great variety of reasons, most of which had little to do with theology, Rome and the four eastern patriarchies parted ways — with disastrous consequences for all, especially for the western church.

Without the pageantry of Antioch, without the song and liturgy of Constantinople, without the dreams of Alexandria, Rome became a very serious place. Even its adaptation of the passion theology of Jerusalem took on elements of the grotesque. We still see the results today: terrible crucifixes, which say nothing about the Lord's paschal mystery and resurrection, still find a place in many of our churches.

But a much more subtle change often went unnoticed. Without the balancing theologies of the East, the gift of law and order — so precious in the ancient church — gradually lost much of its human dimension.

In time, through an almost imperceptible transformation, the western church became better at portraying an authoritarian, highly patriarchal God than in presenting the God of the prodigal son or of the lost sheep — the God, that is, of parables and paradoxes, a God to be discovered in the miracle of life.

It is interesting to note how Cardinal Joseph Ratzinger deflected criticism of his important declaration *Dominus Iesus*. He was "bored" by the "predefined criticism." He noted, "Some proffer criticism with the greatest of ease, because they consider everything that comes out of Rome in the light of politics and the division of power, and they do not tackle the content."

No doubt, the cardinal is right about this criticism; his podium has indeed been weakened by the very centralization of the church institution that has taken place in recent times.

In this regard, it is important to look again at the criticism that Cardinal Walter Kasper, then the Bishop of Rottenberg-Stuttgart, levelled at *Dominus Iesus*. His criticism, he made it clear, was not with the document's content, but with its tone.

The teaching of the Second Vatican Council, Kasper notes, leads to a faith understanding that is open to people of faith and of no faith — an opening that is sensitive to the drama of life in our times. Kasper acknowledges that *Dominus Iesus* reaffirms this teaching of the council — not, however, with joy, but with fear. Ratzinger is afraid that any openness to other religious and/or secular life experiences will relativize the truth about Jesus Christ. The struggle the Roman Congregation for the Doctrine of the Faith had with the theology of Jesuit Father Jacques Dupuis bears this out.

But it is important to recognize that the CDF has backed off from its initial condemnation of "doctrinal error" to the much milder conclusion that Dupuis's work contained "ambiguities."

Far more important, however, was what followed in the Vatican. This January the pope produced a document to mark the opening of the new millennium. Amazingly, the tone and, indeed, the substance of *Novo Millennio Ineunte* is more like the writings of Dupuis than like *Dominus Iesus*.

In this apostolic letter the pope calls for "a relationship and dialogue with the followers of other religions" — a dialogue that will flourish "in the increased cultural and religious pluralism which is expected to mark the society of the new millennium."

There is no way that *Novo Millennio Ineunte* could have been written without crossing the desk of Cardinal Ratzinger. Nor is it conceivable that Bishop Kasper could be named to head the Pontifical Council for Promoting Christian Unity without a green light from the head of the CDF.

Not only has Ratzinger seen Kasper brought into the Roman Curia, he has engaged him publically in perhaps the central theological issue now facing the church, the relationship of the local churches to the universal church.

This theoretical theological debate has enormous practical pastoral ramifications for the church community.

Kasper began his criticism of the current situation on the pastoral level while still the Bishop of Rottenberg-Stuttgart. He criticized the present church centralization as having "gone too far.... The right balance between the universal church and the particular churches has been destroyed. This is not only my own perception; it is the experience and complaint of many bishops from all over the world."

No wonder the U.S.-based *Catholic Family News* saw Kasper's elevation to the College of Cardinals as "a genuine scandal, that is to say, an occasion of sin!" Not so Cardinal Ratzinger. He saw the need for an open dialogue on a central issue facing the church — an issue that could not be fixed by a *Dominus Iesus*-type of decree from the CDF.

This is no place to take sides on, or even to summarize, the two positions. Kasper has taken a more "Aristotelian realistic" stance that gives primacy of place to the local church. The quiet optimism of Thomas Aquinas runs through his presentation. Ratzinger, carefully noting that he does not equate the Roman church with the universal church but, rather, sees it too as a local church, opts for "Platonic idealism."

"The assertion of the inner precedence of God's idea of the one church," Ratzinger maintains, "has nothing whatsoever to do with the problem of centralism."

Ratzinger's tendency toward Platonism moves him away from the optimism of Aquinas's notion of nature toward the moral pessimism of Augustine (and of Luther and the Reformation) — and this certainly plays a part in the fear that so often characterizes his work as head of the CDF.

Perfectly faithful to the Preacher of parables and paradoxes, the bishops at Vatican II repeated the Vatican I teaching that the pope had full and universal authority and then, without a word of explanation, declared that the college of bishops also had full and universal authority. This set the stage for our cardinals duelling on the theoretical level — all the while with their eye on the practical pastoral level — on what role the local bishops should be exercising in the universal church.

In actual fact — if the church is healthy — this debate will go on long after these two cardinals have gone to their eternal reward. God, with wisdom divine, has made ambiguity part and parcel of human existence. In his use of parables and paradoxes, Jesus has taken this human ambiguity and placed it at the centre of his religious thinking.

Many of us are uncomfortable with uncertainty, and so we desire a church without ambiguity, just as we desire a Christ who is perfectly divine — and not "bothered" with human flesh. Just as we are ready to sacrifice the humanity of Christ to "save" his divinity, so we want a faith that can be written in dogmas beyond the influence of anything human.

We want a theology of authority that is beyond ambiguity. The easiest way to achieve this is to place all authority in the pope and only in the pope. Such thinking, of course, has little to do with the Man of parables, and both cardinals know this.

The fact that Cardinals Ratzinger and Kasper are publicly discussing — even arguing about — the exercise of authority in the church is not an embarrassment. It is a necessity.

They both know we will never get it right. The "solution" for one era will be a pastoral problem for the next.

Both cardinals established their reputations as first-rate theologians in the academic world before assuming roles in the highest levels of the magisterium. We rejoice in a church that treasures "duelling cardinals" and it is with great pleasure that we declare them our churchpersons for 2001.

Chapter 11

Revolution by Tradition

By Dr. John Thompson

For nearly 35 years, the *Prairie Messenger* has arrived on Thursday or Friday at our home. For 21 of those years, Father Andrew Britz was editor and editorial writer. Like other *PM* readers, my wife and I considered the weekly editorial an additional Sunday homily.

For more than two decades, Father Andrew reflected on faith, probing church and world. *Truth to Power* makes available fewer than 10 percent of his editorials and as the title suggests, these are forceful words. They are also compassionate. Those who compiled this collection have given us not only a remarkable historical record but also a continuing witness. For two decades these weekly words enabled Prairie Catholics and others to discern the presence of the Lord among us in "the signs of the times." They still do.

How are we to situate these editorials? In distinguishing editorials from news stories, Father Andrew quotes Archbishop John Foley, head of the Pontifical Council for Social Communication: the obligation of the Catholic press is to "report the facts as objectively and as dispassionately as possible: People first ask of us: what we have seen; what have we witnessed; what do we know. Only after that might they ask of us: what do we think." To keep this distinction clear in readers' minds, news stories appear in the first part of the PM, and editorials — what the editors think — in the back pages.

These editorials are a window on the reforms of the Second Vatican Council (1962-65) lived out in the third and fourth decades after the council. They are also a window on what and how Father Andrew thinks about church and world. As an astute and informed observer, he combines historical and theological understanding with knowledge of contemporary church and world — persons, events, issues, politics, culture, and economy. These editorials show an editor's eye sensitive to nuance that also notices who and what are left out and asks why. They look beneath the surface appearances of our times with the eyes of faith. They show an editor who gets it.

How can we characterize these multivalent editorials? I offer five connected ways I hear these editorials at work. My response speaks to why they are still relevant.

Holographic: Like any part of a hologram, each editorial in this collection contains within it an image of the whole. From each editorial, the whole can be seen. Each is imaged in and images God's saving grace in Jesus alive in the People of God. Unified in themes and concerns, they are anchored in the apostolic and patristic faith tradition of early Christian communities and in the reforms and spirit of the Second Vatican Council and the People of God 20 centuries later. In words Pope St. Gregory used to describe St. Benedict — and which Father Andrew uses — these editorials are "seeing the whole world in a single ray of light." Each shows us Jesus among us, fully God and fully human.

Prophetic: These editorials exist within the prophetic tradition of monasticism and the lives of the Benedictine monks of St. Peter's Monastery, who began the newspaper in 1904. They do not foretell the future — though I am struck by how often the editor discerns incipient harmful developments that have since become pervasive. They are prophetic in their penetrating insight — praying "with eyes wide open" — seeing ideologies of power and vested interests being played out, and shutting out the powerless. They are a place to stand to see what is really at stake: to stand against the voices of pessimism and doom; to stand up on behalf of the poor, the powerless, the marginalized, and the planet itself. They are a constant voice raised against the centuries of "the sin of sexism" in the cultures and structures of church and society. They take into account "people of no account" and call to account the powerful in church, society, and world for disregard of human justice. Some of the harshest criticism is levelled at the church, its beliefs and practices — including Church fathers and later theologians — for their negative, dehumanizing views of women. They show critique and courage, unmasking and building up, honesty and humility. The *PM* is prophetic in serving the church in fidelity, openness, honesty, and credibility.

Homiletic/pastoral: These editorials preach the Good News of the Gospel. We are engaged and hear ourselves imaged week after week in the foundational call of our Christian baptism. These editorials possess a pastoral spirit sensitive to the Spirit given to the People of God. We are exhorted to incarnate the Gospel through our engagement in the world where our lived faith experience is recognized as the *sensus fidelium*. Women are respected and appreciated here — religious, single, married — as witnesses of and to the suffering and risen Lord. They are acknowledged as those who for centuries have ensured that the faith has been handed on, including to successive generations of children, and as women who image the Lord fully. These editorials exhibit an embracing pastoral spirit rooted in a call to conversion of heart and ways that match those of Jesus's compassion, shown so tellingly in the story of the Samaritan woman at the well (Jn 4:5-42). Here is the weekly call to share the Eucharist in community symbolizing ourselves as the Body of Christ without distinction "between Jew and Greek, slave and free, male and female" (Gal 3:27).

Vigilant: These editorials watch and call the church to live up to the Vatican II council reforms. They sleuth out the ways in which council reforms — rooted in a return to the Gospels and traditions of the early Christian communities and proclaimed by the council as the highest authority in the church — are being undermined, subverted in Vatican and Curia practices and pronouncements. Readers are made aware of attempts to turn the clock back to pre-Second Vatican Council ways. Against these restorationist efforts, Jesuit Father John O'Malley's books *Vatican II: Did Anything Happen?* (2007) and *What Happened at Vatican II* (2008) provide solid documentation of how the Second Vatican Council undertook major reforms, which are rooted in ancient Christian traditions and involve a profound reorientation of the Catholic Church. These editorials continue to educate readers about the historical and theological bases of the faithful return to tradition represented in the renewal of the Second Vatican Council, which many Catholics did not understand.

Realizing language of faith renewal: These editorials speak in the words, tone, and spirit of the Gospels and reforms of the Second Vatican Council. Readers hear a consistent and holistic language for naming and realizing that renewal. This language shapes our ways of thinking of and talking about our faith experience in the images and words of the council. These editorials are engaging, eloquent, and memorable in their language, subtle humour, and clarity. They are words about the Word that is the Lord among us, with which we fashion ourselves together in the Lord's image as the People of God.

These five features point to a reversal of values that Jesus proclaims in the kingdom of God. The Gospel truth about power is revealed in a paradoxical strength of weakness. God incarnate, flesh and blood among us, Jesus does "not cling to his equality with God but emptied himself to assume the condition of a slave ... he was humbler yet, even to accepting death, death on a cross (Phil 2:6-8). Control, wealth, domination, fame are alluring and illusory temptations that Jesus rejected in the desert and in dying and rising (Lk 4:1-13; Mt 4:1-11).

I will turn now to several themes that recur like motifs in these editorials. These themes focus on what a 1987 editorial entitled "Simple Gospels."

A grounding and enduring question

Based on her own quest and question, Mary Rose O'Reilley concludes that when you go at life with a question and simply try to follow the trail of answers, then all the familiar contours of culture begin to shift. Everything is connected to everything else, and the web shakes with any touch at its farthest margins.
The Peaceable Classroom (1993), pp. 36-37

A question asked repeatedly grounds these editorials: How do we live when we take seriously God coming among us in the person of Jesus, fully God and fully human, "flesh given for the life of the world" (Jn 6:51)? As responses to that question, these editorials are the "trail of answers" that we, as readers, are invited to follow.

This startling incarnation informs these editorials. It drives their exploration into the recesses of culture and our consciousness; it draws them together as a centre. Continually returning to ask and answer this question penetrates everything. This question acts as a lens continually focused on church and world — Benedict's "single ray of light." This central and centring faith question shifts, shapes, and shakes the "familiar contours of culture" — including the church inculturated across 20 centuries and around the world — to reveal the reach, relevance, and call of the divine presence in what appears just mundane.

Anchored in 15 centuries of Benedictine devotion to the prayer of the church, St. Peter's Abbey and the *Prairie Messenger*'s editors have been engaged in "deep listening" to discern the presence of the Lord of the Gospels in the life of the prairie church — as local, national, and universal church. They have listened together in community and also as pastors in parishes throughout the abbacy, a ministry unusual for monks but significant for their sense of the lives and faith of God's people, the *sensus fidelium*. These monks' lives apart have not been flight from the world, but rather a deeper entry into the world through reading, questioning, and listening to God and God's people in the world.

It is the deepening answers to the probing existential question of the meaning of the Incarnation and its continually surprising implications to which these editorials return in an interconnected web that reaches out to the "farthest margins" of our lives together. Taking the Incarnation seriously shows up everywhere. These editorials resound again and again with the answer that God among us in the flesh as one of us changes everything.

Revolution by tradition

In *The Religious Order* (1973), Michael Hill inquires into the renewing force of newly forming religious communities within Christian traditions. Hill draws on the Benedictines in their origins and in their later reforms in his analysis. He summarizes his insight into this energizing spirit of renewal and conversion in the paradoxical phrase "revolution by tradition."

The notion that tradition might be "revolutionary" — that change itself might come from a return to tradition — is a disconcerting surprise, even a contradiction. Change is usually viewed as uprooting and devaluing tradition as the established way of doing things, devaluing tradition as sacred. Change has about it a perceived sense of irreverence or disregard for a revered past.

Changes introduced in the reforms of the Second Vatican Council — changes to liturgical practices, including Mass in the vernacular and communion in the hand, and ecumenism, to pick out only several that were obvious — challenged deeply held views of Catholics. The changes violated a strongly held assumption, one even considered a "mark of the true church" in the minds of Catholics: the Catholic Church does not change because it has not changed. An ahistorical sense of the church as a "perfect society" and hence, by definition, unchangeable left most Catholics ignorant of major historical changes over centuries. They did not — sometimes could not — realize that changes introduced by the Second Vatican Council as a reform were not simply novelty and accommodation to contemporary culture, but rather represented a faithful return to ancient practices, beliefs, and organization — to the full spirit and Spirit — of the apostolic and patristic Christian communities.

These editorials offer readers an understanding of this dynamic of revolution by tradition undertaken by the Second Vatican Council in response to Pope John XXIII's call for *aggiornamento*. This is a dynamic of renewal that communities of religious women have undertaken with prophetic commitment, though with Vatican suspicion and blame, as these editorials point out. Again and again these editorials put past developments of Christianity in the West and in the East — including the rupture itself — into historical perspective of politics and culture, greed and power. We find out how the "accidents" of history and cultural beliefs of societies became the adopted and sacralized patterns of thought and behaviour in later periods — from ways of dressing and exercising power in organizational structures to patterns excluding persons from authority and ministry. These editorials document the recovery of "simple Gospels," a retrieval, however, that is not simple, rooted as it is in the extraordinary and hidden scholarship of theologians who have paid a high personal price of suspicion and silencing. It is well to remember their faithful work of retrieval and the heroic role of theologians as intellectuals and persons of faith, as they are excluded from the magisterium and blamed for dissension in the church. Living out the meaning of the Incarnation in today's world is revolutionary, grounded in the Second Vatican Council's return to the early Christian tradition. Revolution by tradition in "simple Gospels" speaks truth to power in lives lived differently.

Ordinary Time

Prophets do not foretell the future. Prophets see deeply into what is going on now. They call us to pay attention to what is right in front of us — to see beneath appearances. In Paul Ricoeur's words about Jesus's parables, they call us to recognize that "the extraordinary is within the ordinary." The divine is not somewhere else. The sacred is not an escape from the world into a sealed compartment conveniently isolating us from the profane. Inconveniently, our God is present in everyday life — what early Christians, as Father Andrew points out, have called "ordinary time." Only later, after the Peace of Constantine, did Christians adopt sacred time and space, sacred roles, statuses, and hierarchical forms of governance.

These editorials call us back to the experience and faith of early Christians who saw themselves as church, as community, as the Body of Christ, celebrating the Eucharist as offering and receiving themselves back as blessed in the Lord. They themselves were sacred. The Second Vatican Council calls us to discern "the signs of the times," to see the presence and working of the Lord among us. This has meant a significant shift from focusing inward — on our Catholic God and ourselves as the elect — to focusing on Christian communities in the world — God as catholic and universal, inviting our participation for the life of the world. This is the faith stance of The Church in the Modern World, whose Latin title, taken from its opening words, is *Gaudium et Spes* (Joy and hope). "The extraordinary is within the ordinary."

Parables and paradoxes

Throughout these editorials, putting on the mind of Christ (I Cor 2:16; Phil 2:5) means thinking in "parables and paradoxes." We hear this phrase again and again because Jesus chose to speak in parables. As Father Andrew points out, Jesus's parables are as powerful today as when he first told them. Parables show us how central paradoxes were to Jesus's way of understanding, to his way of addressing complex issues, to how he made sense of daily events. Existence itself is paradoxical. In parables, Jesus found a form to tell about the ineffable — his abba's unconditional love for him and for us — and to convey the central paradox of the Gospel: weakness is strength, losing one's life is finding it, the paschal mystery of his suffering, dying, and rising. Telling parables shows Jesus's unwillingness to get sucked into white-and-black ways of thinking and talking, into "lopsided polemics" of legalism, dogmatism, and fundamentalism. Jesus's approach in parables means living with tensions between two truths, turning down the rhetoric of our divisions and controversies, living with the mystery of what we do not yet understand, living with doubt, listening more, letting God be God. Parables don't let us alone. They keep calling us to conversion.

Life of a faithful mind

These editorials exhibit a powerful mind at work — informed, subtle, at home with complexity and uncertainty, compassionate and ethical, clear, and prayerful. These thoughtful editorials show, in Hannah Arendt's book title *The Life of the Mind*, the life of a faithful mind — faithful to knowledge and understanding, faithful to faith, embodied spirit. This Gospel mind brings insight into contemporary issues, employs careful distinctions, confronts difficult issues regularly without trivializing or dodging, sees what is at stake. Extensive knowledge of scripture, history, theology, church and councils, the early Church and the fathers, liturgy, and practice are drawn on to give perspective to present beliefs, practices, and events — both within the Church and beyond. These editorials represent the long Catholic tradition of respect for and valuing of intellectual life — the enduring tension of faith seeking understanding. The 10 topics under which editorials have been grouped show the range and scope of informed and informing reflection.

Concluding words

In concluding my appreciative commentary, I return to the Incarnation — the central and recurring question and call of this work for me. Father Andrew has written, in an editorial not in this collection, that in fully embracing the humanity God has given us, we come into contact with divinity in ways beyond our imagining. His is deep optimism, with "eyes wide open." These editorials celebrate a joyful humanity portrayed in Blessed Pope John XXIII's Italian love of life and the Italian people's delight in his humanity that "celebrated life — and faith." We meet our humanity in Mary, Mother of God. We meet our humanity in Pope John Paul II, who, in later years, found power in his human weakness — debilitating Parkinson's disease — to demonstrate his convictions and call for Christian unity, for a world of peace based on justice. We meet our humanity in the inspiration, courage, and sheer endurance of "heroes of faith" who served us, the People of God. We meet our humanity in Jesus, who calls us to live in compassion and justice within the whole human family.

The words of Micah 6:8 capture for me the question, spirit, and call I hear in reading and listening again to the words of these editorials: "And what does the Lord require of you? To act justly and to love mercy and to walk humbly with your God."

Chapter 12

The Signs of the Times

By Dr. Mary Jo Leddy

The Second Vatican Council issued a deep and far-reaching summons — urging the People of God to "read the signs of the times." It was an invitation to political discernment that was seen as a prerequisite for becoming the church that was in the modern world but not of it.

This was a summons that some, perhaps many, Catholics took very seriously. However, the more we tried to discern the dynamics of sin and grace in the socio-economic context of our time, the more difficult it seemed. It is one thing to articulate fundamental Christian values such as love, peace, and justice and quite another thing to weigh in on the concrete issues of a particular place in time. Reading the signs of the times is perhaps more easily done in an academic context in which the fruits of the discernment are rarely tested by the socio-economic reality or by the community of faith. It is doubly difficult in a Catholic publication in which the reading of the times is done in public and is not without consequence. I know whereof I speak.

I began my work as the editor of *Catholic New Times* a few years before Andrew Britz began his remarkable tenure as the editor of the *Prairie Messenger*. By that time I had become acutely aware of how muddy and messy the most important issues were. There were so many shades of grey that it was tempting to fade away into innocuous pious or political platitudes.

Yet, out of the prairies a voice spoke in a clear and consequential way. Week after week, for 21 years, Andrew Britz wrote editorials that always had something important and helpful to say. This in itself is a remarkable achievement as anyone who has written a regular column will tell you. For most of the readers of the *Prairie Messenger*, he provided a kind of compass, a way of thinking through the issues of turbulent times.

I always felt that he treated his readers like adult Christians who were faithful enough to work their way through the challenges of being in the church and living in North America. Andrew Britz invited his readers to think in consequential ways — about how their faith made a difference, about the effects of theologies, structures, language, and actions.

I was quietly delighted that this consistently prophetic voice rolled out of the prairies. Having been raised in Saskatoon, I had a sense of how that long horizon and pure light helped one to see a little more clearly. On the prairies you must learn to read the weather and this can become an apprenticeship for reading the signs of the times.

It is also significant that this prophetic paper was located within a Benedictine monastery. As the Roman Empire was collapsing, it was the early monastic movement that took what was best in Rome and the Christian tradition and began to build a new form of Christian life, which would provide a bridge into the future. St. Peter's Abbey is a contemporary monastery that has provided a solid base for a newspaper that has articulated the insights that are foundational for the renewal of the church in a time of cultural collapse.

The editorials assembled in this book tackle hot-button topics: birth control, abortion, condoms, clergy abuse, sexism in the church. He entered the public debate on the Tracy Latimer case and the wars of George W. Bush. Andrew Britz weighed in on these issues decisively. However, he did so in a way that gave full weight to the substantial wisdom of the Catholic tradition. He was clearly someone who wrote from within the church community for the sake of this community.

Taken as a whole, this book could be called a textbook in political discernment. Reading the signs of the times is difficult to define. There is no recipe for this multifaceted process, as Vatican II tells us in the document The Church in the Modern World. This discernment involves allowing one's imagination to be transformed by the Scriptures, opening one's mind to the wisdom of a tradition, being touched by the hopes and fears, the griefs, and the anxieties of the people of this age, especially those who are poor or in any way afflicted.

The process of political discernment cannot be defined but it can be described. It is what Andrew Britz did in his editorials over 21 years. How do we determine the signs of the times? Consider the very good example of Andrew Britz.

Epilogue

Pessimism too easy an out   March 20, 2002

We do not live in optimistic times. Indeed, there are many reasons to be downright pessimistic.

The human family is planning to spend more money on armaments this coming year than during any previous year. Even giving present-day dollar equivalents to past expenditures — such as during the height of the Second World War or the Vietnam War — these budgets do not match the current enthusiasm for all things military.

The United States, while giving major tax reductions to the rich and powerful, is planning to spend $400 billion this coming fiscal year on its military. There is every indication that the poor will receive less in social securities. For example, another 5 million Americans are expected to join the ranks of the 32 million (roughly the equivalent of Canada's total population) without any medical insurance.

U.S. President George W. Bush has ambitious plans to accompany this outlay of $400 billion (which is more than the Canadian national debt). He is calling the shots on the world stage; "old" international treaties mean nothing. He is currently dismantling one of the world's most important agreements: the Nuclear Non-Proliferation Treaty. Not only has the United States now pledged to develop nuclear space weaponry, it has also said it is ready to launch nuclear weapons in "pre-emptive first strikes" against the "axis of evil," which includes Iran and Iraq and North Korea.

It is scary when the one superpower in the world starts playing the bully — more so when the Canadian government appears ready to be onside, no matter what.

It is one thing — one thing, however, that Jesus would never do — to reluctantly go to war. It is quite another to relish it. Listening to the media and reading Canada's traditional national newspaper, the *Globe and Mail*, one cannot but conclude that it is wonderful indeed for Canadian soldiers to be finally at war in Afghanistan.

It is important to remember why the Canadian soldiers were sent to flush out pockets of resisters (terrorists in the official lingo). When the Americans used Afghani troops, the belligerents almost all slipped through the net set to trap them. Canadian and American troops, however, have not done much better.

Indeed, not that many terrorists have been caught on the ground — a clear sign that a significant proportion of the Afghan population is co-operating with the "enemy." Carpet bombing, though it has killed many more civilians than members of the military, has been much more "effective."

The Vietnam War quickly came to an end once the American people learned that their government was spending $56 on each poor person at home, while it was costing their nation $300,000 to kill each Viet Cong.

The American people will soon realize that was a real bargain. Three hundred thousand dollars is only a fraction of what America is spending on each Afghan enemy captured or killed.

But Afghan fighters are not the only victims. Refugees around the world are losing their human rights. When any country stops treating its refugees with dignity, that country is the loser. When the world's superpower holds hundreds of men without charge for months on end, and other countries keep silent, they all become more closely identified with the terrorism they have pledged to destroy.

Yes, there is much to be pessimistic about. What can Easter mean in such a world?

Pessimism is the easiest of human responses. In Old Testament times, the people were most downhearted while they pined away on the shores of the rivers of Babylon.

Pessimism holds sway in the Book of Lamentations, and even more so in the Book of Ezekiel. One will look in vain here for one positive statement on the meaning of human existence. Should anyone look deeply into their heart, the common wisdom was that they would discover all was *tohu waw bohu*, a meaningless, empty void (see Gn 1:2).

But the priests at the time would not buy it. In the retelling of the Babylonian creation story, God's spirit has hovered over all creation, bringing it to a unity of purpose. God saw that all was good. Indeed, God created the human person in such a way that everyone, like a mirror, reflected the divine glory. No wonder God took such pleasure in creation, ultimately declaring it "very good."

The apostles, in witnessing the death of Jesus, were filled with fear and made the despondency of the Babylonian captives of old seem almost joyful. Jesus comes into their midst and, in echoing the creation of the first Adam, breathed on them the Holy Spirit and told them to go forth with courage.

Everything remained the same — the Romans were still ruling the world without a moral scruple, the Pharisees were still gathering their brownie points against a judgmental God, women were still counted for very little, and Jesus was still absent from them in the flesh of their daily existence — but Christians started to refute this whole world mindset.

They said that for them all things were made new, that in the risen Lord they had become an altogether new creation. They no longer saw the Roman centurion as the world's power. They baptized Cornelius, a Roman centurion, and said they would have nothing to do with Roman military theory; rather, they would preach forgiveness and non-violence.

They did not see women as second-rate citizens. They taught them to look deeply into their own hearts and find precisely there the waters welling up with eternal life.

They refused to allow blindness to shield anyone in a world of fear. Unlike the parents of the man born blind, who were afraid of being ostracized from religious orthodoxy, they curried favour from no one in power.

They were not afraid to be the Lazaruses at the feet of the rich and powerful, for they knew Jesus would raise them to life everlasting.

Four hundred billion dollars is absolute weakness when compared to the Lamb that was slaughtered who has breathed divine life into our nostrils. The first can but try to bully the world into submission; the second can free the poor, can make cripples dance, can make the mute fill the world with song, and, yes, can make the dead burst forth with the fullness of life.

Appendix

Prairie Messenger Editorial Policy

True to its Catholic tradition, the *Prairie Messenger* seeks to mirror for the church on the Prairies the whole reality of the pilgrim People of God as they seek to better understand, make present, and judge themselves by the Kingdom of God as announced in the liberating and merciful news of Jesus Christ.

In order to reflect truly the total mystery of the church, the *Prairie Messenger* offers opportunity for dialogue and discussion, knowing that the Word of God can only be expressed in limited human words, which means that disagreement, dissent, and diversity will accompany all human efforts to reflect the unity, the faith, and the charity the Spirit offers to the people the Father calls.

Guided by the church's teaching office, and alert to the signs of the times, the *Prairie Messenger* helps to make the People of God aware of their local, national, and international presence and responsibilities, and to keep them informed of the concerns of all the church — its laity, teachers, scholars, and pastors.

In its traditional concern for social justice, the *Prairie Messenger* will continue to reflect upon economic, political, and social processes in the light of the Gospel and of the teachings of the church. In a non-partisan approach, it will challenge its readers to know and live their communal and personal responsibilities in church and society.

In obedience to the Spirit's continual call to reform and renewal, the *Prairie Messenger* places special emphasis on exploring the riches of the Scriptures and of the liturgy, with committed concern for ecumenism and the full catholicity of the Christian message.

To accomplish these goals most effectively, the *Prairie Messenger* will maintain liaison with the dioceses and communities it serves, their people, their organizations, and their leaders, that communication, charity, and truth can best be served in justice and honesty.

Index

A

abortion
   changing minds on, 182-183, 184-185
   John Paul II's view of, 168, 169-170
   and Mother Teresa, 259-260
   polemics behind, 166-167, 250
   as women's issue, 75, 185
abuse of power, 186-187
Accattoli, Luigi, 51-52
Adam and Eve, 188-189
Afghanistan War, 277-278
Africa, 63, 110
AIDS, 177-178, 248
Alexei II, Patriarch, 118
Anglicans, 46-48, 107-109, 150, 155
Annan, Kofi, 206
anointing the sick, 90-91
anti-Semitism, 52-53
apostles, 54-56
Aquinas, Thomas, 77, 251, 265
Archbishop of Canterbury, 142, 235, 256
Arian controversy, 21
ark, 138
assisted suicide, 190-191
   see also euthanasia
Assyrian Orthodox Church, 154
Augustine, St., 35, 66, 77, 223, 224
Avio, Kenneth, 194-195

B

baptism, 57-58, 100, 133-134
Baum, Gregory, 4
Berlin Wall, 200-201
Bernardin, Joseph, 7, 166, 167, 169, 248-250
bible, 82-84
birth control
   bishops and, 44-45, 175, 176
   Cardinals' dispute over, 42, 262
   clergy and laity disagreement on, 172-173, 174-176
   and condoms, 177-178
   and ecumenism, 136-137
   John Paul II's view of, 75, 171
   Paul VI's view of, 172, 174
The Bishop of Rome (book), 257
bishops
   and abortion, 185
   Anglican turning Catholic, 107
   and apostolic tradition, 238
   and birth control, 44-45, 175, 176
   collegiality of, 44, 47-48, 67, 253, 262
   in Czechoslovakia, 104
   and farm subsidies, 203, 204, 205-206
   and foreign aid, 199-200
   and funeral rites, 192
   and lay movements, 66-67
   leadership of, 24, 109
   national meetings of, 253, 255
   popular dislike of, 55-56
   and *Prairie Messenger*, 12, 16
   relationship to local church, 29-30
   role of, 26, 32-35, 125
   search for priests, 100-101
   and Second Vatican Council, 5-6, 47-48, 262

selection of, 24-26, 41, 47-48
and *sensus fidelium*, 41, 46
and sexual abuse, 186-187
and women's concerns, 86-87, 92-93
World Synod of Bishops, 60-61
Blakeney, Allan, 5
Body of Christ, 42, 51
Boniface VIII, Pope, 173
born-again Christians, 36
Borowski, Joseph, 167
Bosnia, 227
Bourassa, Robert, 211
Bright, John, 194
Britz, Andrew
   analysis of *Prairie Messenger* writing, 267-274
   appreciation of, 1, 267, 275-276
   background of, 1-2
   connection to John Paul II, 8
   as editor, 6-7
   other activities of, 8
   and Vatican II, 6, 9
Brusselmans, Christiane, 242-243
Burghardt, Walter, 198
burial customs, 192-193
Bush, George W., 225, 226, 277

C

Callahan, Sidney, 175-176
Camara, Helder, 127, 199, 200, 206, 254-256
canonization, 63-64, 236-237, 238-239
capital punishment, 169, 193-195, 217
capitalism, 116, 127-128, 131, 229, 230-232
Carey, George, 256
Carmelite nuns, 162, 163
Carnley, Peter, 179
Cassidy, Edward, 258
catechism, 45-46, 72, 82-84, 155
CCF (Co-operative Commonwealth Federation), 4-5
celibacy, 38, 58, 64, 97, 107, 108
Chaldean church, 153-154
charisms, 27, 51, 89, 260
Chenu, Marie Dominique, 247

Chittister, Joan, 79-80, 98-99
Christ. *see* Jesus
Christendom, history of, 163-164
Christmas, 23
Christodoulos, Archbishop, 125
Chrysostom, St. John, 77
Clement of Alexandria, St., 77
clergy, 57-58, 172-173, 174-176
   see also bishops; priesthood
Cold War, 115-116, 200-202, 229, 230, 231
colonialism, 202
community, 50-51
condoms, 177-178
confession, 88, 90-91
Congar, Yves, 238, 246-248
Cook, Steven J., 248-249
Coté, Richard, 152
Council of Ephesus, 154
Council of Trent, 45
cremation, 191-193
crime, 216-218
Croteau, Denis, 101
Crusades, 119, 123-124, 125
Curia, 118-119, 126, 130-131, 240
Cyril, St., 62
Czechoslovakia, 104-105

D

Day, Dorothy, 236-237
De Chadarevian, Gabriel, 256
De Lubac, Henri, 241-242
De Roo, Remi, 214
death, 191-193, 261
death penalty. see capital punishment
democracy, 58, 89, 228-229
devil, 188-189
The Disunity of Christians: Principles for Catholic Ecumenism (Congar), 246
Divine Revelation, 237-238
divorce, 93
Dominus Iesus, 264-265
Donovan, Dan, 50
Dulles, Avery, 43-44, 172, 174
Dupuis, Jacques, 262, 265

E

ecumenism
  and baptism, 133-134
  Cardinals' debate over, 264-265
  compared to fundamentalism, 136-137
  and diversity, 153-154
  and Eucharist, 19-20, 155
  and Jesus, 134-135
  J.M. Tillard's work on, 258
  John Paul II's efforts in, 117-118, 119-122, 124-126, 139-140, 144-146, 265
  and language, 155
  and learning from other faiths, 149-150
  Orthodox-Catholic meetings on, 48-49
  and papal primacy, 153
  and polemics, 142-143, 146-148
  and restoring balance, 141, 143-145
  and Second Vatican Council, 136, 144, 149
  teaching of, 17-18
Ehrich, Tom, 71-72, 219, 220
Eisler, Dale, 216
ensoulment, 178-179
episcopalism, 28-30, 41, 109, 253.
  see also bishops
Eucharist
  administration of food, 90-91
  from ancient Iraq, 153-154
  and Christ's humanity, 22
  and ecumenism, 19-20, 155
  expression of, 111-112, 182
  J-M. Tillard's work on, 256
  as most important rite, 100, 109-110
  Pope's encyclical on, 80-81
  and women's place in, 112-113
Eugene de Mazenod, St., 215
euthanasia, 168, 188-189, 190-191, 216
evangelization, 139-140
Exner, Adam, 182
exorcism, 261
Eyt, Pierre, 42-43

F

family, 181
farm subsidies, 204-206, 207
feminism, 13, 80, 91-93
  see also women
festivals, 65-66
filioque controversy, 123
Fineschi, Gianfranco, 129
Fisichella, Rino, 52-53
Flahiff, George, 45
Foley, John P., 13
foreign aid, 199-200, 206-208
forgiveness, 51-54
Free Trade Summit of the Americas, 227-228, 229
fundamentalism, 22, 106, 136-137, 163-164
funeral rites, 192-193

G

Gaillot, Jacques, 26
Genesis, 59
genetically modified (GM) foods, 207-208
Gentilini, Marc, 177
George, Francis E., 147
George, Lloyd, 202
Gervais, Marcel, 256-257
Glemp, Jozef, 162
globalization, 231-232
God, 72, 78-79, 94, 278-279
Gorbachev, Mikhail, 201
Gospels, 81, 93, 234
Grab, Amedee, 221-222
grace, 165-166, 251
Gray, James, 5
Greek Orthodox Church, 118, 119, 124-125
Greeley, Andrew, 224
Gregory I, Pope (Gregory the Great), 15-16, 77
Gregory XVI, Pope, 173
Griffiths, Bede, 243-246
Gulf War, 224-225, 227

H

Hamelin, Jean-Guy, 59
Häring, Bernard, 171, 251-252
Hascal, John, 69
Hayes, James, 182-183
heresies, 148
Hergott, Wilfrid, 3-4
Hermaniuk, Maxim, 262
Hill, Michael, 271
Hippolytus, 90
hockey, 219-220
Holocaust, 163
homosexuality, 147, 186-187, 208-209
Honecker, Erick, 201
Hume, Basil, 253
Husar, Lubomyr, 48
Hussein, Saddam, 224-225

I

Immaculate Conception, 165-166
inculturation, 62-63, 84, 100-102, 152, 157, 214
Innocent I, Pope, 90
international development, 199-200
Iraq War, 225-226
Isaiah, 15
Islam, 163-164, 222
Israel, 161-162, 162-163

J

Jantz, Heidi, 215
Jesus
    attitude towards women, 85-86, 93-94, 113
    and church democracy, 58, 89
    and early church, 23, 137, 138
    effect of ecumenism on, 134-135
    and existence of God, 79
    fear of popularity of, 131-132
    importance of humanity of, 20-23, 234, 252, 266
    as pacifist, 223
    and paradoxes, 18-19, 35-36, 135, 137, 140-141, 159, 263, 273
    and pessimism, 279
    as prophet, 15, 105
    and social justice, 198, 209
    views on modern social issues, 93, 187-188, 189
Jews, 52-53, 54, 85, 160-163
John, St., 60, 87, 150
John Paul II, Pope
    A. Britz's connection to, 8
    and abortion, 168, 169-170
    apologies of, 52, 53, 76, 119, 125
    and birth control, 75, 171
    and capitalism, 116, 127-128, 131, 230
    charismatic leadership of, 124, 131
    and church centralization, 30-32
    and Curia, 118-119
    economic views, 203-204
    and ecumenism, 117-122, 124-126, 139-140, 144-146, 265
    election of, 262
    and euthanasia, 168
    and family, 181
    and fear, 60-61
    and forgiveness, 51-52
    and Greek Orthodox Church, 124-125
    health of, 128-129, 130, 274
    on inclusive language in bible, 83
    and inculturation, 62-63, 101-102, 152
    and J-M. Tillard, 257-258
    and liberation theology, 126-127
    and Mother Teresa, 258
    in northern Canada, 101-102
    and papal primacy, 147-148
    politics of, 115-116, 202, 228, 239-240
    praise for saints, 62
    retirement, 130-131
    and Russian Orthodox Church, 123-124
    and science, 178
    and social justice, 62, 115, 199, 200, 202, 206-208, 250
    and Ukraine, 48, 118, 120, 124, 125-126, 158-159
    and women's place in church, 75-76, 91-93

John the Baptist, 234
John XXIII, Pope
  and F. König, 261, 262
  and Pentecost, 36
  and poverty, 199
  profile of, 233-236
  and Second Vatican Council, 6, 237, 241, 247
Judaism, 160-161
Jung, Carl, 210
Jungmann, Joseph, 143
just wars, 223-226

K

Kasper, Walter, 125, 143, 264-266
Kenny, Michael H., 49
Knights of Columbus, 70-71
Knox, Ronald, 148
König, Franz, 42, 261-262

L

laity
  and birth control, 172-173, 174-176
  canonization of, 236-237
  Congar on, 247
  draft paper on, 57-58
  and ecumenism, 142
  role of, 59, 60
  and Second Vatican Council, 5
  see also lay movements
Last Judgment (Michelangelo), 179-180
Last Supper, 81-82
Latimer, Tracy, 215-216
Latin America
  and Cold War, 202
  and foreign aid, 200
  and Helder Camara, 254-256
  ignored by Church, 99, 158
  and Oscar Romero, 238, 240
  reaching out to, 63, 116, 127, 158
  shortage of priests in, 110
Latin Rite, 120-121, 144, 156-157
lay movements, 29-30, 66-67
Lefebvre, Marcel, 30, 68, 136
Leo I, Pope (Leo the Great), 25, 26, 41
Leo XIII, Pope, 4

Leonard, Graham, 107, 108-109
liberation theology, 126-127
life, beginnings of, 178-179
liturgy, 65, 82-84
Lorscheider, Aloisio, 67
Lubachivsky, Myroslav, 155
Luke, St., 234
Luther, Martin, 35, 146, 151
Lutheran church, 150, 151-152

M

Mahoney, James, 101
Malone, Vincent, 88
Manning, Joanna, 83
Marcinkus-Vatican Bank affair, 162
marriage
  and birth control, 44-45, 175
  and canonization, 63-64
  and Eucharist, 22
  and family, 181
  and priesthood, 101
  and sacraments, 182
  and sex, 22, 59, 72, 77, 180
Martini, Carlo Maria, 41
Martino, Renato, 222
martyrs, 158, 159, 238-239, 240-241
Marx, Paul, 40
Mary, Mother of Jesus, 68-69
Mary Magdalene, St., 81-82
Mass, 111
Matthew, St., 137-138
Mayer, Alfred, 14
McBrien, Richard, 253
McCarrick, Theodore E., 221
McCormick, Richard, 43-44
McGivney, Michael J., 70
media, 11-14
Mennonites, 150, 218
Mercredi, Ovide, 212-213
Merton, Thomas, 150
Methodius, St., 62
Métis, 69
Michelangelo, 179-180
Milord, James E., 68
Milosevic, Slobodan, 228
miracles, 135
monolithism, 54-56

moral theology, 251-252
Morand, Blaise, 210
Morgentaler, Henry, 182
Mount Carmel, 69

N

Natives, 100-101, 102-103, 210-215, 216-217, 218
Nenzel, Augustine, 5
neo-colonialism, 115-116
Nestorianism, 154
northern Canada, 100-101, 102-103, 210
Novo Millennio Ineunte, 265
nuclear weapons, 201-202, 226-227, 248, 277

O

O'Brien, Keith, 177
Oka crisis, 210-212
Opus Dei, 29-30
ordinary time, 64, 65, 66, 272
original sin, 165
Orthodox Christians, 48-49, 123-126, 147-148, 150, 153
  see also
    Assyrian Orthodox Church;
    Greek Orthodox Church;
    Russian Orthodox Church
Ottaviani, Alfredo, 237, 242
Ottenweller, Albert H., 27-28

P

pacifism, 223, 224
papacy
  and leadership, 28-29
  love of, 131
  retirement of, 129-130
  and selecting bishops, 25-26
  universal primacy of, 30-32, 47, 48-49, 147-148, 153, 266
  see also specific popes
Paul, St., 28, 78-79, 91, 93-94, 168, 183-184
Paul VI, Pope, 45, 142, 172, 174, 251, 254

peace, 117-118, 221-222
Peace of Constantine, 88-89
penal reform, 216-218
Pentecost, 36-39, 49
pessimism, 277, 278-279
Peter, St., 37, 132, 137, 138, 223
Pirola, Mavis, 59, 180
Pius IV, Pope, 180
Pius IX, Pope, 233
Pius XI, Pope, 4, 122
Pius XII, Pope, 144, 234, 247
play, 219, 220
pornography, 182
Potter, Philip, 231
poverty
  and A. Britz's interest in, 6
  and feast days, 65-66
  and Helder Camara, 254, 255-256
  J. Sherlock and, 61-62
  John Paul II on, 115, 202
  and Mother Teresa, 259-260
  reaching out to, 63, 102, 119
  and social justice, 197-200
  and taxes, 203
Prairie Messenger
  and CCF, 4-5
  editorial policy, 281-282
  history of, 3-4, 14-15
  how it is structured, 13-14
  and monks, 15-16
  scope and reach of, 7-8
Presbyterian Church, 161
press, 11-14
priesthood
  and Anglican influx, 107-108
  authority of, 27-28, 142-143
  and celibacy, 107, 108
  in Czechoslovakia, 104
  dispute over, 44
  and Eucharist, 20, 109-110
  history of, 89-90
  J. Bernardin on, 250
  and marriage, 100, 101, 103
  in northern Canada, 100-101, 102-103
  recruitment crisis, 96-97, 100-101, 102-103, 105-107, 110
  and sexism, 86-87

women ordained into, 87-88, 104, 107, 147
prophecy/prophets
  Bede Griffiths, 243-246
  and Helder Camara, 256
  and Jesus, 15, 105
  in media, 12
  of *Messenger* editorials, 268, 272-273
  in modern times, 97, 98-99
  unpopularity of, 15
protest, 228-229

Q

Quelch, Peter, 189
Quinn, John R., 48

R

racism, 194-195, 210
Rahner, Karl, 151, 237-238, 248
Raiser, Konrad, 148
Ramsey, Arthur Michael, 235
Ratzinger, Joseph
  and birth control, 262
  and catechism, 45, 46, 169
  and Concilium, 248
  and Czech church, 104
  and debate with W. Kasper, 264-266
  dispute with Cardinals, 41-43
  and ensoulment, 178-179
  and Eucharist, 109, 110
  and inclusive language, 82, 84
  and role of bishops, 32-33, 34, 125
refugees, 278
Resurrection, 81-82
Revelation, 161
Ricci, Matteo, 153
Rite of the Christian Initiation of Adults (RCIA), 84-85, 242
Rittenhouse, 218
Rodriguez, Sue, 190
Romero, Oscar, 238-239, 240
Runcie, Robert, 46-47, 48
Russian Orthodox church, 118, 123-124
Ryan, Tom, 134

S

Sachs, Jeffrey, 207-208
sacraments, 72-73, 182, 243
saints, 58, 62, 122
  see also canonization
Sakharov, Andrei, 194
Salaverri, Joachim, 149
salvation, 159-160
Samaritans, 85
Schillebeeckx, Edward, 109
seamless garment, 7, 167-168
Second Vatican Council
  and A. Britz, 6, 9
  background for, 235
  and bishops' appointment, 5-6, 47-48
  on church's imperfections, 76
  and decentralization, 28, 262
  discussion papers of, 241, 242, 256-257
  and ecumenism, 136, 144, 149
  and episcopal collegiality, 253
  and Latin Rite, 156
  and leadership, 26, 27, 30
  and moral theology, 251-252
  and non-Christian religions, 159-160
  and papal primacy, 266
  Prairie Messenger defence of, 269-270, 271-272
  and revelation, 237
  success of, 5-6, 50-51, 172, 275
  and Y. Congar, 246, 247
sensus fidelium, 26, 40-41, 46, 173, 176
sentencing circles, 218
September 11th, 163, 164, 207, 221-222, 225
sex
  and birth control, 44-45, 174, 175
  and canonization, 64
  and marriage, 22, 59, 72, 77, 180
  and sacrament, 72, 182
  seen as sin, 180-181
  and traditional view of women, 76-77
sexism, 83-84, 86-87, 94
sexual abuse, 24, 186-188, 248
Shamir, Yitzhak, 162

Sherlock, John, 61-62
Shimamoto, Francis Xavier Kaname, 59, 60
Silvestrini, Achille, 152
sin, 86-87, 119, 165, 180-181, 213, 252
Singer, Israel, 117-118
socialism, 4-5, 116
Spence, Francis, 168
sport, 218-221
St. Peter's Abbey, 2-3
stem cells, 179
subsidiarity, 253
Syllabus of Errors, 149, 164, 247
Synod of the Laity, 57-58, 59, 61-62, 67-68

T

Tavard, George, 152
taxes, 202-204, 232
Teilhard de Chardin, Pierre, 241
televangelists, 36
temple messianism, 49
Teresa, Mother, 258-261
Tertullian, 77
Tetzel, John, 35
Thompson, John, 7, 9
Tillard, Jean-Marie, 117, 256-258
Tobin, James, 232
Tomasek, Frantisek, 201
Trautman, Donald W., 83
triumphalism, 71

U

Ukraine
  history of, 155-159
  John Paul II's visit to, 48, 118, 120, 124, 125-126
uniate model, 123, 125, 126, 153
United Church, 161, 166
universal church, 265-266
uranium mining, 201-202
Ut Unum Sint, 32, 121-122, 144, 258

V

vaccination, 173

Vanier, Jean, 191, 198
Vatican, 40, 103
  see also Curia; papacy; Second Vatican Council
Vatican II. *see* Second Vatican Council
Vietnam War, 278
violence, 76, 184-185, 219-220
  see also war
vocations, 95-97
Vsevolod, Archbishop, 48

W

war, 201-202, 210-212, 222-227, 248, 277-278. *see also* Cold War
Ward, Barbara, 199
Weakland, Rembert, 68, 109, 174
Weisgerber, James, 83
Weisner, Gerald, 221
Willebrands, Johannes, 42
women
  and abortion, 75, 185
  among early Christians, 279
  as bar on ecumenism, 147
  debated at Synod of the Laity, 59, 67-68
  defence of, 268, 269
  effect of feminism on, 91-93
  and Eucharist, 112-113
  hearing confessions, 88, 90-91
  history in church, 75-78, 94
  Jesus's attitude toward, 85-86, 93-94, 113
  John Paul II on, 75-76, 91-93
  as ordained priests, 87-88, 104, 107, 147
  and Resurrection, 81-82
  sexism toward, 86-87, 94
  suffering of, 99
  survey on, 78-80
  and use of inclusive language, 155
World Synod of Bishops, 60-61
World Synod on the Laity, 57-58
World War II, 224

X Y Z

Zhirinovsky, Vladimir, 118

About the Authors

Rev. Andrew M. Britz, OSB

Born at Lake Lenore, Saskatchewan, in 1940, Murray Britz entered the Benedictine order in July 1959 receiving the name Andrew. He took his seminary training from 1960 to 1966 at St. John's Abbey, Collegeville, Minn., where he received a Master of Arts degree in liturgy. He was ordained to priesthood in June 1966.

He taught high school and university classes at St. Peter's College in Muenster, Saskatchewan, from 1966 to 1972 and was principal for three years. He undertook doctoral studies in church history (TST, Toronto) from 1972 to 1974 and was called home to resume principalship of the university program where he remained as principal until 1982.

Father Andrew served as editor of the *Prairie Messenger* for twenty-one years until resigning in 2004 due to Parkinson's disease. Since leaving the principal's office, he has continued to perform regular pastoral work. He has, over the years, preached many retreats, both to diocesan priests and to religious, both male and female. He resigned from full-time ministry in 2007.

Dennis Gruending

Dennis Gruending is an Ottawa-based writer and a former Member of Parliament. He has worked as a journalist and radio host and is the author of five books, including the best selling *Great Canadian Speeches*. He attended St. Peter's College, a Benedictine high school at Muenster, Saskatchewan, in the 1960s and has known Father Andrew Britz since that time.

Joan Chittister, OSB

A Benedictine Sister of Erie, Pennsylvania, Joan Chittister is a best-selling author and well-known international lecturer on topics of justice, peace, human rights, women's issues, and contemporary spirituality in the Church and in society. She presently serves as the co-chair of the Global Peace Initiative of Women, a partner organization of the United Nations, facilitating a worldwide network of women peace builders, especially in the Middle East.

Sister Joan's most recent books include *The Way We Were* and *Called to Question* (First Place CPA 2005 award winner). She is founder and executive director of Benetvision, a resource for contemporary spirituality.

Mary Jo Leddy

Mary Jo Leddy is a Canadian writer, speaker, theologian, and social activist widely recognized for her work with refugees at Toronto's Romero House. She began working for the centre as a night manager in 1991 and has been its director since then. After thirty years, as a member of the Roman Catholic Sisters of Our Lady of Sion, she left that congregation in 1994.

In 1973, she was the founding editor of the *Catholic New Times*, an independent Catholic newspaper. She is author of the books *Say to the Darkness We Beg to Differ* (Finalist, City of Toronto Book Award), *Reweaving Religious Life: Beyond the Liberal Model*, *At the Border Called Hope: Where Refugees are Neighbours* (Finalist, Trillium Award), and *Radical Gratitude*.

The recipient of a Ph.D. in philosophy from the University of Toronto, she studied under the direction of Emil Fackenheim. She is currently an adjunct professor at Regis College, the Jesuit theological school at that university. She is active in various human rights and peace groups and is a frequent radio and TV commentator.

John Thompson

Professor Thompson earned his Bachelor of Arts degree in Philosophy at Spring Hill College, Alabama, his Master of Arts in Theology at the University of Santa Clara, California, and his Master of Arts and Doctor of Philosophy degrees in Sociology at the University of California, Santa Barbara.

John and his wife, Patty, moved to Saskatoon in 1975 where he took up a position in sociology at St. Thomas More College (STM), University of Saskatchewan. During thirty years, he taught more than four thousand students at the U of S and St. Peter's College, Muenster. He served as

STM president from 1990 to 2000. His research included studies of marriage and family life, religious movements, the Catholic press, and careers of BA graduates in sociology. In Spring 2004, Thompson received the Master Teacher Award from the U of S.